W9-CCP-147

World Facts

The Earth

AREA: 196,938,000 sq mi (510,066,000 sq km)

LAND: 57,393,000 sq mi (148,647,000 sq km)— 29.1%

WATER: 139,545,000 sq mi (361,419,000 sq km)— 70.9%

POPULATION: 6,624,528,000 people

The Continents

	AREA (sq mi)	(sq km)	Percent of Earth's Land
Asia	17,208,000	44,570,000	30.0
Africa	11,608,000	30,065,000	20.2
North America	9,449,000	24,474,000	16.5
South America	6,880,000	17,819,000	12.0
Antarctica	5,100,000	13,209,000	8.9
Europe	3,841,000	9,947,000	6.7
Australia	2,970,000	7,692,000	5.2

Highest Point On Each Continent

	feet	meters
Mount Everest, Asia	29,035	8,850
Cerro Aconcagua, South America	22,834	6,960
Mount McKinley (Denali), N. America	20,320	6,194
Kilimanjaro, Africa	19,340	5,895
El'brus, Europe	18,510	5,642
Vinson Massif, Antarctica	16,067	4,897
Mount Kosciuszko, Australia	7,310	2,228

Lowest Point On Each Continent

	feet	meters
Dead Sea, Asia	-1,380	-421
Lake Assal, Africa	-512	-156
Laguna del Carbón, South America	-344	-105
Death Valley, North America	-282	-86
Caspian Sea, Europe	-92	-28
Lake Eyre, Australia	-52	-16
Bentley Subglacial Trench, Antarctica (ice covered)	-8,383	-2,555

Ten Longest Rivers

	LENGTH miles	kilometers
Nile, Africa	4,241	6,825
Amazon, South America	4,000	6,437
Yangtze (Chang Jiang), Asia	3,964	6,380
Mississippi-Missouri, North America	3,710	5,971
Yenisey-Angara, Asia	3,440	5,536
Yellow (Huang), Asia	3,395	5,464
Ob-Irtysh, Asia	3,362	5,410
Amur, Asia	2,744	4,416
Lena, Asia	2,734	4,400
Congo, Africa	2,715	4,370

Ten Largest Lakes

	AREA (sq mi)	(sq km)	Greatest Depth (feet)	(meters)
Caspian Sea, Europe-Asia	143,254	371,000	3,363	1,025
Superior, N. America	31,701	82,100	1,332	406
Victoria, Africa	26,836	69,500	269	82
Huron, N. America	23,013	59,600	751	229
Michigan, N. America	22,318	57,800	922	281
Tanganyika, Africa	12,587	32,600	4,823	1,470
Baikal, Asia	12,163	31,500	5,371	1,637
Great Bear, N. America	12,086	31,300	1,463	446
Malawi, Africa	11,159	28,900	2,280	695
Great Slave, N. America	11,043	28,600	2,014	614

Ten Largest Islands

	AREA (sq mi)	(sq km)
Greenland, North America	836,000	2,166,000
New Guinea, Asia-Oceania	306,000	792,500
Borneo, Asia	280,100	725,500
Madagascar, Africa	226,600	587,000
Baffin, North America	196,000	507,500
Sumatra, Asia	165,000	427,300
Honshu, Asia	87,800	227,400
Great Britain, Europe	84,200	218,100
Victoria, North America	83,900	217,300
Ellesmere, North America	75,800	196,200

The Oceans

	AREA (sq mi)	(sq km)	Percent of Earth's Water Area
Pacific	65,436,200	169,479,000	46.8
Atlantic	35,338,500	91,526,400	25.3
Indian	28,839,800	74,694,800	20.6
Arctic	5,390,000	13,960,100	3.9

Deepest Point In Each Ocean

	feet	meters
Challenger Deep, Mariana Trench, Pacific	-35,827	-10,920
Puerto Rico Trench, Atlantic	-28,232	-8,605
Java Trench, Indian	-23,376	-7,125
Molloy Deep, Arctic	-18,599	-5,669

Ten Largest Seas

	AREA (sq mi)	(sq km)	Average Depth (feet)	(meters)
Coral Sea	1,615,260	4,183,510	8,107	2,471
South China Sea	1,388,570	3,596,390	3,871	1,180
Caribbean Sea	1,094,330	2,834,290	8,517	2,596
Bering Sea	972,810	2,519,580	6,010	1,832
Mediterranean Sea	953,320	2,469,100	5,157	1,572
Sea of Okhotsk	627,490	1,625,190	2,671	814
Gulf of Mexico	591,430	1,531,810	5,066	1,544
Norwegian Sea	550,300	1,425,280	5,801	1,768
Greenland Sea	447,050	1,157,850	4,734	1,443
Sea of Japan (East Sea)	389,290	1,008,260	5,404	1,647

Earth's Extremes

HOTTEST PLACE: Dalol, Danakil Desert, Ethiopia; annual average temperature— 93°F (34°C)

COLDEST PLACE: Plateau Station, Antarctica; annual average temperature— -70°F (-57°C)

WETTEST PLACE: Mawsynram, Assam, India; annual average rainfall— 467 in (1,187 cm)

DRIEST PLACE: Atacama Desert, Chile; rainfall barely measurable

HIGHEST WATERFALL: Angel Falls, Venezuela— 3,212 ft (979 m)

LARGEST HOT DESERT: Sahara, Africa— 3,475,000 sq mi (9,000,000 sq km)

LARGEST ICE DESERT: Antarctica— 5,100,000 sq mi (13,209,000 sq km)

LARGEST CANYON: Grand Canyon, Colorado River, Arizona; 277 mi (446 km) long along river, 600 ft (180 m) to 18 mi (29 km) wide, about 1.1 mi (1.8 km) deep

LONGEST REEF: Great Barrier Reef, Australia— 1,429 mi (2,300 km)

GREATEST TIDAL RANGE: Bay of Fundy, Nova Scotia, Canada— 52 ft (16 m)

MOST PREDICTABLE GEYSER: Old Faithful, Wyoming, U.S.; annual average interval— 66 to 80 minutes

LARGEST CAVE SYSTEM: Mammoth Cave, Kentucky, U.S.; over 330 mi (530 km) of passageways mapped

Abbreviations

COUNTRY NAMES

ARM.	Armenia
AZERB.	Azerbaijan
B. & H.; BOSN. & HERZG.	Bosnia and Herzegovina
BELG.	Belgium
CRO.	Croatia
EST.	Estonia
HUNG.	Hungary
KOS.	Kosovo
LATV.	Latvia
LIECH.	Liechtenstein
LITH.	Lithuania
LUX.	Luxembourg
MACED.	Macedonia
MOLD.	Moldova
MONT.	Montenegro
N.Z.	New Zealand
NETH.	Netherlands
SLOV.	Slovenia
SWITZ.	Switzerland
U.A.E.	United Arab Emirates
U.K.	United Kingdom
U.S.	United States

PHYSICAL FEATURES

I.-s.	Island-s
L.	Lake
Mt.-s.	Mont, Mount-ain-s
R.	River

OTHER

ALA.	Alabama
ARK.	Arkansas
CONN.	Connecticut
D.C.	District of Columbia
Eq.	Equatorial
FLA.	Florida
ILL.	Illinois
IND.	Indiana
KY.	Kentucky
LA.	Louisiana
MASS.	Massachusetts
MD.	Maryland
MINN.	Minnesota
MISS.	Mississippi
N.H.	New Hampshire
N.Y.	New York
PA.	Pennsylvania
P.E.I.	Prince Edward Island
Pop.	Population
Rep.	Republic
R.I.	Rhode Island
St.-e.	Saint-e
TENN.	Tennessee
VA.	Virginia
VT.	Vermont
WASH.	Washington
WIS.	Wisconsin
W.VA.	West Virginia
&	and

STUDENT
ATLAS OF THE
WORLD

THIRD EDITION

YOU are the world! ➤

WASHINGTON, D.C.

TABLE OF CONTENTS

North America:
Floods, page 68

South America:
Three-toed sloth,
page 78

Asia:
Terraced rice
fields, page 90

Antarctica: Whale, page 123

Africa: Giraffe, page 108

BACK OF THE BOOK

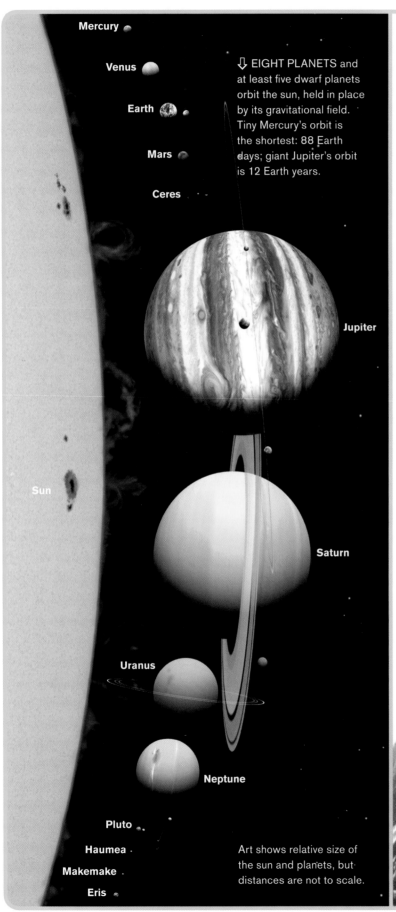

Mercury

Venus

Earth

Mars

Ceres

⇩ EIGHT PLANETS and at least five dwarf planets orbit the sun, held in place by its gravitational field. Tiny Mercury's orbit is the shortest: 88 Earth days; giant Jupiter's orbit is 12 Earth years.

Jupiter

Sun

Saturn

Uranus

Neptune

Pluto

Haumea

Makemake

Eris

Art shows relative size of the sun and planets, but distances are not to scale.

Earth in Space

At the center of our solar system is the sun, a huge mass of hot gas that is the source of both light and warmth for Earth. Third in a group of 13 planets that revolve around the sun, Earth is a terrestrial, or mostly rocky, planet. So are Mercury, Venus, and Mars. Earth is about 93 million miles (150 million kilometers) from the sun, and its journey, or revolution, around the sun takes 365¼ days. Farther away from the sun, four more planets—Jupiter, Saturn, Uranus, and Neptune (all made up primarily of gases)—plus at least five "dwarf" planets (Ceres, Pluto, Haumea, Makemake, and Eris) complete the main bodies of our solar system. The solar system, in turn, is part of the Milky Way galaxy.

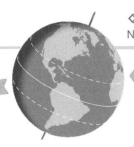

⇐ SPRING
Northern Hemisphere

⇨ WINTER
Northern Hemisphere

EARTH'S SEASONS change throughout the year because the planet tilts 23.5° on its axis as it revolves around the sun. For example, when the Northern Hemisphere is tilted toward the sun, summer occurs there; when it's tilted away from the sun, it experiences winter.

⇐ SUMMER
Northern Hemisphere

⇨ FALL
Northern Hemisphere

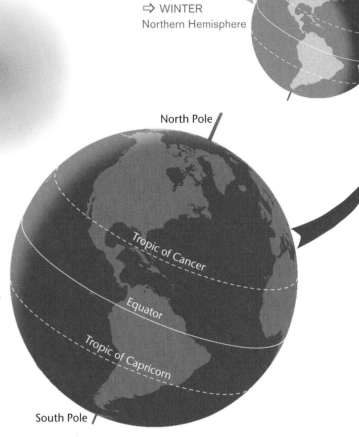

North Pole

Tropic of Cancer

Equator

Tropic of Capricorn

South Pole

⬇ AN ENVELOPE OF AIR surrounds Earth. Called the atmosphere, it is made up of a mix of nitrogen, oxygen, and other gases. It is 300 miles (483 km) thick. The troposphere, which extends upward as much as 10 miles (16 km) from Earth's surface, is called the zone of life. The combination of gases, moderate temperatures, and water in this layer supports plants, animals, and other forms of life on Earth.

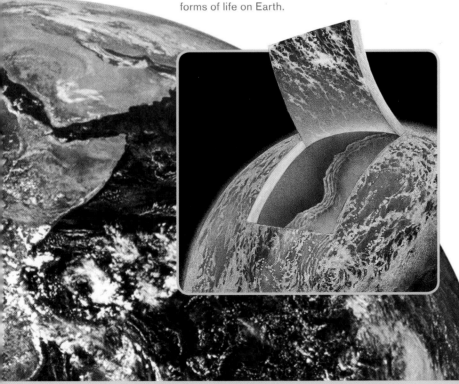

⇧ EARTH ROTATES WEST TO EAST on its axis, an imaginary line that runs through Earth's center from Pole to Pole. Each rotation takes 24 hours, or one full cycle of day and night. One complete rotation equals one Earth day. One complete revolution around the sun equals one Earth year.

Map Projections

Maps tell a story about physical and human systems, places and regions, patterns and relationships. This atlas is a collection of maps that tell a story about Earth.

Understanding that story requires a knowledge of how maps are made and a familiarity with the special language used by cartographers, the people who create maps.

Globes present a model of Earth as it is—a sphere—but they are bulky and can be difficult to use and store. Flat maps are much more convenient, but certain problems result from transferring Earth's curved surface to a flat piece of paper, a process called projection. There are many different types of projections, all of which involve some form of distortion: area, distance, direction, or shape.

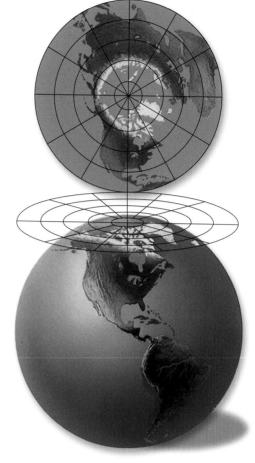

⇧ AZIMUTHAL MAP PROJECTION. This kind of map is made by projecting a globe onto a flat surface that touches the globe at a single point, such as the North Pole. These maps accurately represent direction along any straight line extending from the point of contact. Away from the point of contact, shape is increasingly distorted.

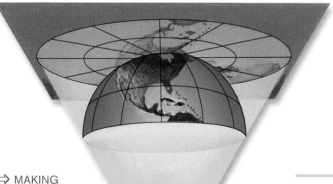

⇨ MAKING A PROJECTION. Imagine a globe that has been cut in half as this one has. If a light is shined into it, the lines of latitude and longitude and the shapes of the continents will cast shadows that can be "projected" onto a piece of paper, as shown here. Depending on how the paper is positioned, the shadows will be distorted in different ways.

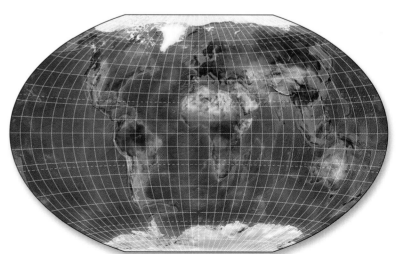

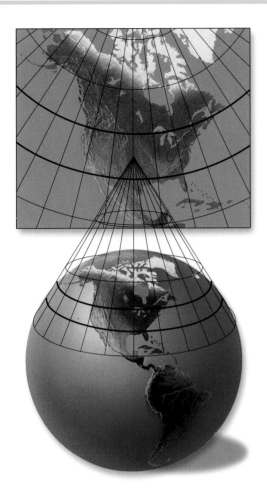

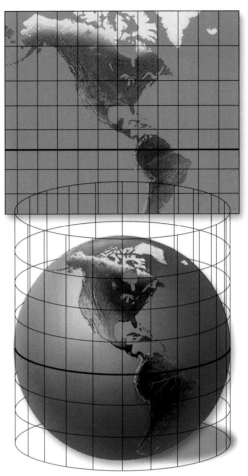

⇧ CONIC MAP PROJECTION. This kind of map is made by projecting a globe onto a cone. The part of Earth being mapped touches the sides of the cone. Lines of longitude appear as straight lines; lines of latitude appear as parallel arcs. Conic projections are often used to map mid-latitude areas with great east-west extent, such as North America.

⇧ CYLINDRICAL MAP PROJECTION. A cylindrical projection map is made by projecting a globe onto a cylinder that touches Earth's surface along the Equator. Latitude and longitude lines on this kind of map show true compass directions, which makes it useful for navigation. But there is great distortion in the size of high-latitude landmasses.

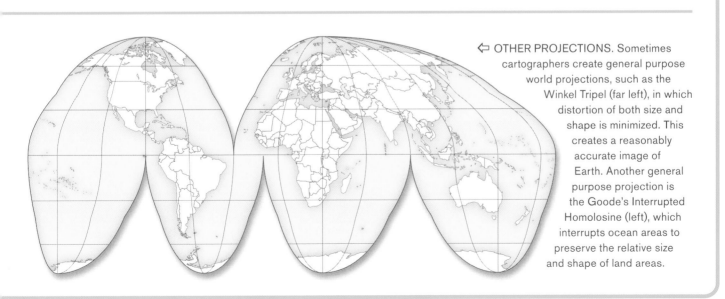

⇦ OTHER PROJECTIONS. Sometimes cartographers create general purpose world projections, such as the Winkel Tripel (far left), in which distortion of both size and shape is minimized. This creates a reasonably accurate image of Earth. Another general purpose projection is the Goode's Interrupted Homolosine (left), which interrupts ocean areas to preserve the relative size and shape of land areas.

Reading Maps

People can use maps to find locations, to determine direction or distance, and to understand information about places. Cartographers rely on a special graphic language to communicate through maps.

An imaginary system of lines, called the global grid, helps us locate particular points on Earth's surface. The global grid is made up of lines of latitude and longitude that are measured in degrees, minutes, and seconds. The point where these lines intersect identifies the absolute location of a place. No other place has the exact same address.

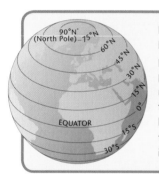

LATITUDE. Lines of latitude—also called parallels because they are parallel to the Equator—run east to west around the globe and measure location north or south of the Equator. The Equator is 0° latitude.

LONGITUDE. Lines of longitude, also called meridians, run from Pole to Pole and measure location east or west of the prime meridian. The prime meridian is 0° longitude, and it runs through Greenwich, near London, England.

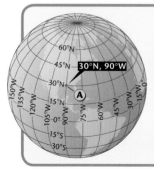

GLOBAL GRID. When used together, latitude and longitude form a grid that provides a system for determining the exact, or absolute, location of every place on Earth. For example, the absolute location of point A is 30°N, 90°W.

⬆ DIRECTION. Cartographers put a north arrow or a compass rose, which shows the four cardinal directions—north, south, east, and west—on a map. On this map, point **B** is northwest (NW) of point **A**. Northwest is an example of an intermediate direction, which means it is between two cardinal directions. Grid lines can also be used to indicate north.

⇨ SCALE. A map represents a part of Earth's surface, but that part is greatly reduced. Cartographers include a map scale to show what distance on Earth is represented by a given length on the map. Scale can be graphic (a bar), verbal, or a ratio.

To determine how many miles point **A** is from point **B**, place a piece of paper on the map above and mark the distance between **A** and **B**. Then compare the marks on the paper with the bar scale on the map.

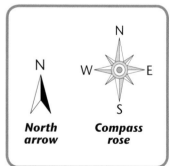

North arrow   **Compass rose**

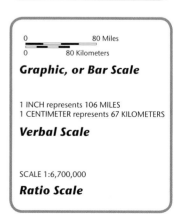

Graphic, or Bar Scale

1 INCH represents 106 MILES
1 CENTIMETER represents 67 KILOMETERS

Verbal Scale

SCALE 1:6,700,000

Ratio Scale

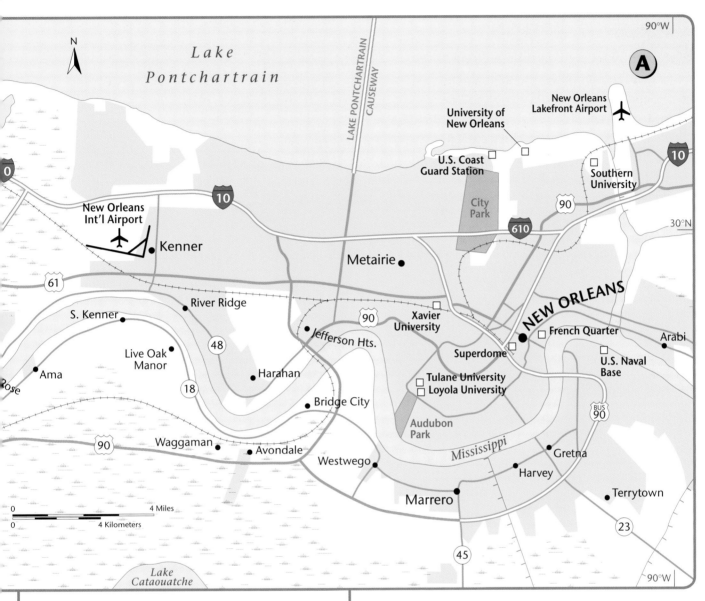

Lake Pontchartrain

LAKE PONTCHARTRAIN CAUSEWAY

University of New Orleans

New Orleans Lakefront Airport

U.S. Coast Guard Station

Southern University

City Park

90°W

A

New Orleans Int'l Airport

Kenner

61

Metairie

River Ridge

S. Kenner

48

Jefferson Hts.

Live Oak Manor

Harahan

18

Bridge City

Ama

Rose

90

Waggaman

Avondale

Westwego

Marrero

90

90

610

30°N

Xavier University

NEW ORLEANS

French Quarter

Arabi

Superdome

U.S. Naval Base

Tulane University

Loyola University

Audubon Park

Mississippi

BUS 90

Gretna

Harvey

Terrytown

23

45

90°W

0   4 Miles
0   4 Kilometers

Lake Cataouatche

⇩ SYMBOLS. Finally, cartographers use a variety of symbols, which are identified in a map key or legend, to tell us more about the places represented on the map. There are three general types of symbols:

● ● POINT SYMBOLS show exact location of places (such as cities) or quantity (a large dot can mean a more populous city).

┼┼┼┼ LINE SYMBOLS show boundaries or connections (such as roads, canals, and other trade links).

▭ AREA SYMBOLS show the form and extent of a feature (such as a lake, park, or swamp).

Additional information may be coded in color, size, and shape.

⇧ PUTTING IT ALL TOGETHER. We already know from the map on page 8 which states A and B are located in. But to find out more about city A, we need a larger scale map—one that shows a smaller area in more detail (see above).

MAP LEGEND

▭ Metropolitan area	━━ Road
▭ Lake or river	┼┼┼┼ Railroad
� Park	╲╱ Runway
∴ Swamp	✈ Airport
⊥⊤⊥ Canal	▢ Point of interest
══ Highway	● ● ● Town

Types of Maps

This atlas includes many different types of maps so that a wide variety of information about Earth can be presented. Three of the most commonly used types of maps are physical, political, and thematic.

A **physical map** identifies natural features, such as mountains, deserts, oceans, and lakes. Area symbols of various colors and shadings may indicate height above sea level or, as in the example here, ecosystems. Similar symbols could also show water depth.

A **political map** shows how people have divided the world into countries. Political maps can also show states, counties, or cities within a country. Line symbols indicate boundaries, and point symbols show the locations and sometimes sizes of cities.

Thematic maps use a variety of symbols to show distributions and patterns on Earth. For example, a choropleth map uses shades of color to represent different values. The example here shows the amount of energy consumed each year by various countries. Thematic maps can show many different things, such as patterns of vegetation, land use, and religions.

A **cartogram** is a special kind of thematic map in which the size of a country is based on some statistic other than land area. In the cartogram at far right, population size determines the size of each country. This is why Nigeria—the most populous country in Africa—appears much larger than Sudan, which has more than double the land area of Nigeria (see the political map). Cartograms allow for a quick visual comparison of countries in terms of a selected statistic.

⇨ THIS GLOBE is useful for showing Africa's position and size relative to other landmasses, but very little detail is possible at this scale. By using different kinds of maps, mapmakers can show a variety of information in more detail.

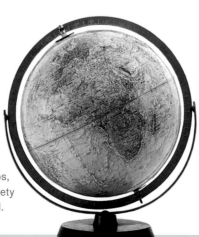

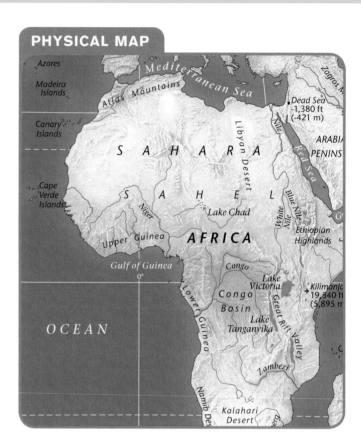

PHYSICAL MAP

Azores • Mediterranean Sea • Zagros M.
Madeira Islands • Atlas Mountains • Dead Sea -1,380 ft (-421 m)
Canary Islands • SAHARA • Libyan Desert • Nile • Red Sea • ARABIA PENINS
Cape Verde Islands • SAHEL • Niger • Lake Chad • White Nile • Blue Nile • Ethiopian Highlands
Upper Guinea • AFRICA
Gulf of Guinea 0° • Congo • Lake Victoria • Kilimanj. 19,340 ft (5,895 m)
Lower Guinea • Congo Basin • Lake Tanganyika • Great Rift Valley
OCEAN • Zambezi
Namib Des. • Kalahari Desert

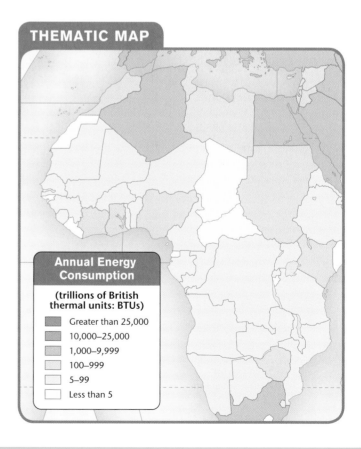

THEMATIC MAP

Annual Energy Consumption

(trillions of British thermal units: BTUs)

	Greater than 25,000
	10,000–25,000
	1,000–9,999
	100–999
	5–99
	Less than 5

POLITICAL MAP

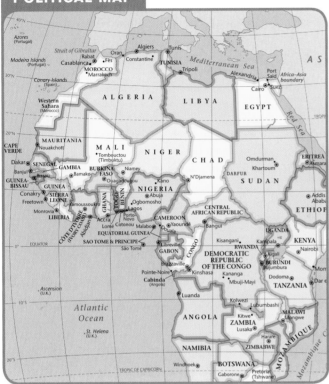

CARTOGRAM

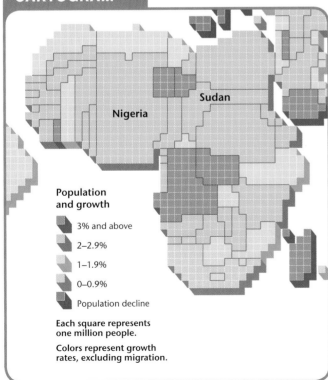

Nigeria

Sudan

Population and growth

- 3% and above
- 2–2.9%
- 1–1.9%
- 0–0.9%
- Population decline

Each square represents one million people.

Colors represent growth rates, excluding migration.

SATELLITE IMAGE MAPS

Satellites orbiting Earth transmit images of the surface to computers on the ground. These computers translate the information into special maps (below) that use colors to show various characteristics. Such maps are valuable tools for identifying patterns or comparing changes over time.

⬇ CLOUD COVERAGE

⬇ TOPOGRAPHY/BATHYMETRY

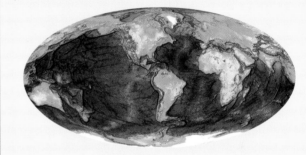

⬇ SEA LEVEL VARIABILITY

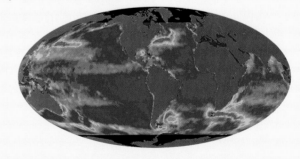

⬇ SEA SURFACE TEMPERATURE

Time Zones

The *Fiji Times*, a newspaper published in Suva, capital of the Fiji Islands, carries the message "The First Newspaper Published in the World Today" on the front page of each edition. How can this newspaper from a small island country make such a claim? Fiji lies west of the date line, an invisible boundary designated to mark the beginning of each new day. The date line is just part of the system we have adopted to keep track of the passage of days.

For most of human history, people determined time by observing the position of the sun in the sky. Slight differences in time did not matter until, in the mid-19th century, the spread of railroads and telegraph lines changed forever the importance of time. High-speed transportation and communications required schedules, and schedules required that everyone agree on the time.

In 1884, an international conference, convened in Washington, D.C., established an international system of 24 time zones based on the fact that Earth turns from west to east 15 degrees of longitude every hour. Each time zone has a central meridian and is 15 degrees wide, 7½ degrees to either side of the named central meridian.

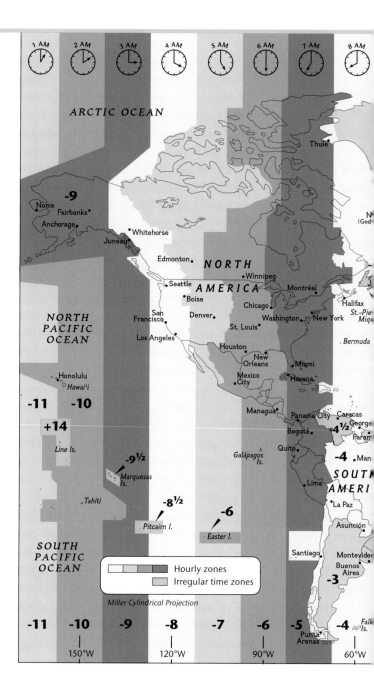

← WORLD TIME CLOCK, in Alexanderplatz in Berlin, Germany, features a large cylinder that is marked with the world's 24 time zones and major cities found in each zone. The cylinder rises almost 33 feet (10 m) above the square and weighs 16 tons.

⇧ A SYSTEM OF STANDARD TIME put trains on schedules, which helped reduce the chance of collisions and the loss of lives and property caused by them.

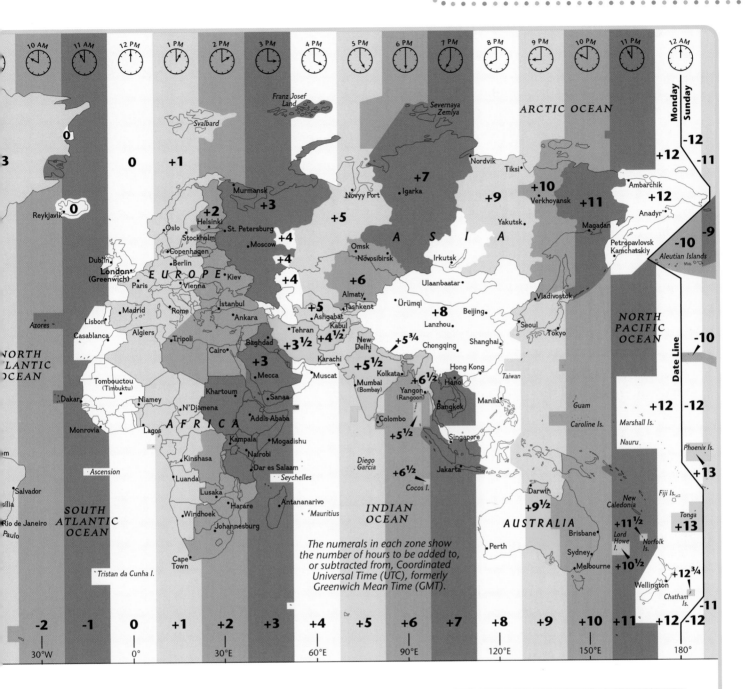

10 AM 11 AM 12 PM 1 PM 2 PM 3 PM 4 PM 5 PM 6 PM 7 PM 8 PM 9 PM 10 PM 11 PM 12 AM

Monday
Sunday

ARCTIC OCEAN

Franz Josef Land
Svalbard
Severnaya Zemlya

0   **0**   **+1**   **+3**

+7   **+10**   **+12**

Nordvik   •Tiksi   •Ambarchik
Novyy Port   •Igarka   Verkhoyansk   **+11**   **+12**
+2   **+5**   **+9**   Anadyr'
•Murmansk   **+3**   A S I A   Magadan   **-9**
Helsinki   St. Petersburg   Yakutsk•   Petropavlovsk   **-10**
Oslo•   Stockholm   •Moscow   **+4**   Omsk   **+6**   Irkutsk•   Kamchatskiy
Reykjavik•   **0**   Copenhagen   **+4**   Novosibirsk   Ulaanbaatar •   Vladivostok•   Aleutian Islands
Dublin•   Berlin   Kiev   **+4**   Almaty   Ürümqi   Seoul•   NORTH PACIFIC OCEAN
London   EUROPE   Vienna   **+5**   Tashkent•   **+8**   Beijing•   Tokyo•   **-10**
(Greenwich)   Paris   Istanbul   Ashgabat   Kabul   Lanzhou•   Date Line
Madrid•   Rome•   Ankara•   Tehran•   **+4½**   New   Chongqing•   Shanghai•
Azores   Lisbon•   **+3½**   Delhi   **+5¾**   Hong Kong   **+12**   **-12**
Casablanca•   Algiers•   Baghdad•   Karachi•   Kolkata•   Taiwan   Guam•   Marshall Is.
NORTH ATLANTIC OCEAN   Tripoli•   Cairo•   **+3**   •Mecca   **+5½**   Mumbai   **+6½**   Hanoi•   Manila•   Caroline Is.   Nauru•
Tombouctou   Muscat•   (Bombay)   Yangon   Bangkok•
(Timbuktu)   Khartoum•   •Sanaa   (Rangoon)   Phoenix Is.
Dakar•   Niamey•   Colombo•   Singapore•   **+12**   **+13**
Monrovia•   N'Djamena•   AFRICA   •Addis Ababa   **+5½**   Jakarta•   Darwin•   Fiji Is.
Lagos•   Kampala•   •Mogadishu   Diego   New Caledonia
•Kinshasa   Nairobi•   Garcia   **+6½**   AUSTRALIA   **+9½**   **+11½**   Tonga   **+13**
Ascension   Luanda•   Dar es Salaam•   •Seychelles   Cocos I.   Brisbane•   Lord   Norfolk
Salvador•   Lusaka•   Antananarivo•   INDIAN   Howe   Is.   **+12¾**
Rio de Janeiro•   Harare•   •Mauritius   OCEAN   Perth•   Sydney•   I.   **+10½**
Paulo•   SOUTH ATLANTIC OCEAN   Windhoek•   Johannesburg•   Melbourne•   Wellington•
Cape   Tristan da Cunha I.   Chatham Is.   **-11**
Town•

The numerals in each zone show the number of hours to be added to, or subtracted from, Coordinated Universal Time (UTC), formerly Greenwich Mean Time (GMT).

-2   **-1**   **0**   **+1**   **+2**   **+3**   **+4**   **+5**   **+6**   **+7**   **+8**   **+9**   **+10**   **+11**   **+12**
30°W   0°   30°E   60°E   90°E   120°E   150°E   180°

-12   **-11**   **+12**   **-12**   **-10**   **-9**   **-12**   **+13**   **-11**   **-12**

THE DATE LINE (180°) is directly opposite the prime meridian (0°). As Earth rotates, each new day officially begins as the 180° line passes 12 midnight. If you travel west across the date line, you advance one day; if you travel east across the date line, you fall back one day. Notice on the map how the line zigs to the east as it passes through the South Pacific so that the islands of Fiji will not be split between two different days. Also notice that India is 5½ hours ahead of Coordinated Universal Time (formerly Greenwich Mean Time), and China has only one time zone, even though the country spans more than 60 degrees of longitude. These differences are the result of decisions made at the country level.

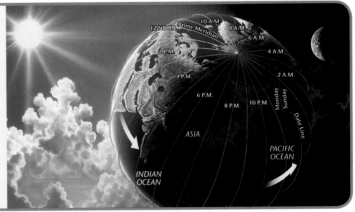

The Physical World

Realms of land and water make up the physical world. More than two-thirds of Earth's surface is covered by water: oceans, lakes, and rivers. The rest is land: continents and islands. People inhabit every continent except Antarctica, which lies frozen beneath a vast ice cap at Earth's South Pole. Each continent is unique, but all show evidence of dynamic forces at work. Some forces build up mountains such as the Rockies, the Andes, and the Himalaya; other forces wear down Earth's surface, creating vast sedimentary plains and lowlands. Powerful rivers such as the Mississippi, the Congo, and the Yangtze (Chang) cut through the land and empty billions of gallons of freshwater into the oceans and seas each day.

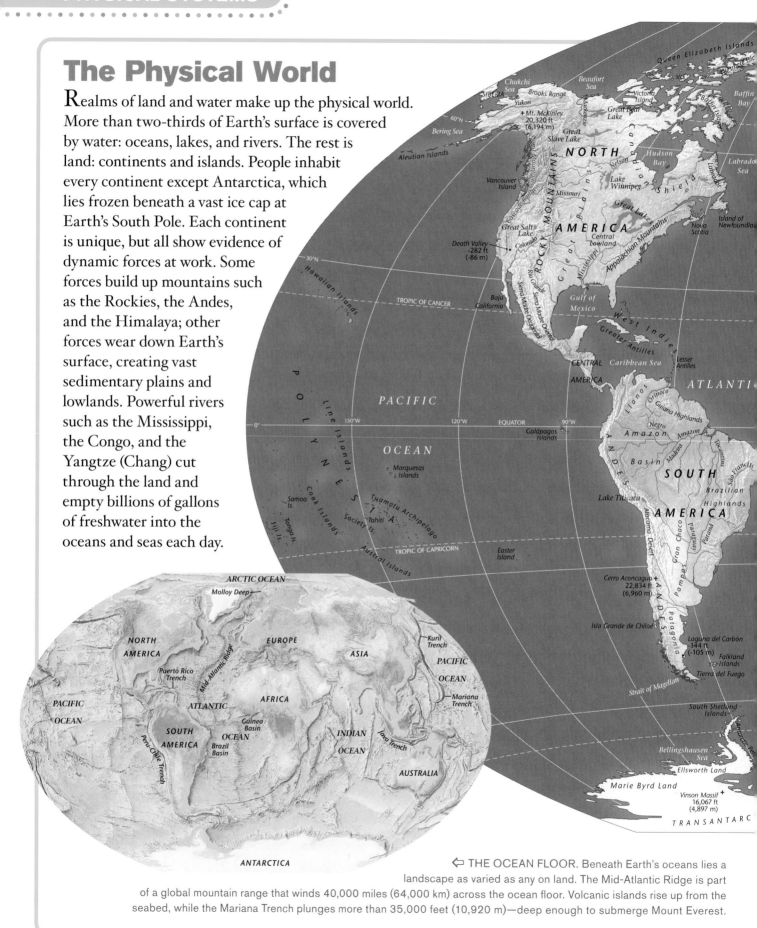

⇦ THE OCEAN FLOOR. Beneath Earth's oceans lies a landscape as varied as any on land. The Mid-Atlantic Ridge is part of a global mountain range that winds 40,000 miles (64,000 km) across the ocean floor. Volcanic islands rise up from the seabed, while the Mariana Trench plunges more than 35,000 feet (10,920 m)—deep enough to submerge Mount Everest.

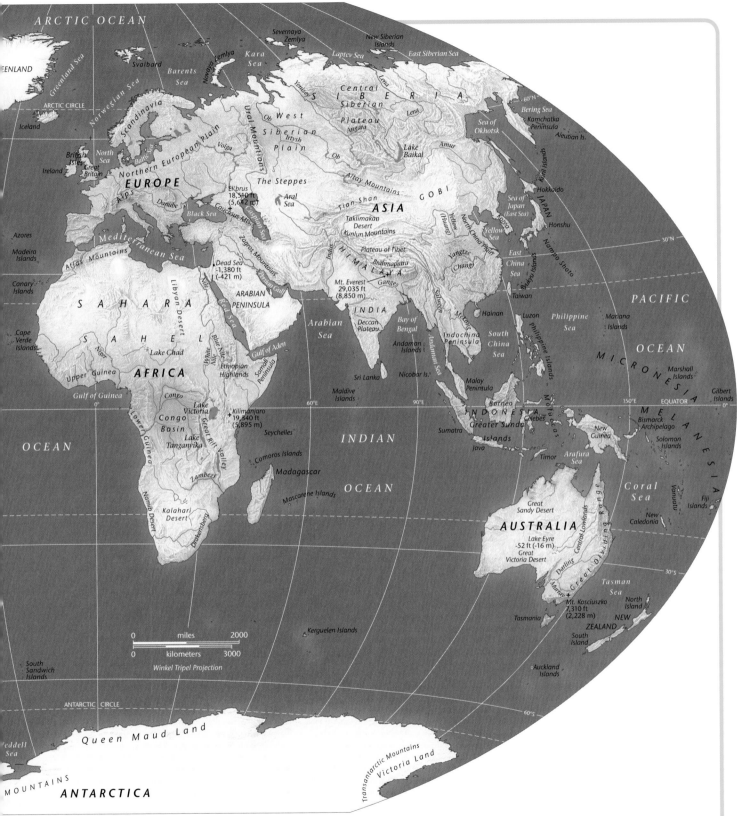

⇧ THE PHYSICAL WORLD. Great landmasses called
continents break Earth's global ocean into four smaller ones. Each continent is
unique in terms of the landforms and rivers that etch its surface and the ecosystems
that lend colors ranging from the deep greens of the tropical forests of northern South America and southeastern Asia
to the browns and yellows of the arid lands of Africa and Australia. Most of Antarctica's features are hidden beneath its ice cap.

Earth's Geologic History

Earth is a dynamic planet. Its outer shell, or crust, is broken into huge pieces called plates. These plates ride on the slowly moving molten rock, or magma, that lies beneath the crust. Their movement constantly changes Earth's surface. For instance, along one convergent boundary—a place where two plates meet—the Indian Plate moves northward, colliding with the Eurasian Plate and heaving up the still growing mountains of the Himalaya. Along another convergent boundary, the Nasca Plate dives beneath the South American Plate in a process called subduction. Volcanoes and underwater earthquakes may occur along subduction zones, sometimes triggering giant waves called tsunamis. Along transform zones, such as California's San Andreas Fault, plates grind past each other, resulting in destructive earthquakes. The Mid-Atlantic Ridge is a divergent boundary where plates are pulling apart, allowing rising molten rock to form new ocean floor.

⬇ OUR CHANGING PLANET. The Latin phrase *terra firma* implies planet Earth is solid and unchanging. However, Earth's surface has been anything but unchanging. Geologic evidence suggests that moving plates have collided and moved apart more than once over the course of the planet's long history. As the main map shows, the forces of change show no signs of stopping.

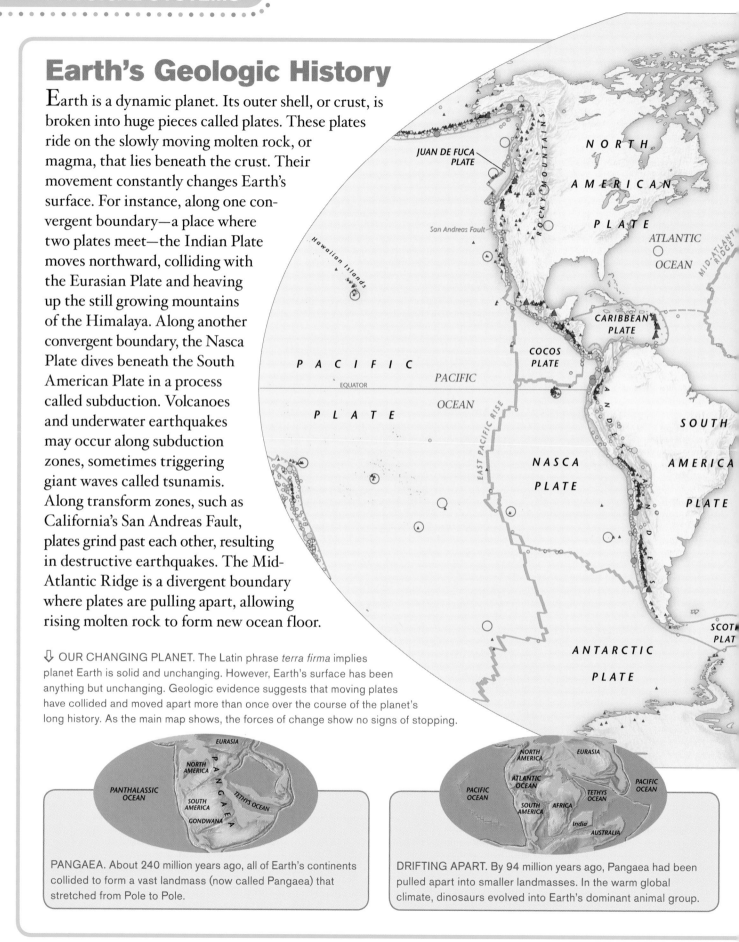

PANGAEA. About 240 million years ago, all of Earth's continents collided to form a vast landmass (now called Pangaea) that stretched from Pole to Pole.

DRIFTING APART. By 94 million years ago, Pangaea had been pulled apart into smaller landmasses. In the warm global climate, dinosaurs evolved into Earth's dominant animal group.

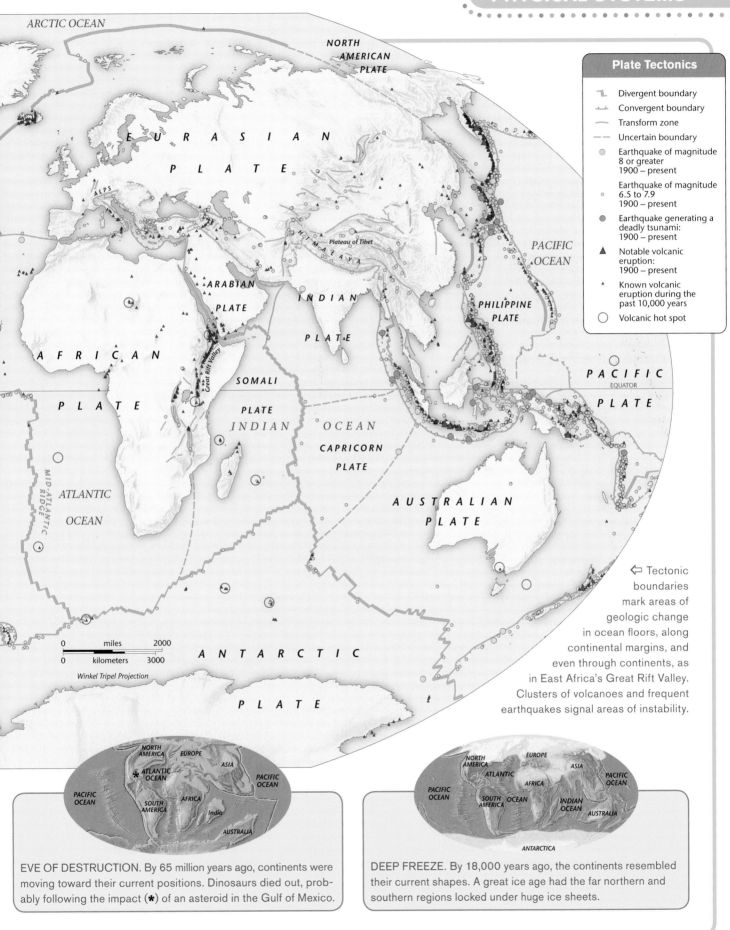

ARCTIC OCEAN

NORTH AMERICAN PLATE

EURASIAN PLATE

ALPS

ARABIAN PLATE

HIMALAYA

Plateau of Tibet

INDIAN PLATE

PACIFIC OCEAN

PHILIPPINE PLATE

AFRICAN PLATE

Great Rift Valley

SOMALI PLATE

INDIAN OCEAN

CAPRICORN PLATE

PACIFIC PLATE

EQUATOR

MID-ATLANTIC RIDGE

ATLANTIC OCEAN

AUSTRALIAN PLATE

ANTARCTIC PLATE

0   miles   2000
0   kilometers   3000

Winkel Tripel Projection

Plate Tectonics

- Divergent boundary
- Convergent boundary
- Transform zone
- Uncertain boundary
- ○ Earthquake of magnitude 8 or greater 1900 – present
- · Earthquake of magnitude 6.5 to 7.9 1900 – present
- ● Earthquake generating a deadly tsunami: 1900 – present
- ▲ Notable volcanic eruption: 1900 – present
- ▲ Known volcanic eruption during the past 10,000 years
- ○ Volcanic hot spot

← Tectonic boundaries mark areas of geologic change in ocean floors, along continental margins, and even through continents, as in East Africa's Great Rift Valley. Clusters of volcanoes and frequent earthquakes signal areas of instability.

NORTH AMERICA   EUROPE   ASIA

ATLANTIC OCEAN   PACIFIC OCEAN

PACIFIC OCEAN   AFRICA   SOUTH AMERICA   India   AUSTRALIA

EVE OF DESTRUCTION. By 65 million years ago, continents were moving toward their current positions. Dinosaurs died out, probably following the impact (✱) of an asteroid in the Gulf of Mexico.

NORTH AMERICA   EUROPE   ASIA

ATLANTIC   AFRICA   PACIFIC OCEAN

PACIFIC OCEAN   SOUTH AMERICA   OCEAN   INDIAN OCEAN   AUSTRALIA

ANTARCTICA

DEEP FREEZE. By 18,000 years ago, the continents resembled their current shapes. A great ice age had the far northern and southern regions locked under huge ice sheets.

Earth's Land and Water Features

The largest land and water features on Earth are the continents and the oceans, but many other features—large and small—make each place unique. Mountains, plateaus, and plains give texture to the land. The Rockies and the Andes rise high above the lowlands of North and South America. In Asia, the Himalaya and the Plateau of Tibet form the rugged core of Earth's largest continent. These features are the result of powerful forces within Earth pushing up the land. Other landforms, such as canyons and valleys, are created when weathering and erosion wear down parts of Earth's surface.

Dramatic features are not limited to the land. Submarine mountains, appearing like pale blue threads against the deep blue on the satellite map, rise from the seafloor and trace zones of underwater geologic activity. Deep trenches form where plates collide, causing one to dive beneath the other.

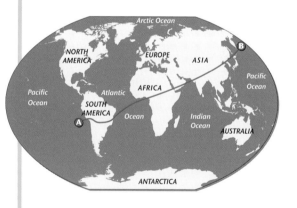

⇩ A SLICE OF EARTH. This cross section of Earth's surface extends from Lake Titicaca near South America's Pacific coast to the Kuril Islands in the northwestern Pacific Ocean. It shows towering mountains, eroded highlands, broad coastal plains, and deep ocean basins.

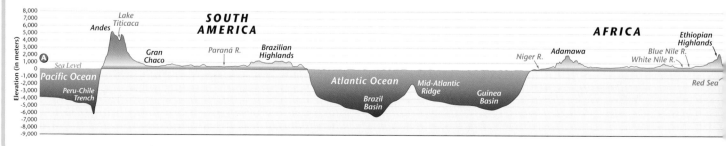

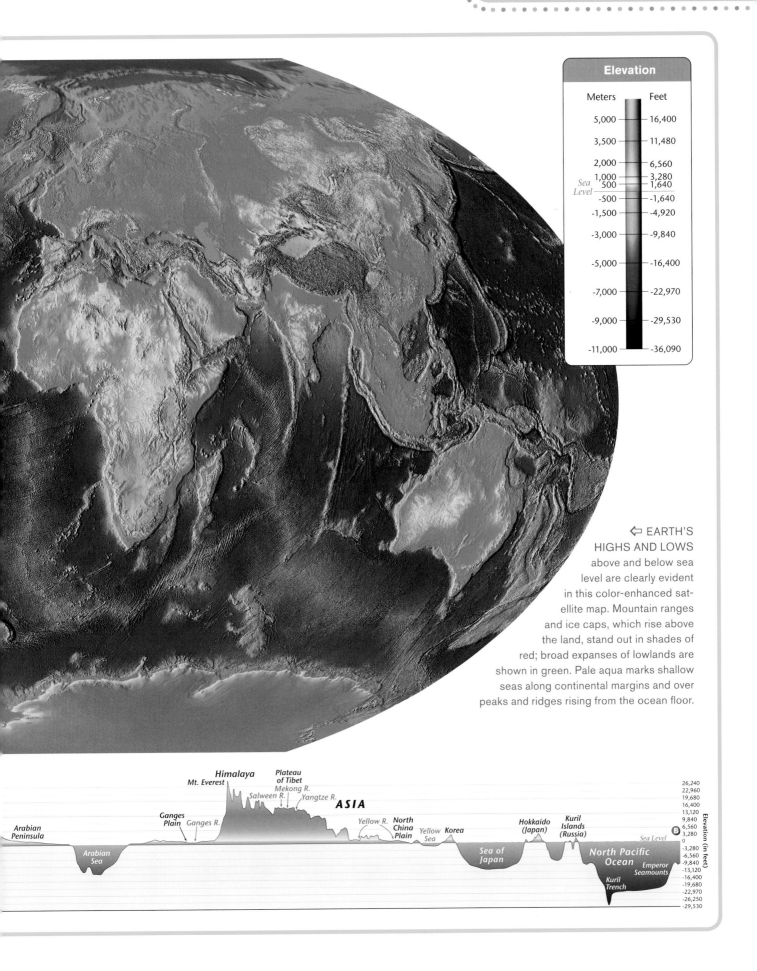

Elevation

Meters	Feet
5,000	16,400
3,500	11,480
2,000	6,560
1,000	3,280
500	1,640
Sea Level	
-500	-1,640
-1,500	-4,920
-3,000	-9,840
-5,000	-16,400
-7,000	-22,970
-9,000	-29,530
-11,000	-36,090

⇐ EARTH'S HIGHS AND LOWS above and below sea level are clearly evident in this color-enhanced satellite map. Mountain ranges and ice caps, which rise above the land, stand out in shades of red; broad expanses of lowlands are shown in green. Pale aqua marks shallow seas along continental margins and over peaks and ridges rising from the ocean floor.

Elevation (in feet)

26,240
22,960
19,680
16,400
13,120
9,840
6,560
3,280
0
Sea Level
-3,280
-6,560
-9,840
-13,120
-16,400
-19,680
-22,970
-26,250
-29,530

Ⓑ

Himalaya
Mt. Everest
Plateau of Tibet
Mekong R.
Salween R.
Yangtze R.
ASIA
Ganges Plain
Ganges R.
Yellow R.
North China Plain
Yellow Sea
Korea
Hokkaido (Japan)
Kuril Islands (Russia)
Arabian Peninsula
Arabian Sea
Sea of Japan
North Pacific Ocean
Emperor Seamounts
Kuril Trench

Earth's Climates

Climate is not the same as weather. Climate is the long-term average of conditions in the atmosphere at a particular location on Earth's surface. Weather refers to the momentary conditions of the atmosphere. Climate is important because it influences vegetation and soil development. It also influences people's choices about how and where to live.

There are many different systems for classifying climates. One commonly used system was developed by Russian-born climatologist Wladimir Köppen and later modified by American climatologist Glenn Trewartha. Köppen's system identifies five major climate zones based on average precipitation and temperature, and a sixth zone for highland, or high elevation, areas. Except for continental climate, all climate zones occur in mirror image north and south of the Equator.

↓ CLIMATE GRAPHS. A climate graph is a combination bar and line graph that shows monthly averages of precipitation and temperature for a particular place. The bar graph shows precipitation in inches and centimeters; the line graph shows temperature in degrees Fahrenheit and Celsius. The graphs below are typical for places in the climate zone represented by their background color. The seeming inversion of the temperature lines for Alice Springs and McMurdo reflects the reversal of seasons south of the Equator, where January is midsummer. The abbreviations for months are across the bottom of each graph.

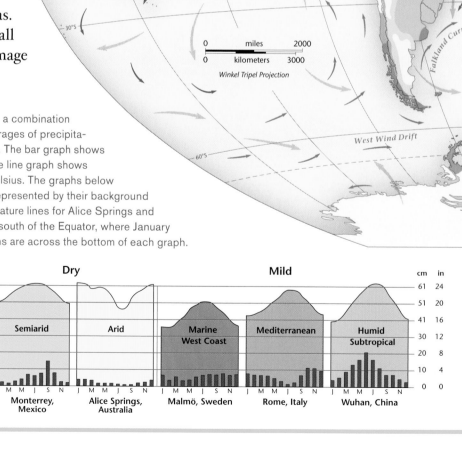

Tropical

Tropical Wet — Belém, Brazil

Tropical Dry — Kumasi, Ghana

Dry

Semiarid — Monterrey, Mexico

Arid — Alice Springs, Australia

Mild

Marine West Coast — Malmö, Sweden

Mediterranean — Rome, Italy

Humid Subtropical — Wuhan, China

°F °C
80 27
60 14
40 4
20 -7
0 -18
-20 -29
-40 -40

cm in
61 24
51 20
41 16
30 12
20 8
10 4
0 0

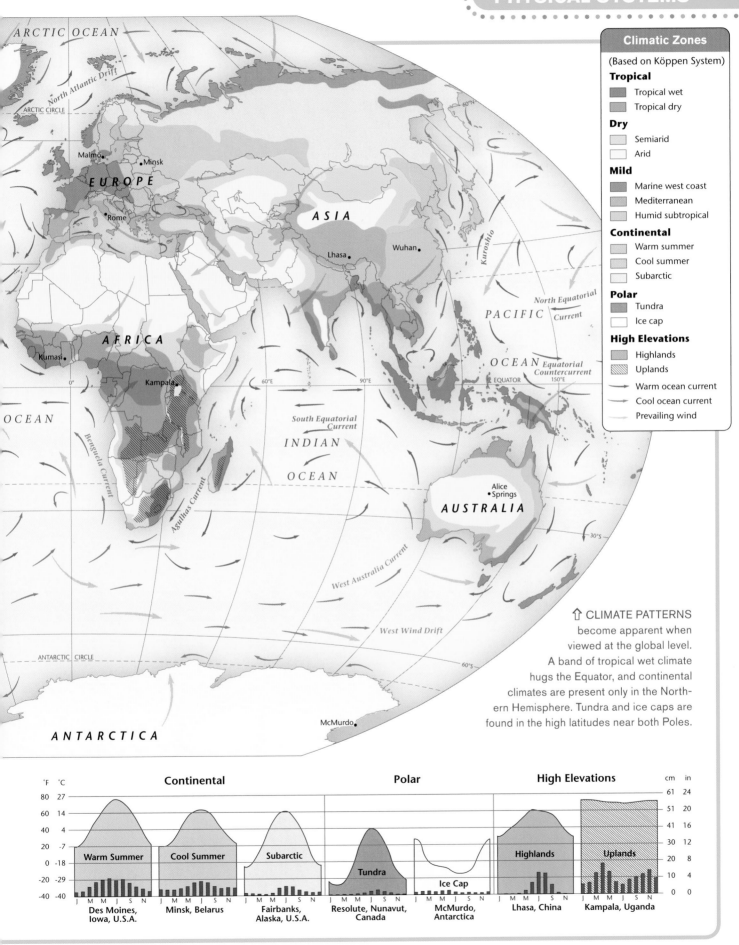

Climatic Zones

(Based on Köppen System)

Tropical
- Tropical wet
- Tropical dry

Dry
- Semiarid
- Arid

Mild
- Marine west coast
- Mediterranean
- Humid subtropical

Continental
- Warm summer
- Cool summer
- Subarctic

Polar
- Tundra
- Ice cap

High Elevations
- Highlands
- Uplands

→ Warm ocean current
→ Cool ocean current
→ Prevailing wind

⇧ CLIMATE PATTERNS become apparent when viewed at the global level. A band of tropical wet climate hugs the Equator, and continental climates are present only in the Northern Hemisphere. Tundra and ice caps are found in the high latitudes near both Poles.

ARCTIC OCEAN

North Atlantic Drift

ARCTIC CIRCLE

Malmö

Minsk

EUROPE

Rome

ASIA

Lhasa

Wuhan

Kuroshio

AFRICA

Kumasi

Kampala

PACIFIC

North Equatorial Current

OCEAN

Equatorial Countercurrent

EQUATOR

150°E

60°E

90°E

OCEAN

Benguela Current

South Equatorial Current

INDIAN

OCEAN

Agulhas Current

AUSTRALIA

Alice Springs

30°S

West Australia Current

West Wind Drift

ANTARCTIC CIRCLE

60°S

McMurdo

ANTARCTICA

60°N

0°

Continental

Warm Summer — Des Moines, Iowa, U.S.A.

Cool Summer — Minsk, Belarus

Subarctic — Fairbanks, Alaska, U.S.A.

Polar

Tundra — Resolute, Nunavut, Canada

Ice Cap — McMurdo, Antarctica

High Elevations

Highlands — Lhasa, China

Uplands — Kampala, Uganda

°F °C
80 27
60 14
40 4
20 -7
0 -18
-20 -29
-40 -40

cm in
61 24
51 20
41 16
30 12
20 8
10 4
0 0

J M M J S N

Climate Controls

The patterns of climate vary widely. Some climates, such as those near the Equator and the Poles, are nearly constant year-round. Others experience great seasonal variations, such as the wet and dry patterns of the tropical dry zone and the monthly average temperature extremes of the subarctic.

Climate patterns are not random. They are the result of complex interactions of basic climate controls: **latitude, elevation, prevailing winds, ocean currents, landforms,** and **location.**

These controls combine in various ways to create the bands of climate that can be seen on the world climate map on pages 20–21 and on the climate maps in the individual continent sections of this atlas. At the local level, however, special conditions may create microclimates that differ from those that are more typical of the region.

ELEVATION

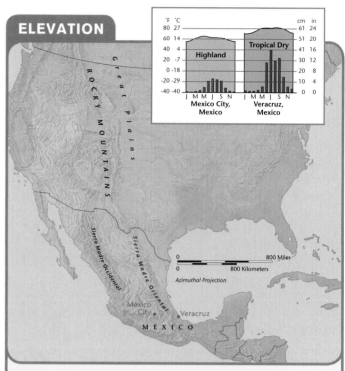

Not all locations at the same latitude experience similar climates. Air at higher elevations is cooler and holds less moisture than air at lower elevations. This explains why the climate at Veracruz, Mexico, which is near sea level, is warm and wet, and the climate at Mexico City, which is more than 7,000 feet (2,100 m) above sea level, is cooler and drier.

LATITUDE

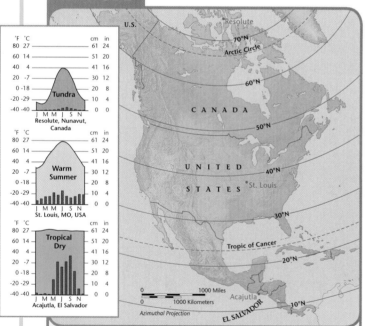

Energy from the sun strikes the Equator at a right angle. As latitude (distance north or south of the Equator) increases, the angle becomes increasingly oblique, or slanted. Less energy is received from the sun, and annual average temperatures fall. Therefore, the annual average temperature decreases as latitude increases from Acajutla, El Salvador, to St. Louis, Missouri, to Resolute, Canada.

LANDFORMS

When air carried by prevailing winds blows across a large body of water, such as the ocean, it picks up moisture. If that air encounters a mountain when it reaches land, it is forced to rise and the air becomes cooler, causing precipitation on the windward side of the mountain (see Portland graph). When air descends on the side away from the wind—the leeward side—the air warms and absorbs available moisture. This creates a dry condition known as rain shadow (see Wallowa graph).

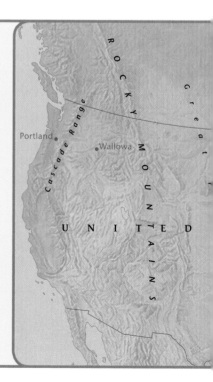

PREVAILING WINDS AND OCEAN CURRENTS

Earth's rotation combined with heat energy from the sun creates patterns of movement in Earth's atmosphere called prevailing winds. In the oceans, similar movements of water are called currents. Prevailing winds and ocean currents bring warm and cold temperatures to land areas. They also bring moisture or take it away. The Gulf Stream and the North Atlantic Drift, for example, are warm-water currents that influence average temperatures in eastern North America and northern Europe. Prevailing winds—trade winds, polar easterlies, and westerlies—also affect temperature and precipitation averages.

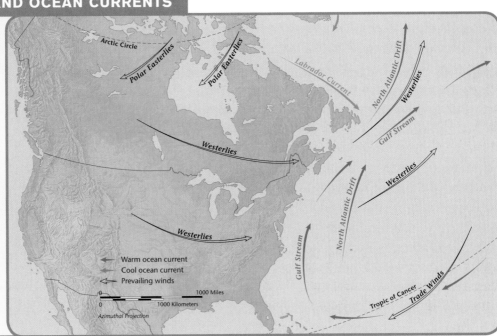

LOCATION

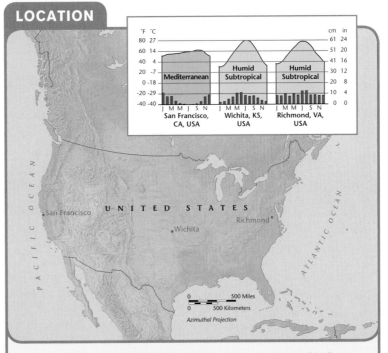

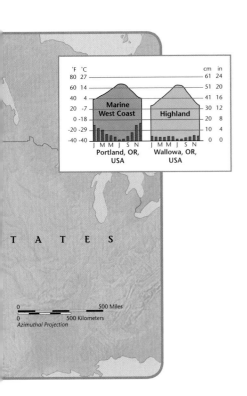

Marine locations—places near large bodies of water—have mild climates with little temperature variation because water gains and loses heat slowly (see San Francisco graph). Interior locations—places far from large water bodies—have much more extreme climates. There are great temperature variations because land gains and loses heat rapidly (see Wichita graph). Richmond, which is relatively near the Atlantic Ocean but which is also influenced by prevailing westerly winds blowing across the land, has moderate characteristics of both conditions.

Earth's Natural Vegetation

Natural vegetation is plant life that would be found in an area if it were undisturbed by human activity. Natural vegetation varies widely depending on climate and soil conditions. In rain forests, trees tower as much as 200 feet (60 m) above the forest floor. In the humid mid-latitudes, deciduous trees shed their leaves during the cold season, while coniferous trees remain green throughout the year. Areas receiving too little rainfall to support trees have grasses. Dry areas have plants such as cacti that tolerate long periods without water. In the tundra, dwarf species of shrubs and flowers are adaptations to harsh conditions at high latitudes and high elevations.

Vegetation is important to human life. It provides oxygen, food, fuel, products with economic value, even lifesaving medicines. Human activities, however, have greatly affected natural vegetation (see pages 28–29). Huge forests have been cut to provide fuel and lumber. Grasslands have yielded to the plow as people extend agricultural lands. As many as one in eight plants may become extinct due to human interference.

⇩ TYPES OF VEGETATION. Vegetation creates a mosaic of colors and textures across Earth's surface. Grasslands dominate in places where there is too little precipitation to support trees. In the wet conditions of the tropics, rain forests and mangroves flourish. Desert shrubs are adapted to dry climates, and tundra plants survive a short growing season. These photographs show some of the plants found in various vegetation regions. Each is keyed to the map by color and number.

TUNDRA

NORTHERN CONIFEROUS FOREST

TEMPERATE BROADLEAF FOREST

TEMPERATE GRASSLAND

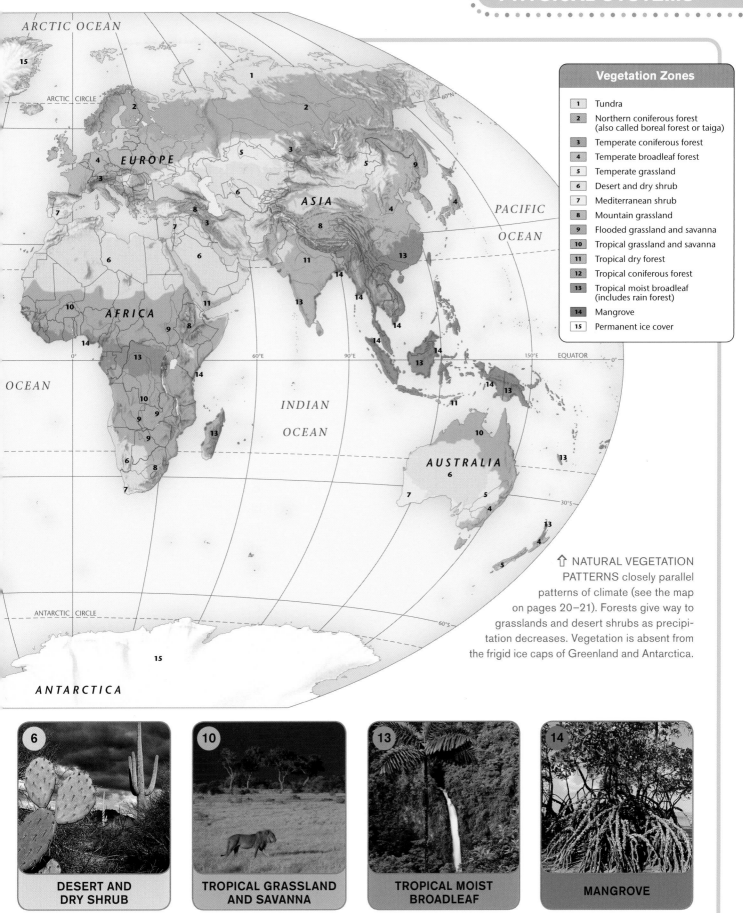

Vegetation Zones

1 Tundra
2 Northern coniferous forest (also called boreal forest or taiga)
3 Temperate coniferous forest
4 Temperate broadleaf forest
5 Temperate grassland
6 Desert and dry shrub
7 Mediterranean shrub
8 Mountain grassland
9 Flooded grassland and savanna
10 Tropical grassland and savanna
11 Tropical dry forest
12 Tropical coniferous forest
13 Tropical moist broadleaf (includes rain forest)
14 Mangrove
15 Permanent ice cover

⇧ NATURAL VEGETATION PATTERNS closely parallel patterns of climate (see the map on pages 20–21). Forests give way to grasslands and desert shrubs as precipitation decreases. Vegetation is absent from the frigid ice caps of Greenland and Antarctica.

6 DESERT AND DRY SHRUB

10 TROPICAL GRASSLAND AND SAVANNA

13 TROPICAL MOIST BROADLEAF

14 MANGROVE

Earth's Water

Water is essential for life and is one of Earth's most valuable natural resources. It is even more important than food. More than 70 percent of Earth's surface is covered with water in the form of oceans, lakes, rivers, and streams, but most of it—about 97 percent—is salty, and without treatment is unusable for drinking or growing crops. The remaining 3 percent is fresh, but most of this is either trapped in glaciers or ice caps or lies too deep underground to be tapped economically.

Water is a renewable resource. We can use it over and over because the hydrologic, or water, cycle purifies water as it moves through the processes of evaporation, condensation, precipitation, runoff, and infiltration. But like other natural resources, water is unevenly distributed on Earth. Some regions have large drainage areas, called watersheds, that provide ample water for the population living there, while other more densely populated regions have only limited supplies of freshwater (see map at right). In addition, careless use can diminish the supply of usable freshwater. Water may become polluted as a result of dumping from industries, runoff of fertilizers or pesticides from cultivated fields, and sewage released from urban areas.

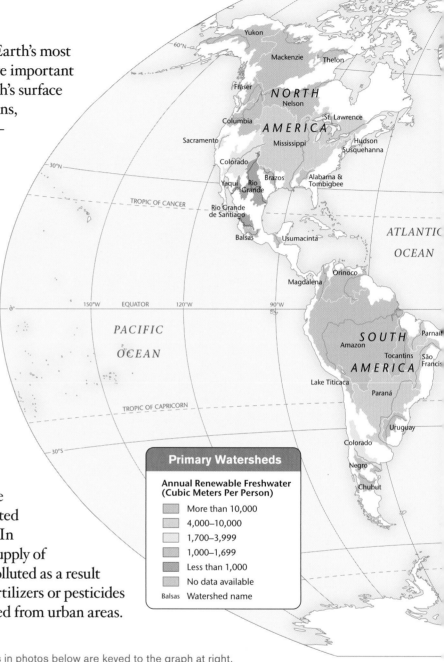

Primary Watersheds

Annual Renewable Freshwater
(Cubic Meters Per Person)

- More than 10,000
- 4,000–10,000
- 1,700–3,999
- 1,000–1,699
- Less than 1,000
- No data available

Balsas   Watershed name

WATER USES

Note: Color blocks in photos below are keyed to the graph at right.

DOMESTIC. In many less developed regions, women, such as these in Central America, haul water for daily use.

AGRICULTURAL. Irrigation has made agriculture possible in dry areas such as the San Pedro Valley in Arizona, shown here.

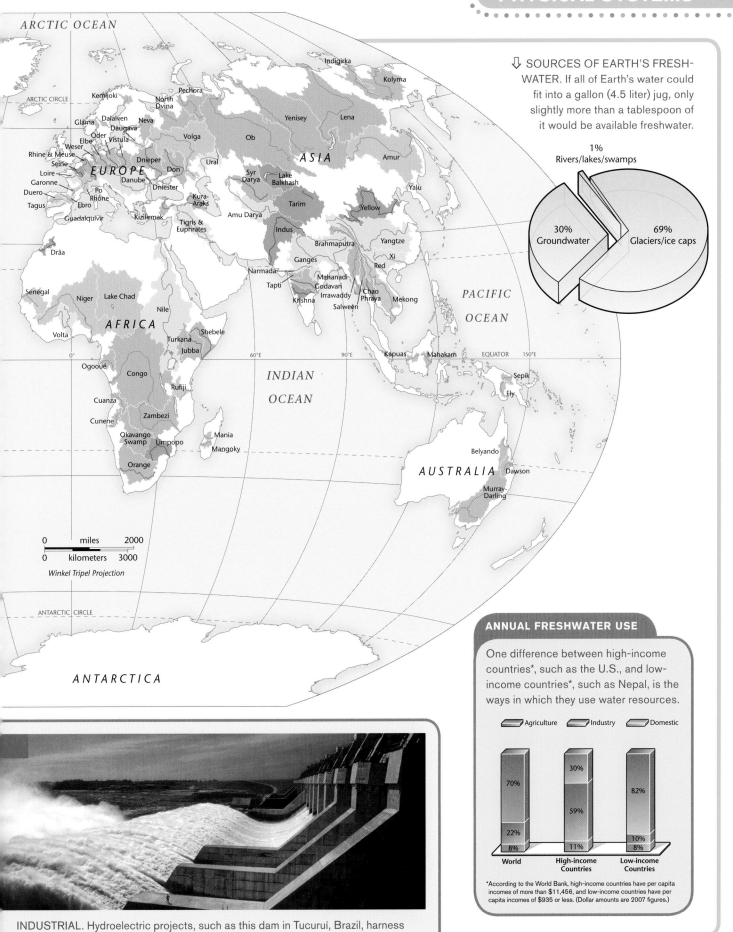

⇩ SOURCES OF EARTH'S FRESH-WATER. If all of Earth's water could fit into a gallon (4.5 liter) jug, only slightly more than a tablespoon of it would be available freshwater.

1% Rivers/lakes/swamps

30% Groundwater

69% Glaciers/ice caps

ARCTIC OCEAN

ARCTIC CIRCLE

EUROPE

ASIA

AFRICA

PACIFIC OCEAN

INDIAN OCEAN

EQUATOR

AUSTRALIA

ANTARCTIC CIRCLE

ANTARCTICA

0 miles 2000
0 kilometers 3000

Winkel Tripel Projection

ANNUAL FRESHWATER USE

One difference between high-income countries*, such as the U.S., and low-income countries*, such as Nepal, is the ways in which they use water resources.

◢ Agriculture ◢ Industry ◢ Domestic

	World	High-income Countries	Low-income Countries
Agriculture	70%	30%	82%
Industry	22%	59%	10%
Domestic	8%	11%	8%

*According to the World Bank, high-income countries have per capita incomes of more than $11,456, and low-income countries have per capita incomes of $935 or less. (Dollar amounts are 2007 figures.)

INDUSTRIAL. Hydroelectric projects, such as this dam in Tucuruí, Brazil, harness running water to generate electricity that powers industry.

Environmental Hot Spots

As Earth's human population increases, pressures on the natural environment also increase. In industrialized countries, landfills overflow with the volume of trash produced. Industries generate waste and pollution that foul the air and water. Farmers use chemical fertilizers and pesticides that run off into streams and groundwater. Cars release exhaust fumes that pollute the air and perhaps also contribute to global climate change.

In less developed countries, forests are cut and not replanted, making the land vulnerable to erosion. Fragile grasslands turn to deserts when farmers and herders move onto marginal land as they try to make a living. And cities struggle with issues such as water safety, sanitation, and basic services that accompany the explosive urban growth that characterizes many less developed countries.

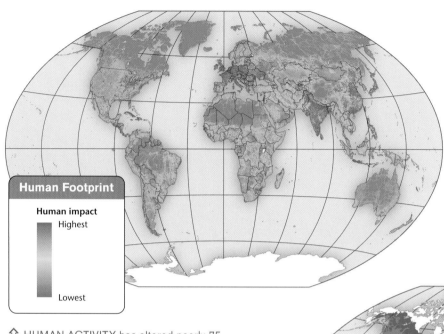

Human Footprint

Human impact

Highest

Lowest

⇧ HUMAN ACTIVITY has altered nearly 75 percent of Earth's habitable surface. Referred to as the "human footprint," this disturbance is greatest in areas of high population.

⇨ FORESTS PLAY a critical role in Earth's natural systems. They regulate water flow, release oxygen and retain carbon, cycle nutrients, and build soils. But humans have cut, burned, altered, and replaced half of all forests that stood 8,000 years ago.

Fragile Forests

Current frontier forest (large, relatively undisturbed forest)

Current non-frontier forest (degraded, regrown, replanted, plantation, or other forest areas)

Estimated extent of frontier forest 8,000 years ago

POLLUTED WATER is a part of life in this New Delhi slum where people bathe and wash clothes in the Yamuna River. More than 25 percent of the city's 16 million residents lack access to piped water, putting them at risk of water-borne diseases.

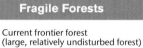

AN OIL SPILL off the coast of California closed this beach. Clean-up workers are attempting to reduce the amount of damage to the environment.

DEFORESTATION, resulting from logging, slash-and-burn agriculture, and forest fires, threatens Borneo's rain forests, once a rich storehouse of biodiversity.

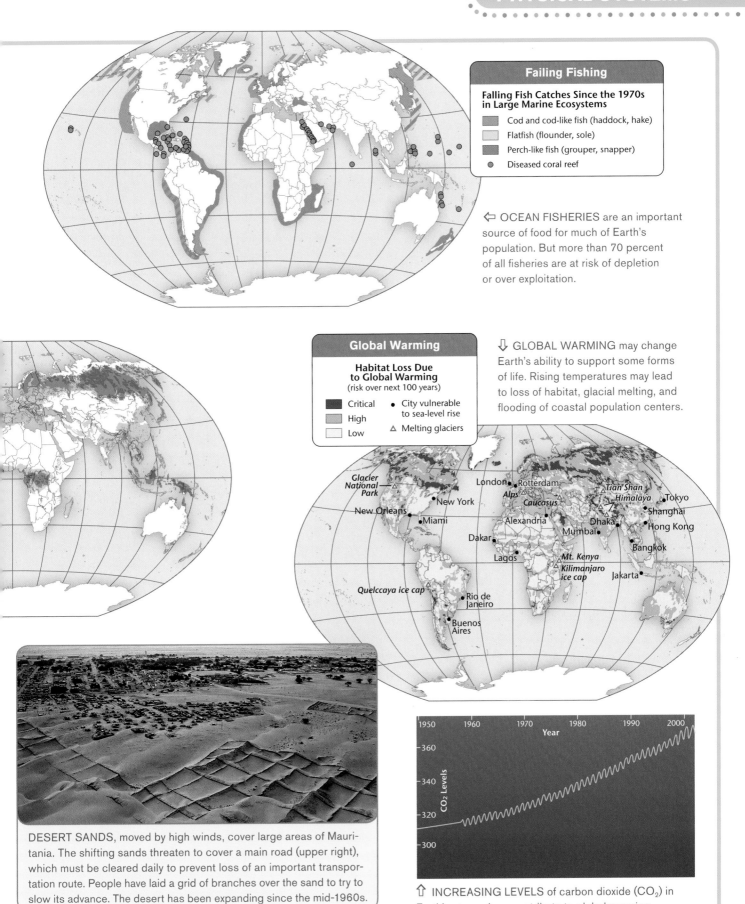

Failing Fishing

Falling Fish Catches Since the 1970s in Large Marine Ecosystems

- Cod and cod-like fish (haddock, hake)
- Flatfish (flounder, sole)
- Perch-like fish (grouper, snapper)
- Diseased coral reef

⇐ OCEAN FISHERIES are an important source of food for much of Earth's population. But more than 70 percent of all fisheries are at risk of depletion or over exploitation.

Global Warming

Habitat Loss Due to Global Warming
(risk over next 100 years)

- Critical
- High
- Low
- City vulnerable to sea-level rise
- △ Melting glaciers

⇓ GLOBAL WARMING may change Earth's ability to support some forms of life. Rising temperatures may lead to loss of habitat, glacial melting, and flooding of coastal population centers.

Glacier National Park · London · Rotterdam · Alps · Tian Shan · Himalaya · Tokyo · New York · Caucasus · Shanghai · New Orleans · Miami · Alexandria · Dhaka · Hong Kong · Dakar · Mumbai · Bangkok · Lagos · Mt. Kenya · Kilimanjaro ice cap · Jakarta · Quelccaya ice cap · Rio de Janeiro · Buenos Aires

DESERT SANDS, moved by high winds, cover large areas of Mauritania. The shifting sands threaten to cover a main road (upper right), which must be cleared daily to prevent loss of an important transportation route. People have laid a grid of branches over the sand to try to slow its advance. The desert has been expanding since the mid-1960s.

⇑ INCREASING LEVELS of carbon dioxide (CO_2) in Earth's atmosphere contribute to global warming.

The Political World

A map with the names and boundaries of countries shows the political world. Boundaries—some arrived at peacefully, others after years of conflict and war—carve up the land into 194 independent units, or countries, early in the 21st century. Boundaries are dynamic, meaning they change over time as political power shifts. For example, in 1990, West and East Germany became one country, removing a boundary that had separated them since 1949. In 1993 a new boundary divided Czechoslovakia into two separate countries, the Czech Republic and Slovakia.

Countries vary in size. Russia, the largest, stretches across northern Asia into Europe. Other countries are small enough to fit inside another country. For instance, the country of Lesotho lies entirely within the country of South Africa.

⇨ THE SCALE OF THIS MAP makes it impossible to name all 194 independent countries and their capital cities. For a complete listing, refer to pages 126–133 or use the place-name index and the political maps in each continent section.

⇨ VIEW FROM THE NORTH POLE. Ocean, not land, surrounds the area of the North Pole, so there are no political boundaries there. The Arctic Ocean, icebound much of the year, is part of the coastal waters of Earth's northernmost countries.

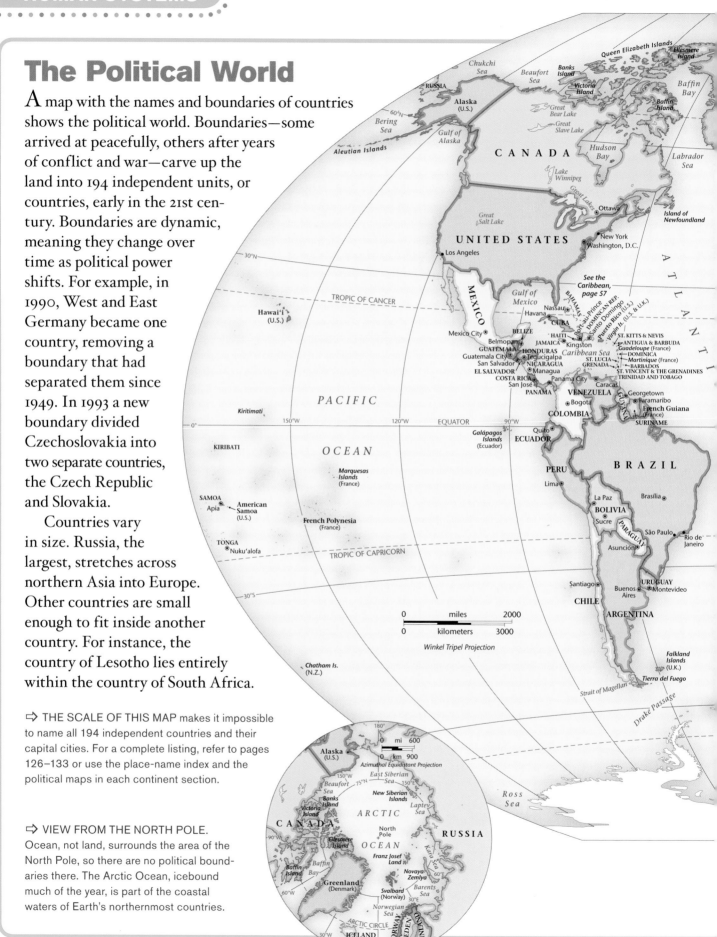

Cities

⊛ Country capital

• Urban area with more than 10 million people

ARCTIC OCEAN

Greenland Sea

enland
(mark)

Barents Sea

Svalbard
(Norway)

Franz Josef
Land

Severnaya
Zemlya

New Siberian
Islands

Kara
Sea

Novaya
Zemlya

Laptev Sea

East
Siberian
Sea

Norwegian
Sea

ARCTIC CIRCLE

ICELAND
Reykjavik

60°N

Bering
Sea

Sea of
Okhotsk

Kamchatka
Peninsula

R U S S I A

Sakhalin

Oslo

Helsinki

Lake
Baikal

Hokkaido

UNITED
KINGDOM

North
Sea

Stockholm

EST.

Astana ⊛

Ulaanbaatar ⊛

NORTH
KOREA

Honshu

JAPAN

Dublin

Copenhagen

Minsk

LATV.
LITH.

Moscow ⊛

Tokyo

IRELAND

DENMARK

Warsaw

BELARUS

KAZAKHSTAN

MONGOLIA

Pyongyang

Seoul

Osaka

London

Berlin

POLAND

Kiev

Beijing ⊛

SOUTH
KOREA

Kyushu

See Europe,
pp. 82-83

NETH.
BELG.

GERMANY
CZECH
REP.

UKRAINE

Aral
Sea

UZBEKISTAN

Bishkek

KYRGYZSTAN

C H I N A

FRANCE

SWITZ.

SLOVAKIA
HUNG.
ROMANIA

Black Sea

Tashkent

Dushanbe

TAJIKISTAN

Shanghai

30°N

Paris

SLO.

MOLD.

TURKMENISTAN

TAIWAN

ITALY

CRO.

SERBIA

GEORGIA
ARM.

Ashgabat

The People's Republic of China
claims Taiwan as its 23rd province.
Taiwan's government (Republic of
China) maintains that there are
two political entities.

PACIFIC

ores
rtugal)

PORTUGAL

Madrid

Rome

MONTENEGRO
ALBANIA

MACED.
BULGARIA

Istanbul

AZER.

Tehran ⊛

Kabul ⊛

Islamabad ⊛

Taipei

Lisbon

SPAIN

Athens

Ankara

Baghdad

Taiwan

Madeira Is.
(Portugal)

TUNIS

GREECE

TURKEY

SYRIA

IRAQ

IRAN

AFGHANISTAN

New
Delhi

NEPAL

Thimphu

Kathmandu

BHUTAN

OCEAN

Rabat

Algiers

CYPRUS
LEBANON
ISRAEL

Kolkata
(Calcutta)

BANGLADESH
Dhaka

Hanoi

Hainan

South
China
Sea

Philippine
Sea

Northern
Mariana
Islands
(U.S.)

MOROCCO

ALGERIA

LIBYA

EGYPT

Cairo ⊛

JORDAN

KUWAIT

BAHRAIN

QATAR

Riyadh

U.A.E.

Karachi

PAKISTAN

I N D I A

Mumbai
(Bombay)

MYANMAR
(BURMA)

Yangon

LAOS

Vientiane

THAILAND

Bangkok

CAMBODIA

VIETNAM

Luzon

Manila

PHILIPPINES

Guam
(U.S.)

MARSHALL
ISLANDS

Western
Sahara
(Morocco)

Tripoli

Muscat

Bay
of
Bengal

nary Is.
(Spain)

MAURITANIA

CAPE
VERDE

Nouakchott

SENEGAL

GAMBIA

MALI

NIGER

CHAD

SAUDI
ARABIA

Khartoum

ERITREA

YEMEN

Sanaa

OMAN

Arabian
Sea

Socotra
(Yemen)

Phnom Penh

Mindanao

PALAU

FEDERATED STATES
OF MICRONESIA

KIRIBATI

Dakar

Niamey

N'Djamena

Addis Ababa

DJIBOUTI

Colombo

SRI
LANKA

BRUNEI

Bandar Seri Begawan

Bamako

BURKINA
FASO

NIGERIA

Asmara

SUDAN

Male

MALDIVES

Kuala Lumpur

MALAYSIA

GUINEA-
BISSAU

Ouagadougou

Abuja

CENTRAL
AFRICAN
REPUBLIC

ETHIOPIA

SOMALIA

Mogadishu

60°E

90°E

Sumatra

SINGAPORE

Borneo

150°E

EQUATOR

0°

Bissau

GHANA
BENIN

GUINEA

Conakry

Lagos

Freetown

SIERRA
LEONE

Monrovia

Accra

Lomé

CAMEROON

Yaoundé

Bangui

UGANDA

Kampala

Rwanda

KENYA

Nairobi

I N D O N E S I A

Celebes

New
Guinea

PAPUA
NEW GUINEA

NAURU

SOLOMON
ISLANDS

Honiara

TUVALU

Yamoussoukro

CÔTE D'IVOIRE
(IVORY COAST)

LIBERIA

EQ.
GUINEA

GABON

Libreville

DEMOCRATIC
REPUBLIC
OF THE CONGO

CONGO

Kigali

BURUNDI

Bujumbura

Dodoma

Dar es Salaam

SEYCHELLES

Jakarta

Java

TIMOR-LESTE
(EAST TIMOR)

Port
Moresby

Brazzaville

Kinshasa

TANZANIA

INDIAN

Coral
Sea

VANUATU

FIJI
ISLANDS

CABINDA
(Angola)

Luanda

ANGOLA

ZAMBIA

MALAWI

Lilongwe

COMOROS

Moroni

Port-Vila

Suva

New Caledonia
(France)

Lusaka

Harare

Antananarivo

MAURITIUS
Port Louis

OCEAN

30°S

OCEAN

NAMIBIA

ZIMBABWE

MOZAMBIQUE

MADAGASCAR

Réunion
(France)

Windhoek

BOTSWANA

Gaborone

Pretoria (Tshwane)

SWAZILAND

A U S T R A L I A

Kerguelen Islands
(France)

eddell
Sea

Bloemfontein

Maputo

LESOTHO

Great
Australian
Bight

Canberra

Tasman
Sea

North
Island

Cape Town

SOUTH
AFRICA

ANTARCTIC CIRCLE

Tasmania

NEW
ZEALAND

Wellington

South
Island

Meridian of Greenwich (London)

A N T A R C T I C A

Ross Sea

60°S

30°W

0°

ATLANTIC
OCEAN

ANTARCTIC CIRCLE

30°E

60°W

Weddell
Sea

60°E

Ronne
Ice
Shelf

ANTARCTICA

INDIAN
OCEAN

90°W

West
Antarctica

South
Pole

East
Antarctica

90°E

⇨ **VIEW FROM THE SOUTH POLE.** Covered by ice, the continent of
Antarctica has been set aside by treaty for scientific research. It has no
permanent population and no political boundaries, although 7 countries claim
territory there and 19 operate year-round research stations (see map page 125).

120°W

Ross
Ice
Shelf

PACIFIC
OCEAN

Ross
Sea

120°E

0   mi   600

0   km   900

150°W

180°

150°E

Azimuthal Equidistant Projection

World Population

Late in 1999 the United Nations announced that Earth's population had surpassed six billion. Although more than 80 million people are added each year, the rate, or annual percent, at which the population is growing is gradually decreasing. Earth's population has very uneven distribution, with huge clusters in Asia and in Europe. Population density, the number of people living in each square mile (or square kilometer) on average, is high in these regions. For example, on average there are more than 2,680 people per square mile (1,035 per sq km) in Bangladesh. Other areas, such as deserts and Arctic tundra, have less than 2 people per square mile (1 person per sq km).

⇩ CROWDED STREETS, like this one in Shanghai, China, may become commonplace as Earth's population continues to increase and as more people move to urban areas.

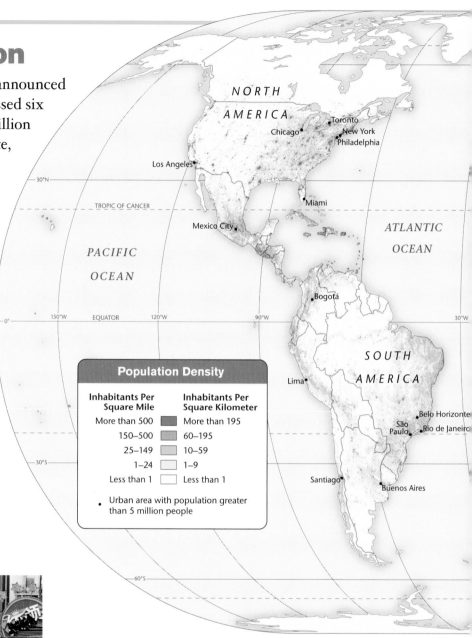

Population Density

Inhabitants Per Square Mile	Inhabitants Per Square Kilometer
More than 500	More than 195
150–500	60–195
25–149	10–59
1–24	1–9
Less than 1	Less than 1

• Urban area with population greater than 5 million people

POPULATION GROWTH OVER TIME

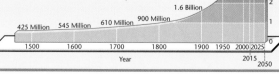

The population's rate of increase—the percent by which it changes each year—was slow until industrial and scientific discoveries in the 1800s brought improved health, a more reliable food supply, and other changes that improved the quality of life. Earth's population began to increase rapidly. Although the rate of increase has begun to slow, the United Nations projects that Earth's population will reach almost 9.2 billion by 2050.

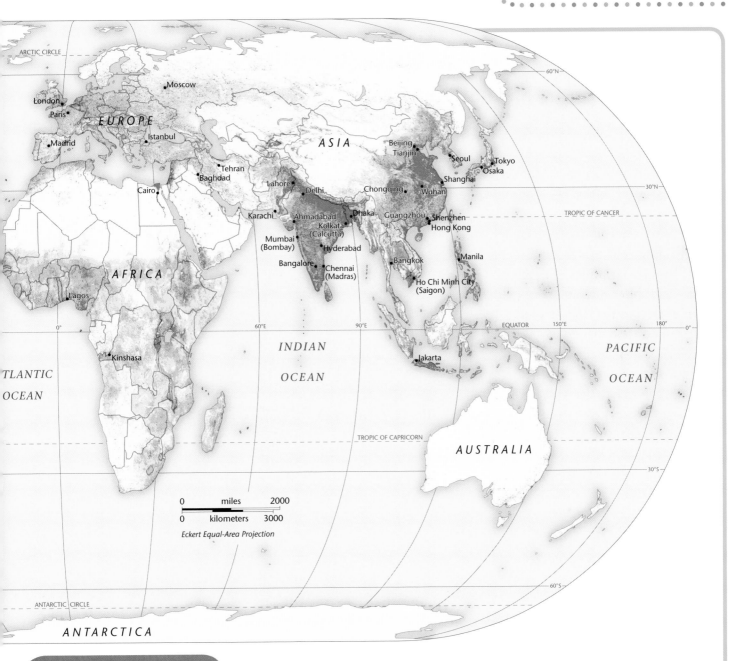

THREE POPULATION PYRAMIDS

A population pyramid is a special type of bar graph that shows the distribution of a country's population by sex and age. Italy has a very narrow pyramid, which shows that most people are in middle age. Its population is said to be aging, meaning the median age is increasing. The United States also has a narrow pyramid, but one that shows some growth due to a median age of about 37 years and a young immigrant population. By contrast, Nigeria's pyramid has a broad base, showing it has a young population. Almost half of its people are younger than 15 years.

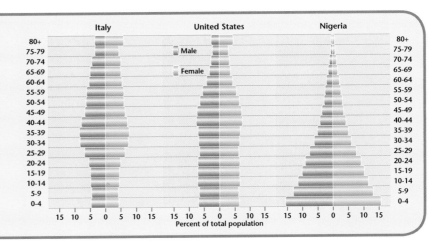

Italy | United States | Nigeria

Male
Female

| 80+ | 75-79 | 70-74 | 65-69 | 60-64 | 55-59 | 50-54 | 45-49 | 40-44 | 35-39 | 30-34 | 25-29 | 20-24 | 15-19 | 10-14 | 5-9 | 0-4 |

15 10 5 0 5 10 15   15 10 5 0 5 10 15   15 10 5 0 5 10 15
Percent of total population

World Refugees

Every day, people relocate to new cities, new states, even new countries. Most move by choice, but some people, called refugees, move to escape war and persecution that make it impossible to remain where they are. Such forced movement creates severe hardship for families who have to leave behind their possessions. They may find themselves in a new place where they do not speak the local language, where customs are unfamiliar, and where basic necessities, such as food, shelter, and medical care, are in short supply.

An agency of the United Nations, the Office of the High Commissioner for Refugees (UNHCR), is responsible for the safety and well-being of refugees worldwide and for protection of their rights. UNHCR works to find solutions to refugee situations through voluntary return to home countries, integration in a host country, or resettlement to another country.

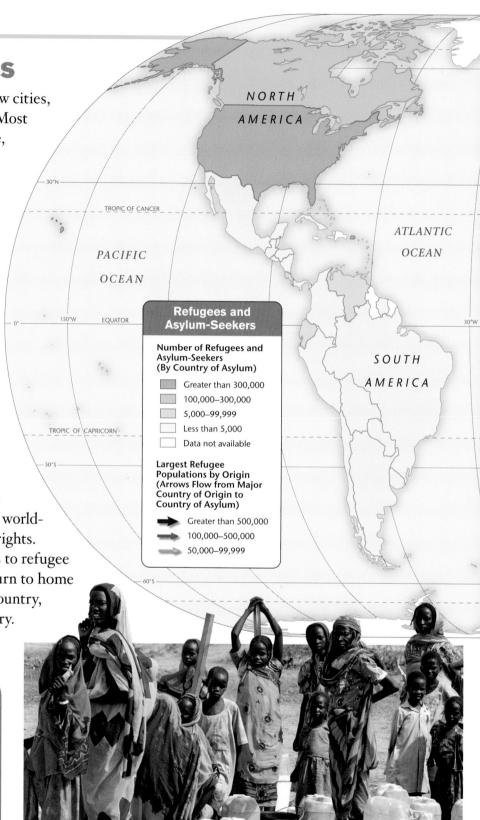

Refugees and Asylum-Seekers

Number of Refugees and Asylum-Seekers (By Country of Asylum)

- Greater than 300,000
- 100,000–300,000
- 5,000–99,999
- Less than 5,000
- Data not available

Largest Refugee Populations by Origin (Arrows Flow from Major Country of Origin to Country of Asylum)

- Greater than 500,000
- 100,000–500,000
- 50,000–99,999

REFUGEE HOSTING COUNTRIES

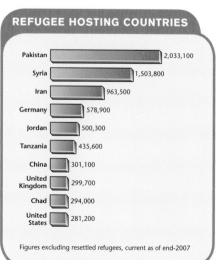

Country	Refugees
Pakistan	2,033,100
Syria	1,503,800
Iran	963,500
Germany	578,900
Jordan	500,300
Tanzania	435,600
China	301,100
United Kingdom	299,700
Chad	294,000
United States	281,200

Figures excluding resettled refugees, current as of end-2007

⇧ THOUSANDS OF SUDANESE refugees have been forced to leave their homes. Some, called internally displaced persons, or IDPs (above), remain in camps within Sudan. Others are refugees who have crossed into Chad to escape rebel forces attacking their villages.

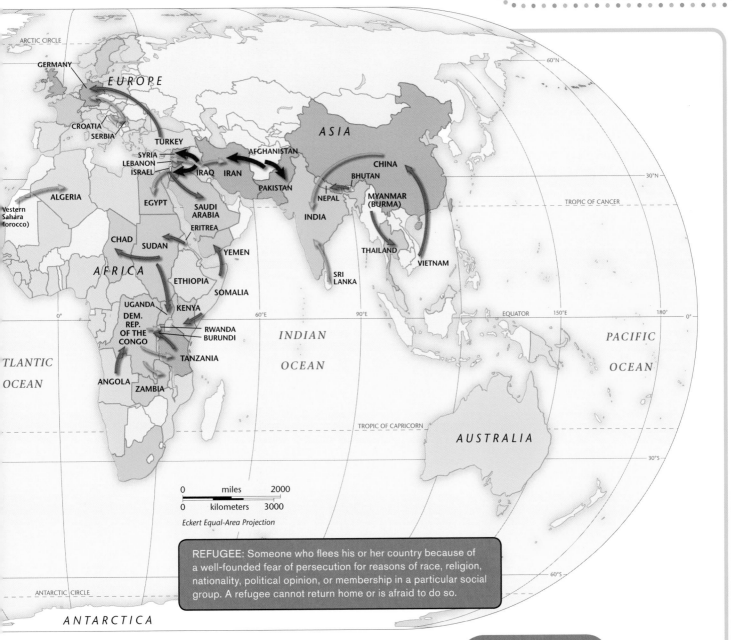

ARCTIC CIRCLE

60°N

GERMANY

EUROPE

ASIA

CROATIA
SERBIA

TURKEY

AFGHANISTAN

CHINA

30°N

SYRIA
LEBANON
ISRAEL

IRAQ   IRAN

BHUTAN

PAKISTAN

NEPAL

MYANMAR
(BURMA)

TROPIC OF CANCER

ALGERIA

EGYPT

SAUDI
ARABIA

INDIA

Western
Sahara
(Morocco)

ERITREA

CHAD

YEMEN

THAILAND

SUDAN

VIETNAM

AFRICA

ETHIOPIA

SRI
LANKA

SOMALIA

UGANDA
DEM.
REP.
OF THE
CONGO

KENYA

0°   60°E   90°E   EQUATOR   150°E   180°   0°

RWANDA
BURUNDI

INDIAN

PACIFIC

TANZANIA

OCEAN

OCEAN

ATLANTIC

OCEAN

ANGOLA

ZAMBIA

TROPIC OF CAPRICORN

AUSTRALIA

```
0       miles     2000
0     kilometers  3000
```
Eckert Equal-Area Projection

30°S

REFUGEE: Someone who flees his or her country because of
a well-founded fear of persecution for reasons of race, religion,
nationality, political opinion, or membership in a particular social
group. A refugee cannot return home or is afraid to do so.

60°S

ANTARCTIC CIRCLE

ANTARCTICA

⇧ MANY KURDS, a people who live mainly in Iraq and Turkey, fled to the remote
mountains of northern Iraq to escape spreading hostilities. This region, referred
to as Kurdistan, is the traditional homeland of these stateless people.

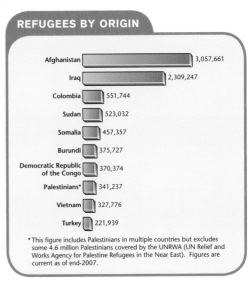

REFUGEES BY ORIGIN

Origin	Refugees
Afghanistan	3,057,661
Iraq	2,309,247
Colombia	551,744
Sudan	523,032
Somalia	457,357
Burundi	375,727
Democratic Republic of the Congo	370,374
Palestinians*	341,237
Vietnam	327,776
Turkey	221,939

*This figure includes Palestinians in multiple countries but excludes
some 4.6 million Palestinians covered by the UNRWA (UN Relief and
Works Agency for Palestine Refugees in the Near East). Figures are
current as of end-2007.

World Cities

Throughout most of history, people have lived spread across the land, first as hunters and gatherers, later as farmers. But urban geographers—people who study cities—have determined that by 2010 the percentage of people living in urban areas will be 50.6 percent. Urban areas include one or more cities and their surrounding suburbs. People living there are employed primarily in industry or in service-related jobs. Large urban areas are sometimes called metropolitan areas. In some countries, such as Belgium, almost all the population lives in cities. But throughout much of Africa and Asia, only about 40 percent of the people live in urban areas. Even so, some of the world's fastest growing urban areas are towns and small cities in Africa and Asia.

MOST POPULOUS URBAN AREAS

In 1950 New York was the larger of just two cities with a population of 10 million or more. By 2007 New York had dropped behind Tokyo, just slightly ahead of Mexico City and Mumbai (Bombay), India, in a list of 19 cities with populations of at least 10 million. By 2025, the list is projected to include 27 cities.

Cities with populations greater than ten million for the years:

▱ 1950   ▱ 1975   ▱ 2007   ▱ 2025

US/Canada   Latin America   Europe   Africa   Asia   Australia/ Oceania

⬆ CENTRAL TOKYO, viewed from the special observation deck of Tokyo Tower, 820 feet (250 m) above crowded city streets, contains a mix of modern high-rise and older low-rise buildings. With almost 13 million people, Tokyo is Japan's largest and most densely populated city and one of the world's largest cities.

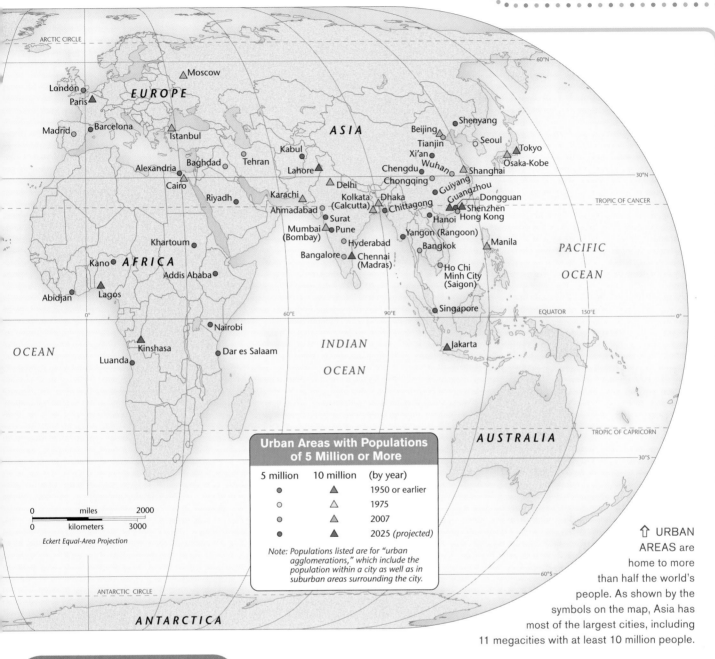

ARCTIC CIRCLE

EUROPE

London
Paris

Moscow

Madrid
Barcelona
Istanbul

ASIA

Kabul

Beijing
Tianjin

Shenyang

Seoul

Tokyo
Osaka-Kobe

Alexandria
Baghdad
Tehran

Xi'an
Chengdu
Chongqing

Wuhan
Shanghai

Cairo

Lahore

Riyadh

Karachi

Delhi

Guiyang
Guangzhou
Dongguan
Shenzhen
Hong Kong

Ahmadabad

Kolkata
(Calcutta)

Dhaka
Chittagong

TROPIC OF CANCER

Khartoum

Surat

Mumbai
(Bombay)

Pune

Hanoi

Yangon (Rangoon)

AFRICA

Kano

Addis Ababa

Hyderabad

Bangalore

Chennai
(Madras)

Bangkok

Manila

PACIFIC
OCEAN

Abidjan
Lagos

Ho Chi
Minh City
(Saigon)

Nairobi

Singapore

EQUATOR

OCEAN

Kinshasa

Dar es Salaam

INDIAN

Jakarta

Luanda

OCEAN

**Urban Areas with Populations
of 5 Million or More**

5 million	10 million	(by year)
●	▲	1950 or earlier
○	△	1975
●	▲	2007
●	▲	2025 (projected)

*Note: Populations listed are for "urban
agglomerations," which include the
population within a city as well as in
suburban areas surrounding the city.*

AUSTRALIA

TROPIC OF CAPRICORN

0   miles   2000
0   kilometers   3000

Eckert Equal-Area Projection

⇧ URBAN
AREAS are
home to more
than half the world's
people. As shown by the
symbols on the map, Asia has
most of the largest cities, including
11 megacities with at least 10 million people.

ANTARCTIC CIRCLE

ANTARCTICA

URBAN AND RURAL POPULATIONS

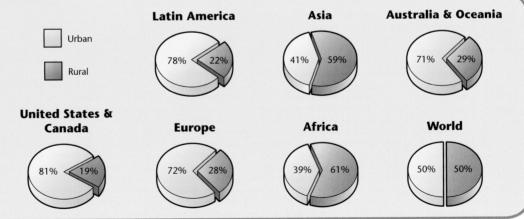

These graphs show the percentages of people living in urban and rural areas in the world and its various regions. Only Asia and Africa are pre-dominantly rural, although both are experiencing rapid urban growth. Asia, which had just one city of 10 million or more people in 1950, now has 11.

Urban
Rural

Latin America
78% 22%

Asia
41% 59%

Australia & Oceania
71% 29%

**United States &
Canada**
81% 19%

Europe
72% 28%

Africa
39% 61%

World
50% 50%

World Languages

Culture is all the shared traits that make different groups of people around the world unique. For example, customs, food and clothing preferences, housing styles, and music and art forms are all a part of each group's culture. Language is one of the most defining characteristics of culture.

Language reflects what people value and the way they understand the world. It also reveals how certain groups of people may have had common roots at some point in history. For example, English and German are two very different languages, but both are part of the same Indo-European language family. This means that these two languages share certain characteristics that suggest they have evolved from a common ancestor language.

Patterns on the world language families map (right) offer clues to the diffusion, or movement, of groups of people. For example, the widespread use of English, extending from the United States to India, reflects the far-reaching effects of British colonial empires. Today, English is the main language of the Internet.

About 5,000 languages are spoken in the world today, but experts think many may become extinct as more people become involved in global trade, communications, and travel.

⇨ THE GOLDEN ARCHES icon would help you identify this restaurant in Moscow even if you didn't know how to read the Cyrillic alphabet of the Russian language.

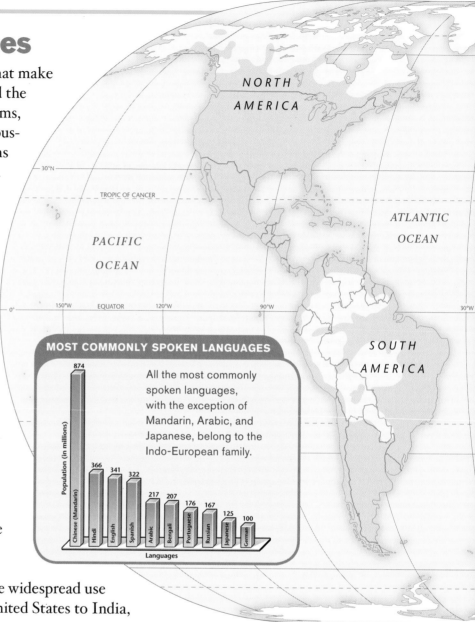

MOST COMMONLY SPOKEN LANGUAGES

All the most commonly spoken languages, with the exception of Mandarin, Arabic, and Japanese, belong to the Indo-European family.

Bar chart — Population (in millions) by Languages:
- Chinese (Mandarin): 874
- Hindi: 366
- English: 341
- Spanish: 322
- Arabic: 217
- Bengali: 207
- Portuguese: 176
- Russian: 167
- Japanese: 125
- German: 100

Map labels: NORTH AMERICA, SOUTH AMERICA, PACIFIC OCEAN, ATLANTIC OCEAN, 30°N, TROPIC OF CANCER, EQUATOR, 150°W, 120°W, 90°W, 30°W, 0°

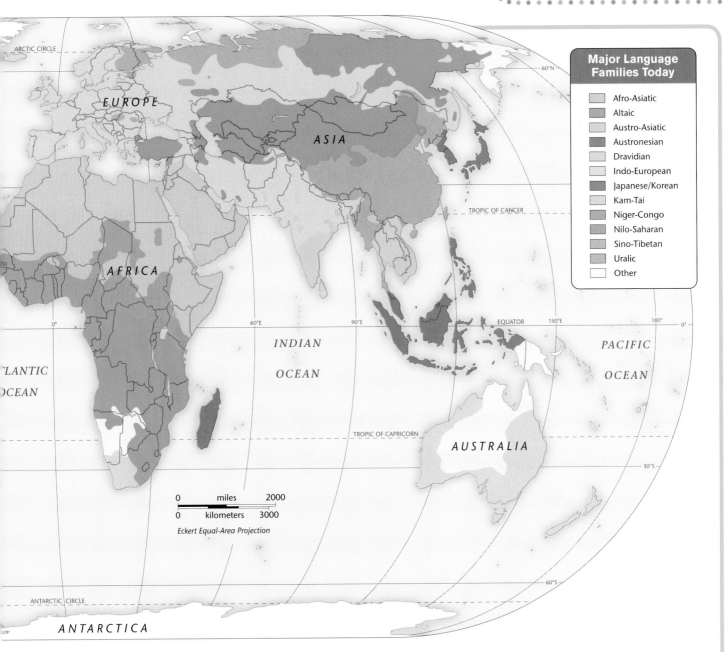

Major Language Families Today

- Afro-Asiatic
- Altaic
- Austro-Asiatic
- Austronesian
- Dravidian
- Indo-European
- Japanese/Korean
- Kam-Tai
- Niger-Congo
- Nilo-Saharan
- Sino-Tibetan
- Uralic
- Other

Eckert Equal-Area Projection

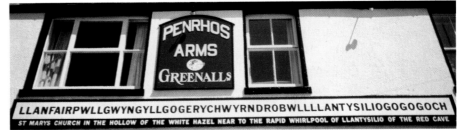

LLANFAIRPWLLGWYNGYLLGOGERYCHWYRNDROBWLLLLANTYSILIOGOGOGOCH

ST MARYS CHURCH IN THE HOLLOW OF THE WHITE HAZEL NEAR TO THE RAPID WHIRLPOOL OF LLANTYSILIO OF THE RED CAVE

⇑ SOME WORDS TELL A STORY, like this place name on the island of Anglesey in Wales. Welsh is an ancient Gaelic language. The alphabet may look familiar, but it has a few more letters than English and different pronunciations.

⇐ BENGALI, a language derived from ancient Sanskrit, appears on the walls of a women's health clinic in Kolkata (Calcutta), India. It is just one of the many languages that make up the Indo-European language family.

World Religions

Religious beliefs are a central element of culture. Religious beliefs and practices help people deal with the unknown. But people in different places have developed a variety of belief systems.

Universalizing religions, such as Christianity, Islam, and Buddhism, seek converts. They have spread throughout the world from their origins in Asia. Other religions, including Judaism, Hinduism, and Shinto—called ethnic religions—tend to be associated with particular groups of people and are concentrated in certain places. Some groups, especially indigenous, or native, people living in the tropical forests of Africa and South America, believe that spirits inhabit all things in the natural world. Such belief systems are known as animistic religions.

Places of worship are often a distinctive part of the cultural landscape. A cathedral, mosque, or temple can reveal much about the people who live in a particular place.

There are almost a million more Jews living in the United States than there are in Israel.

The United States also has almost as many Muslims as Jews, approximately 5 million each.

Christianity dominates in the Americas as a result of large-scale European colonization.

Dominant Religion

	Buddhism	Christianity	Hinduism	Islam (Muslim)	Judaism	Ethno-religionism
80% and above						
50%–79.9%						
Below 50%						

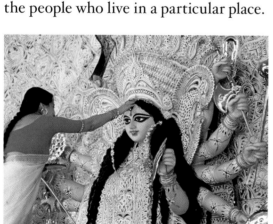

⇧ MOST OF HINDUISM'S 900 million followers live in India and other countries of South Asia. The goddess Durga (above) is regarded as Mother of the Universe and protector of the righteous.

⇩ JERUSALEM IS HOLY to Muslims, Christians, and Jews, a fact that has led to tension and conflict. Below, a Russian orthodox church is silhouetted against the Wailing Wall, while sunlight reflects off the Dome of the Rock mosque.

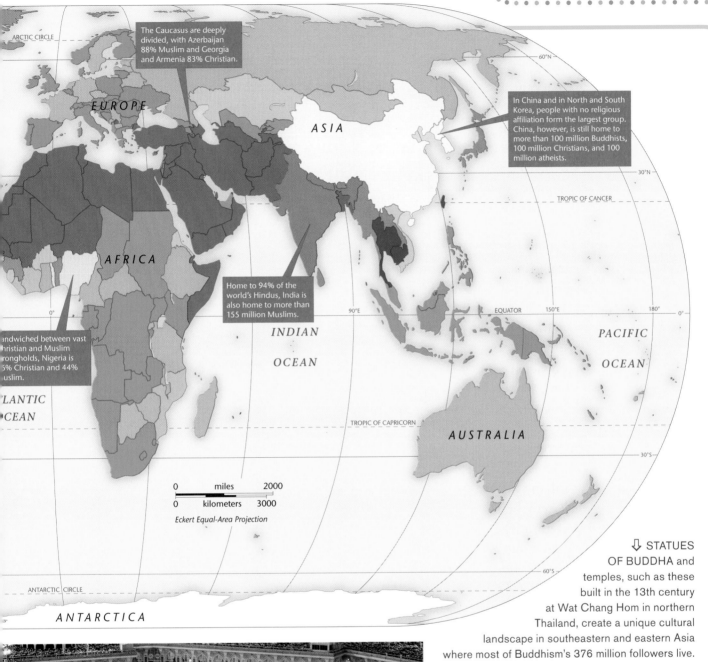

The Caucasus are deeply divided, with Azerbaijan 88% Muslim and Georgia and Armenia 83% Christian.

In China and in North and South Korea, people with no religious affiliation form the largest group. China, however, is still home to more than 100 million Buddhists, 100 million Christians, and 100 million atheists.

Home to 94% of the world's Hindus, India is also home to more than 155 million Muslims.

andwiched between vast hristian and Muslim rongholds, Nigeria is 5% Christian and 44% uslim.

ARCTIC CIRCLE

EUROPE

ASIA

AFRICA

ATLANTIC
OCEAN

INDIAN
OCEAN

PACIFIC
OCEAN

AUSTRALIA

ANTARCTIC CIRCLE

ANTARCTICA

60°N

30°N

TROPIC OF CANCER

EQUATOR

TROPIC OF CAPRICORN

30°S

60°S

0°   90°E   150°E   180°   0°

```
0        miles        2000
0      kilometers      3000
```
Eckert Equal-Area Projection

⇩ STATUES OF BUDDHA and temples, such as these built in the 13th century at Wat Chang Hom in northern Thailand, create a unique cultural landscape in southeastern and eastern Asia where most of Buddhism's 376 million followers live.

⇧ MUSLIM WORSHIPPERS surround the sacred Kaaba stone, which lies shrouded in black cloth at the center of the Grand Mosque in Mecca. Each year two million Muslims make a hajj, or pilgrimage, here to Islam's holiest shrine.

Predominant World Economies

Economic activities are the many different ways that people generate income to meet their needs and wants. Long ago most people lived by hunting and gathering. Today most engage in a variety of activities that can be grouped into three categories, or sectors: agriculture, as well as other primary activities such as fishing and forestry; industry, which includes manufacturing and processing activities; and services that range from banking and medicine to information exchange and e-commerce—buying and selling over the Internet. Services and industry, which generate higher incomes, are predominant in more developed countries, while many less developed countries still rely on agriculture.

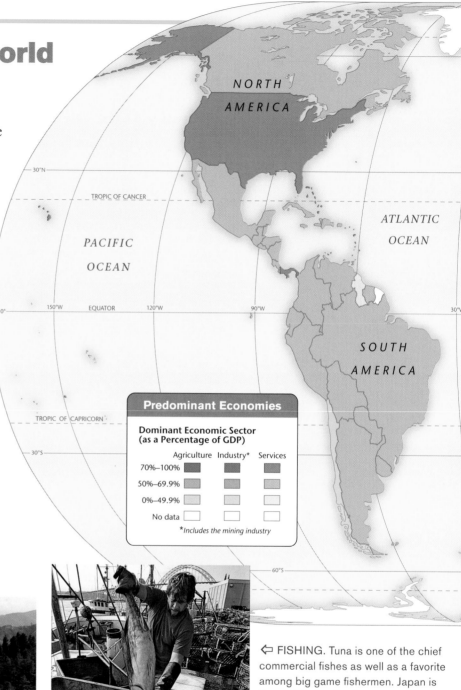

Predominant Economies

Dominant Economic Sector (as a Percentage of GDP)

	Agriculture	Industry*	Services
70%–100%			
50%–69.9%			
0%–49.9%			
No data			

Includes the mining industry

⇧ SUBSISTENCE AGRICULTURE. Many people in developing countries, such as these farmers in Bhutan, use traditional methods to grow crops for their daily food requirements rather than for commercial sale.

⇦ FISHING. Tuna is one of the chief commercial fishes as well as a favorite among big game fishermen. Japan is the world's leading harvester of tuna. Albacore, shown here, is one of the top commercial varieties.

⇨ LOGGING. Workers ready logs to float down the Columbia River in Washington State. Processing plants will turn the logs into paper products or cut them into lumber for the construction industry.

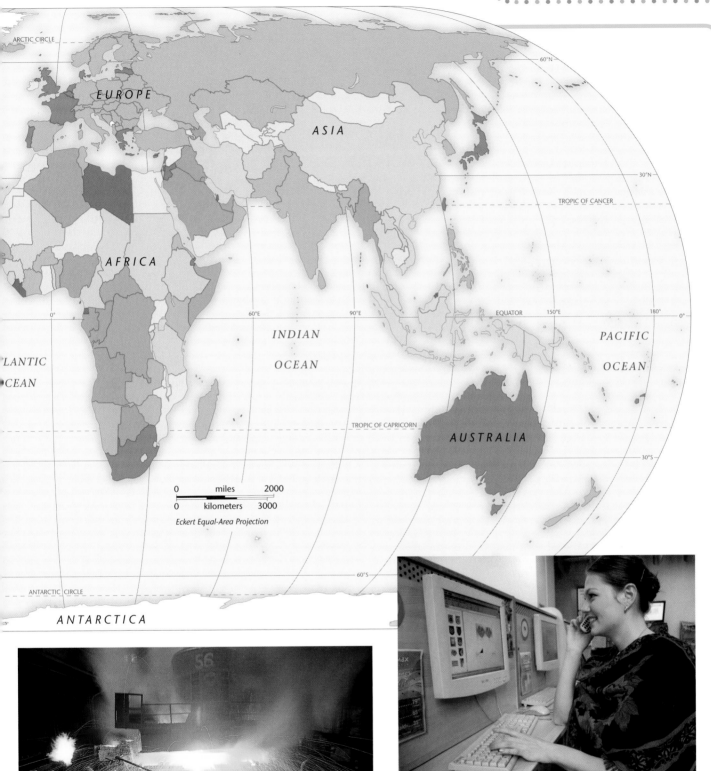

ARCTIC CIRCLE

EUROPE

ASIA

60°N

30°N

TROPIC OF CANCER

AFRICA

0°

60°E

90°E

EQUATOR

150°E

180°

0°

INDIAN

OCEAN

PACIFIC

OCEAN

ATLANTIC

OCEAN

TROPIC OF CAPRICORN

AUSTRALIA

30°S

0   miles   2000
0   kilometers   3000
Eckert Equal-Area Projection

60°S

ANTARCTIC CIRCLE

ANTARCTICA

⇧ MANUFACTURING. This mill in Slovakia processes raw materials—coal and iron ore—to make steel, which in turn is used by other industries to produce cars, machinery, and other kinds of manufactured goods.

⇧ COMMUNICATIONS AND THE INTERNET. A computer and mobile phone link this cybercafé in St. Petersburg, Russia, to the world. The Internet and new technologies have opened a whole new way of exchanging information. E-mail connects people in places near and far, while e-commerce allows them to buy and sell products without ever leaving home.

World Food

In 2008, the world's population surpassed 6.7 billion people—all needing to be fed. However, the productive potential of Earth's surface varies greatly from place to place. Some areas are good for growing crops; some are best used for grazing animals; but large expanses have little or no agricultural potential at all. Grains, such as rice, corn, and wheat, are the main sources of food calories for most of the world's people.

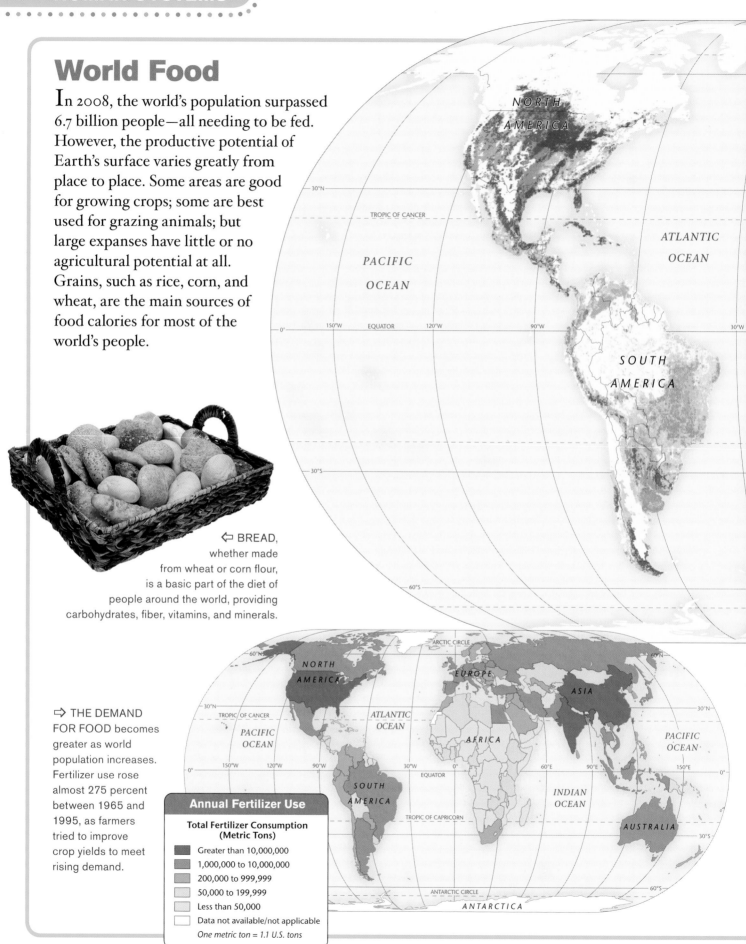

⇦ BREAD, whether made from wheat or corn flour, is a basic part of the diet of people around the world, providing carbohydrates, fiber, vitamins, and minerals.

⇨ THE DEMAND FOR FOOD becomes greater as world population increases. Fertilizer use rose almost 275 percent between 1965 and 1995, as farmers tried to improve crop yields to meet rising demand.

Annual Fertilizer Use

Total Fertilizer Consumption (Metric Tons)
- Greater than 10,000,000
- 1,000,000 to 10,000,000
- 200,000 to 999,999
- 50,000 to 199,999
- Less than 50,000
- Data not available/not applicable

One metric ton = 1.1 U.S. tons

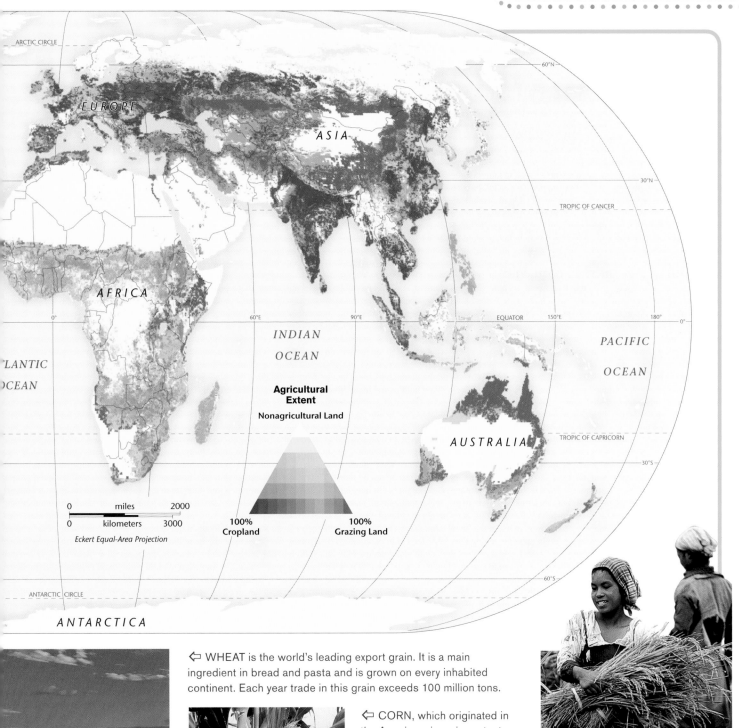

ARCTIC CIRCLE

60°N

EUROPE

ASIA

30°N

TROPIC OF CANCER

0°   60°E   90°E   EQUATOR   150°E   180°   0°

AFRICA

INDIAN
OCEAN

PACIFIC
OCEAN

**Agricultural
Extent**

Nonagricultural Land

ATLANTIC
OCEAN

AUSTRALIA

TROPIC OF CAPRICORN

30°S

**100%
Cropland**

**100%
Grazing Land**

| 0 | miles | 2000 |
| 0 | kilometers | 3000 |

Eckert Equal-Area Projection

60°S

ANTARCTIC CIRCLE

ANTARCTICA

⇦ WHEAT is the world's leading export grain. It is a main
ingredient in bread and pasta and is grown on every inhabited
continent. Each year trade in this grain exceeds 100 million tons.

⇦ CORN, which originated in
the Americas, is an important
food grain for both people
and livestock.

⇨ RICE is an important staple
food crop, especially in eastern
and southern Asia. Although China
produces about one-third of the
world's rice, it is also a major im-
porter of rice to feed its population
of more than a billion people.

World Energy & Mineral Resources

Beginning in the 19th century, as the Industrial Revolution spread across Europe and around the world, the demand for energy and mineral resources skyrocketed. Fossil fuels—first coal, then oil—provided the energy that kept the wheels of industry turning. Minerals such as iron ore (essential for the production of steel) and copper (used for electrical wiring) became increasingly important.

Energy and minerals, like all nonrenewable resources, are in limited supply and are unevenly distributed. Countries with major deposits play an important role in the global economy. For example, the Organization of Petroleum Exporting Countries (OPEC) influences the world supply of oil and, therefore, fuel prices.

⇩ RENEWABLE ENERGY, including energy from the sun, wind, running water, and heat from within Earth, is an important alternative to fossil fuels, supplies of which are rapidly being depleted.

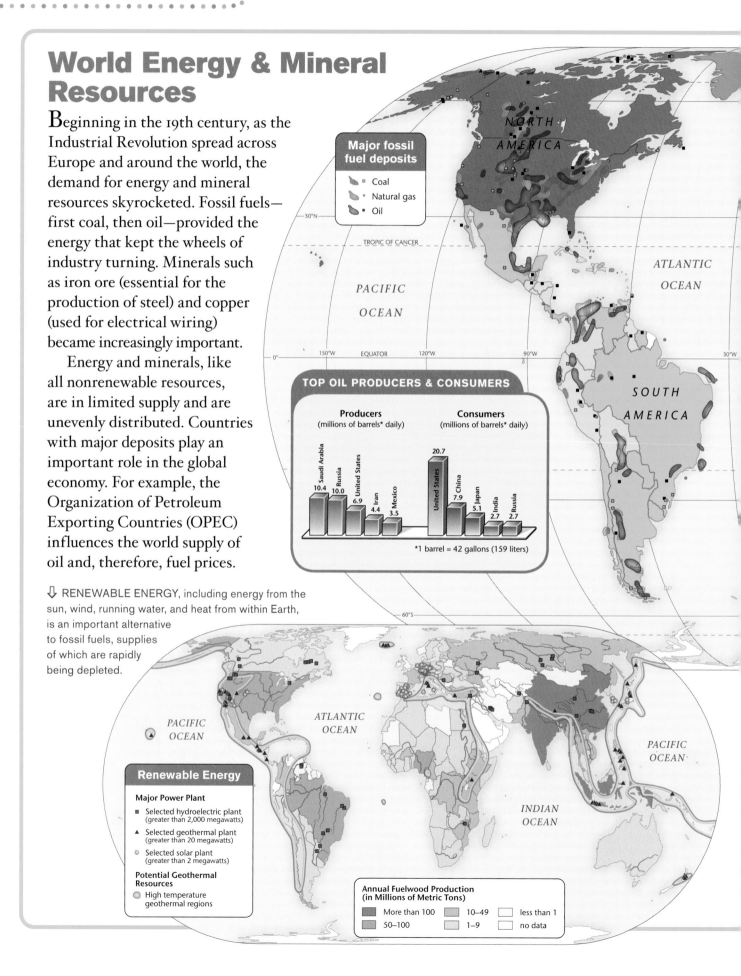

Major fossil fuel deposits
- Coal
- Natural gas
- Oil

TOP OIL PRODUCERS & CONSUMERS

Producers (millions of barrels* daily)
- Saudi Arabia 10.4
- Russia 10.0
- United States 6.9
- Iran 4.4
- Mexico 3.5

Consumers (millions of barrels* daily)
- United States 20.7
- China 7.9
- Japan 5.1
- India 2.7
- Russia 2.7

*1 barrel = 42 gallons (159 liters)

Renewable Energy

Major Power Plant
- ■ Selected hydroelectric plant (greater than 2,000 megawatts)
- ▲ Selected geothermal plant (greater than 20 megawatts)
- ✷ Selected solar plant (greater than 2 megawatts)

Potential Geothermal Resources
- High temperature geothermal regions

Annual Fuelwood Production (in Millions of Metric Tons)
- More than 100
- 50–100
- 10–49
- 1–9
- less than 1
- no data

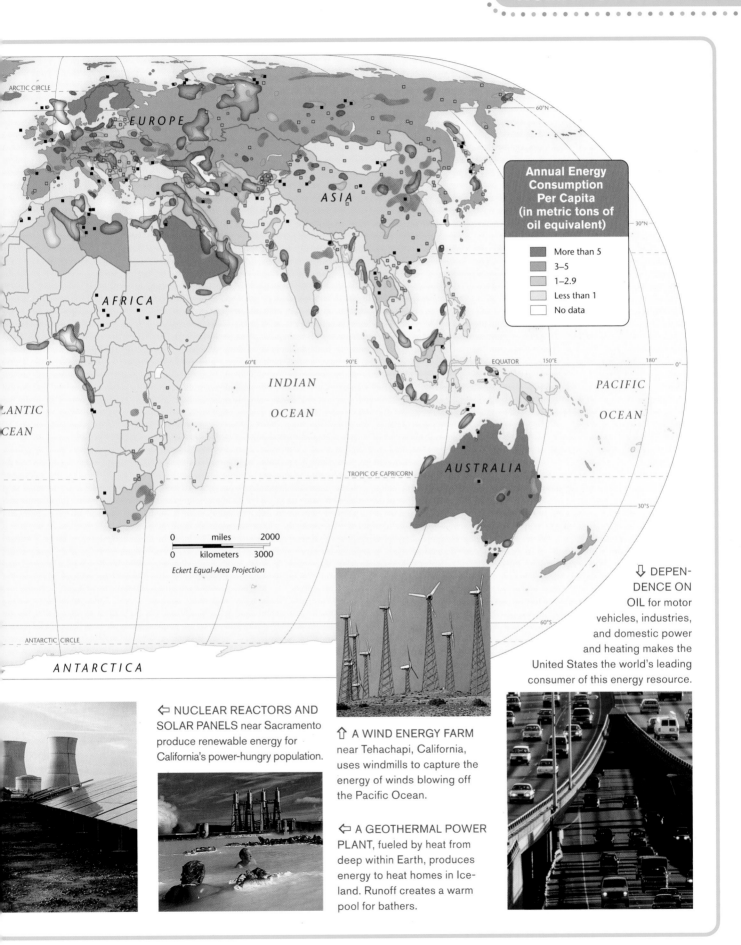

ARCTIC CIRCLE

EUROPE

ASIA

AFRICA

ATLANTIC
OCEAN

INDIAN
OCEAN

PACIFIC
OCEAN

EQUATOR

TROPIC OF CAPRICORN

AUSTRALIA

ANTARCTIC CIRCLE

ANTARCTICA

60°N

30°N

0° 60°E 90°E 150°E 180°

30°S

60°S

Annual Energy Consumption Per Capita (in metric tons of oil equivalent)

- More than 5
- 3–5
- 1–2.9
- Less than 1
- No data

0 miles 2000
0 kilometers 3000

Eckert Equal-Area Projection

⬇ DEPEN-
DENCE ON
OIL for motor
vehicles, industries,
and domestic power
and heating makes the
United States the world's leading
consumer of this energy resource.

⬅ NUCLEAR REACTORS AND
SOLAR PANELS near Sacramento
produce renewable energy for
California's power-hungry population.

⬆ A WIND ENERGY FARM
near Tehachapi, California,
uses windmills to capture the
energy of winds blowing off
the Pacific Ocean.

⬅ A GEOTHERMAL POWER
PLANT, fueled by heat from
deep within Earth, produces
energy to heat homes in Iceland. Runoff creates a warm
pool for bathers.

Globalization

The close of the 20th century saw a technology revolution that changed the way people and countries relate to each other. This revolution in technology is part of a process known as globalization.

Globalization refers to the complex network of interconnections linking people, companies, and places together without regard for national boundaries. Although it began when countries became increasingly active in international trade, the process of globalization has gained momentum in recent years.

Improvements in communications and transportation have enabled companies to employ workers in distant countries. Some workers make clothing; some perform accounting tasks; and others work in call centers answering inquiries about product services. Technology also allows banking transactions to take place faster and over greater distances than ever before. Companies that have offices and conduct business in multiple countries around the world are called transnational companies.

One important aspect of today's global communications system is the Internet, a vast system of computer networks that allows people to access information and to communicate around the world in just seconds. While most Internet users are in North America and Europe, ideas and images travel over the Internet to distant places, introducing change and making places more and more alike.

⇨ MAQUILADORAS, foreign-owned assembly plants located in Mexico, import parts and materials duty-free to produce finished goods for consumers in the U.S. and around the world. Maquiladoras, such as this one in Ciudad Juarez, employ a large work force.

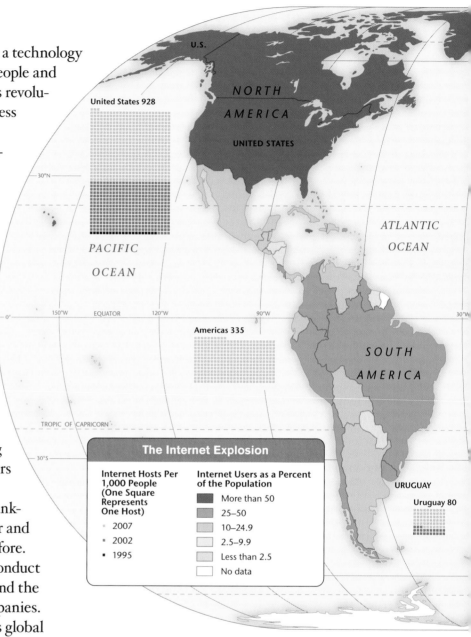

United States 928

Americas 335

URUGUAY

Uruguay 80

The Internet Explosion

Internet Hosts Per 1,000 People (One Square Represents One Host)
- 2007
- 2002
- 1995

Internet Users as a Percent of the Population
- More than 50
- 25–50
- 10–24.9
- 2.5–9.9
- Less than 2.5
- No data

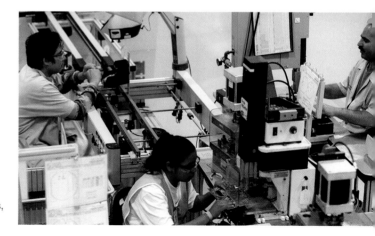

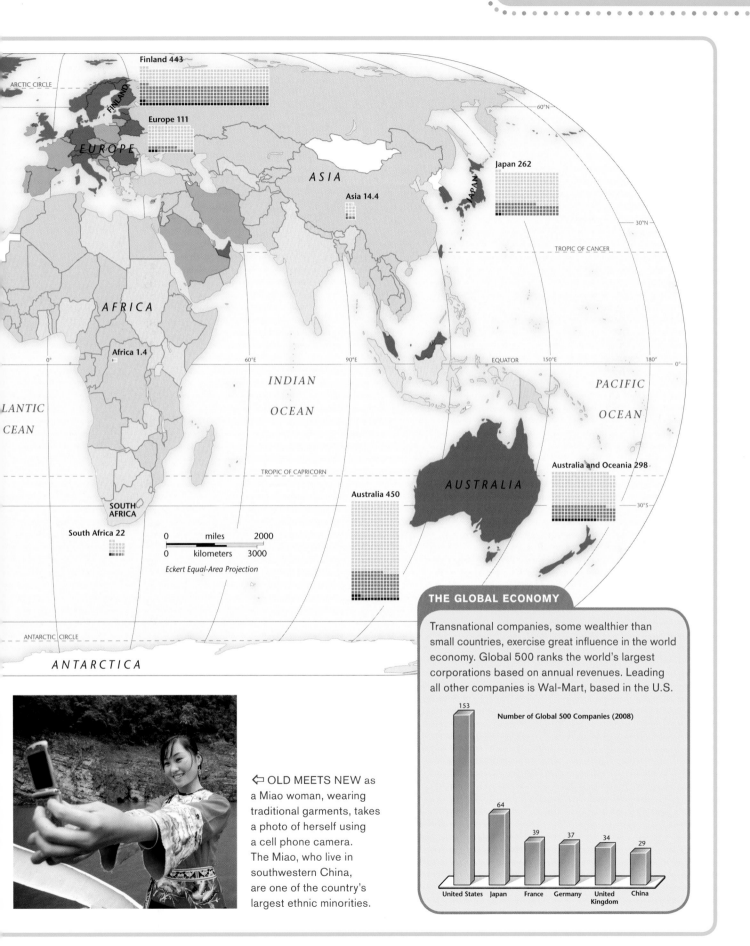

Finland 443

ARCTIC CIRCLE

FINLAND

Europe 111

EUROPE

ASIA

Japan 262

JAPAN

Asia 14.4

60°N

30°N

TROPIC OF CANCER

AFRICA

Africa 1.4

0°   60°E   90°E

INDIAN

OCEAN

EQUATOR   150°E   180°   0°

PACIFIC

OCEAN

LANTIC
CEAN

Australia and Oceania 298

TROPIC OF CAPRICORN

AUSTRALIA

30°S

SOUTH
AFRICA

Australia 450

South Africa 22

0   miles   2000
0   kilometers   3000

Eckert Equal-Area Projection

THE GLOBAL ECONOMY

ANTARCTIC CIRCLE

ANTARCTICA

Transnational companies, some wealthier than
small countries, exercise great influence in the world
economy. Global 500 ranks the world's largest
corporations based on annual revenues. Leading
all other companies is Wal-Mart, based in the U.S.

Number of Global 500 Companies (2008)

153 — United States
64 — Japan
39 — France
37 — Germany
34 — United Kingdom
29 — China

⬅ OLD MEETS NEW as
a Miao woman, wearing
traditional garments, takes
a photo of herself using
a cell phone camera.
The Miao, who live in
southwestern China,
are one of the country's
largest ethnic minorities.

Cultural Diffusion

In the past, when groups of people lived in relative isolation, cultures varied widely from place to place. Customs, styles, and preferences were handed down from one generation to the next.

Today, as a result of high-speed communication, trade, and travel, cultures all around the world are encountering and adopting new ideas. New customs, clothing and music trends, food habits, and lifestyles are being introduced into cultures everywhere at almost the same time. Some people are concerned that this trend in popular culture may result in a loss of cultural distinctiveness that makes places unique. For example, fast food chains once found only in the United States can now be seen in major cities around the world. And denim jeans, once a distinctively American clothing style, are worn by young people everywhere in place of more traditional clothing.

An important key to the spread, or diffusion, of popular culture is the increasing contact between people and places around the world. Cellular telephones, satellite television, and cyber-cafés have opened the world to styles and trends popular in Western countries. And tourists, traveling to places that were once considered remote and isolated, carry with them new ideas and fashions that become catalysts for bringing about cultural change.

⇨ THE INFLUENCE OF IMMIGRANT CULTURES on the American landscape is evident in ethnic communities such as Chinatown in the heart of New York City.

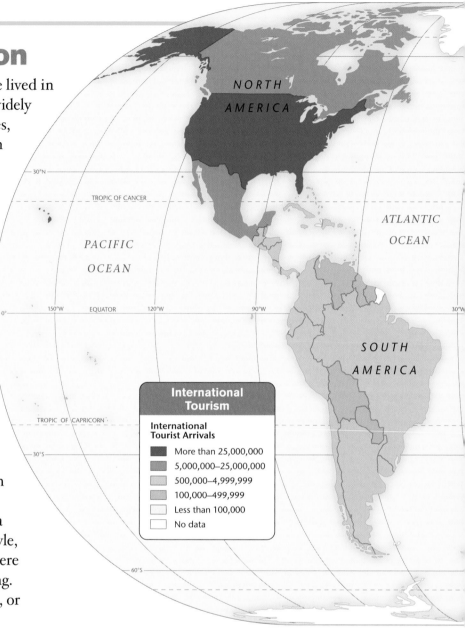

NORTH AMERICA

TROPIC OF CANCER

ATLANTIC OCEAN

PACIFIC OCEAN

EQUATOR

SOUTH AMERICA

TROPIC OF CAPRICORN

International Tourism

International Tourist Arrivals

More than 25,000,000
5,000,000–25,000,000
500,000–4,999,999
100,000–499,999
Less than 100,000
No data

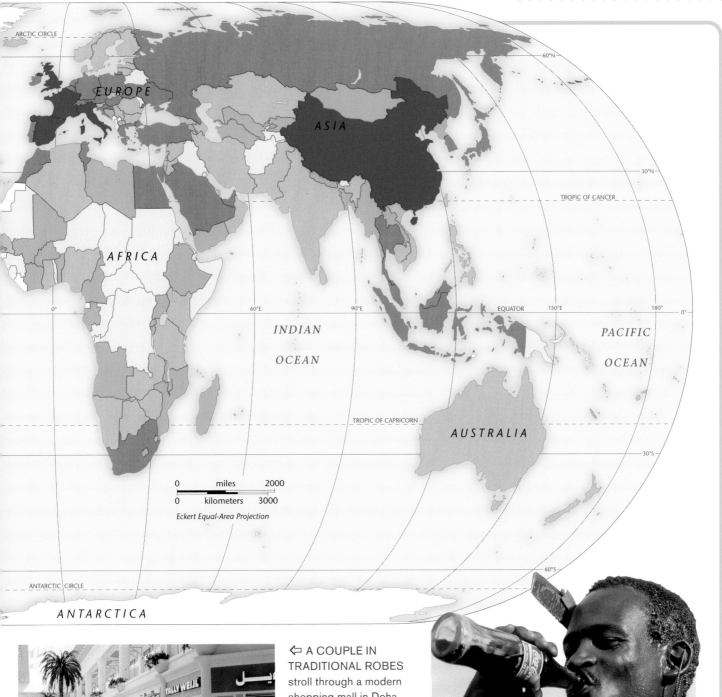

ARCTIC CIRCLE

60°N

EUROPE

ASIA

30°N

TROPIC OF CANCER

AFRICA

0°   60°E   90°E   EQUATOR   150°E   180°

INDIAN

OCEAN

PACIFIC

OCEAN

TROPIC OF CAPRICORN

AUSTRALIA

30°S

0   miles   2000
0   kilometers   3000
Eckert Equal-Area Projection

60°S

ANTARCTIC CIRCLE

ANTARCTICA

⇐ A COUPLE IN TRADITIONAL ROBES stroll through a modern shopping mall in Doha, Qatar. Stores and movie theaters bring Western fashions, technologies, and ideas into contact with Arab culture and values.

⇨ TAKING A BREAK from a traditional ceremony, a Maasai warrior in Kenya enjoys a soft drink that was once uniquely American.

World Conflicts

The world map reveals a complex mosaic of people and cultures. However, when two groups claim the same territory or when major cultural differences overlap, previously peaceful people may turn to violence. Political differences, opposing value systems, or competition for resources can also create tensions.

Some conflicts are relatively short-lived, while others last years. For example, when the country of Yugoslavia broke into several new countries, conflict in Slovenia, which is culturally homogeneous, did not last very long. But Bosnia and Herzegovina faced years of civil war, as groups with different languages, religions, and traditions struggled for control. In the Middle East, territorial disputes between Muslim Palestinians and Jewish Israelis have been a source of turmoil for more than 50 years. And in eastern Asia, ethnic minorities in Myanmar, Indonesia, and the Philippines frequently protest, sometimes violently, domination by the majority group.

Since the 2001 attack on the United States by the terrorist network known as al Qaeda, American military forces have been engaged in wars in Afghanistan and Iraq. In Africa, a region with a turbulent post-colonial history, long-standing tensions between ethnic groups in Kenya erupted into open conflict following disputed elections in late 2007. And around the world the United Nations maintains 19 multi-national peacekeeping missions in places such as Sudan, Liberia, and Haiti.

Political Violence

- Political violence in a localized region
- Political violence affecting population generally
- Recently-ended or low-level political violence
- Location of terrorist attack(s) resulting in 50 or more deaths, 2000 to 2008

Based on data collection and analysis by the Center for Systemic Peace. Countries or areas color-coded on this map are—or recently have been—directly involved in sustained warfare resulting in at least 500 combat deaths.

⬆ ARMED GUERRILLAS, members of Colombia's largest rebel group, FARC, maintain a checkpoint southwest of Bogotá. Civil war has plagued the country for decades.

⬇ ETHNIC TENSIONS turned into open conflict following disputed elections in Kenya in late 2007. Smoldering ruins are all that remain of a housing block in the Nairobi slum of Mathare.

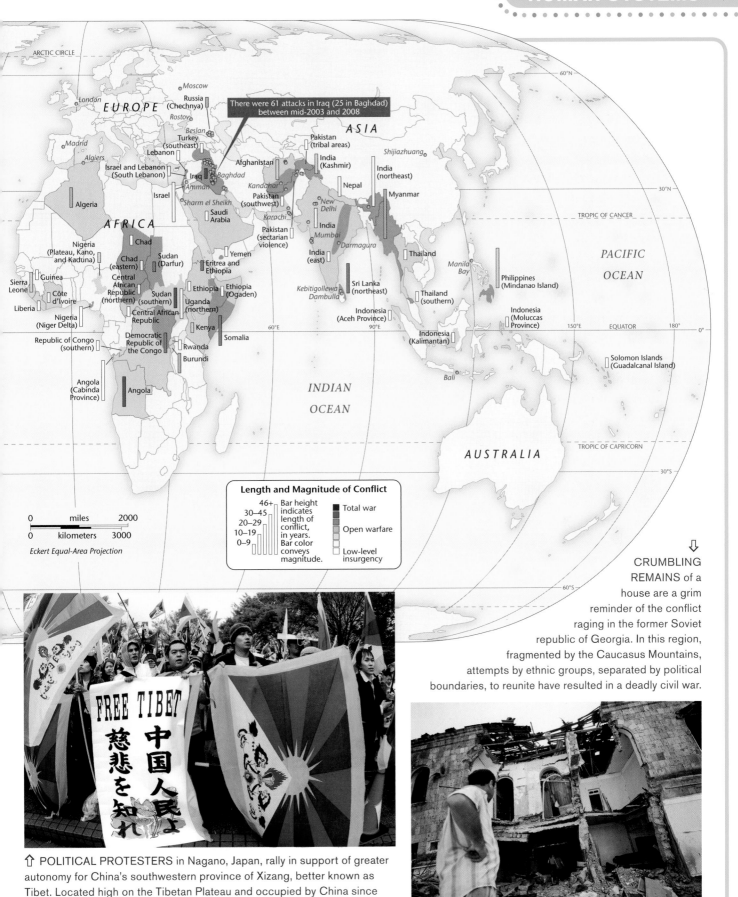

There were 61 attacks in Iraq (25 in Baghdad) between mid-2003 and 2008

ARCTIC CIRCLE

EUROPE
London
Moscow
Madrid
Russia (Chechnya)
Rostov
Algiers
Beslan
Turkey (southeast)
Lebanon
AFRICA
Israel and Lebanon (South Lebanon)
Iraq
Baghdad
Amman
Israel
Sharm el Sheikh
Algeria
Saudi Arabia
ASIA
Afghanistan
Kandahar
Pakistan (southwest)
Karachi
Pakistan (tribal areas)
India (Kashmir)
Shijiazhuang
India (northeast)
Nepal
New Delhi
India
Mumbai
Pakistan (sectarian violence)
Darmagura
Myanmar
Nigeria (Plateau, Kano, and Kaduna)
Chad
Chad (eastern)
Sudan (Darfur)
Yemen
Eritrea and Ethiopia
India (east)
Thailand
PACIFIC OCEAN
Sierra Leone
Guinea
Côte d'Ivoire
Liberia
Central African Republic (northern)
Sudan (southern)
Ethiopia
Ethiopia (Ogaden)
Kebitigollewa
Dambulla
Sri Lanka (northeast)
Manila Bay
Thailand (southern)
Philippines (Mindanao Island)
Nigeria (Niger Delta)
Central African Republic
Uganda (northern)
Kenya
Somalia
Indonesia (Aceh Province)
Indonesia (Moluccas Province)
Republic of Congo (southern)
Democratic Republic of the Congo
Rwanda
Burundi
Indonesia (Kalimantan)
Bali
Angola (Cabinda Province)
Angola
INDIAN OCEAN
Solomon Islands (Guadalcanal Island)
AUSTRALIA

60°N
30°N
TROPIC OF CANCER
60°E
90°E
150°E
EQUATOR
180°
0°
TROPIC OF CAPRICORN
30°S
60°S

0 — miles — 2000
0 — kilometers — 3000
Eckert Equal-Area Projection

Length and Magnitude of Conflict

	Bar height indicates length of conflict, in years. Bar color conveys magnitude.	
46+		■ Total war
30–45		Open warfare
20–29		
10–19		
0–9		□ Low-level insurgency

⇩ CRUMBLING REMAINS of a house are a grim reminder of the conflict raging in the former Soviet republic of Georgia. In this region, fragmented by the Caucasus Mountains, attempts by ethnic groups, separated by political boundaries, to reunite have resulted in a deadly civil war.

⇧ POLITICAL PROTESTERS in Nagano, Japan, rally in support of greater autonomy for China's southwestern province of Xizang, better known as Tibet. Located high on the Tibetan Plateau and occupied by China since 1950, the region is led by the Dalai Lama, who lives in exile.

FREE TIBET
中国人民よ
慈悲を知れ

THE CONTINENT: NORTH AMERICA

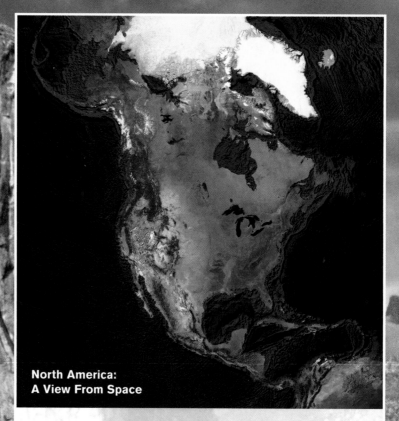

**North America:
A View From Space**

Viewed from high above, North America stretches from the frozen expanses of the Arctic Ocean and Greenland to the lush green of Panama's tropical forests. Hudson Bay and the Great Lakes, fingerprints of long-departed glaciers, dominate the continent's East, while the brown landscapes of the West and Southwest tell of dry lands where water is scarce.

A view of El Capitan mountain and Bridalveil Falls at Yosemite National Park, California

THE CONTINENT: NORTH AMERICA

North America

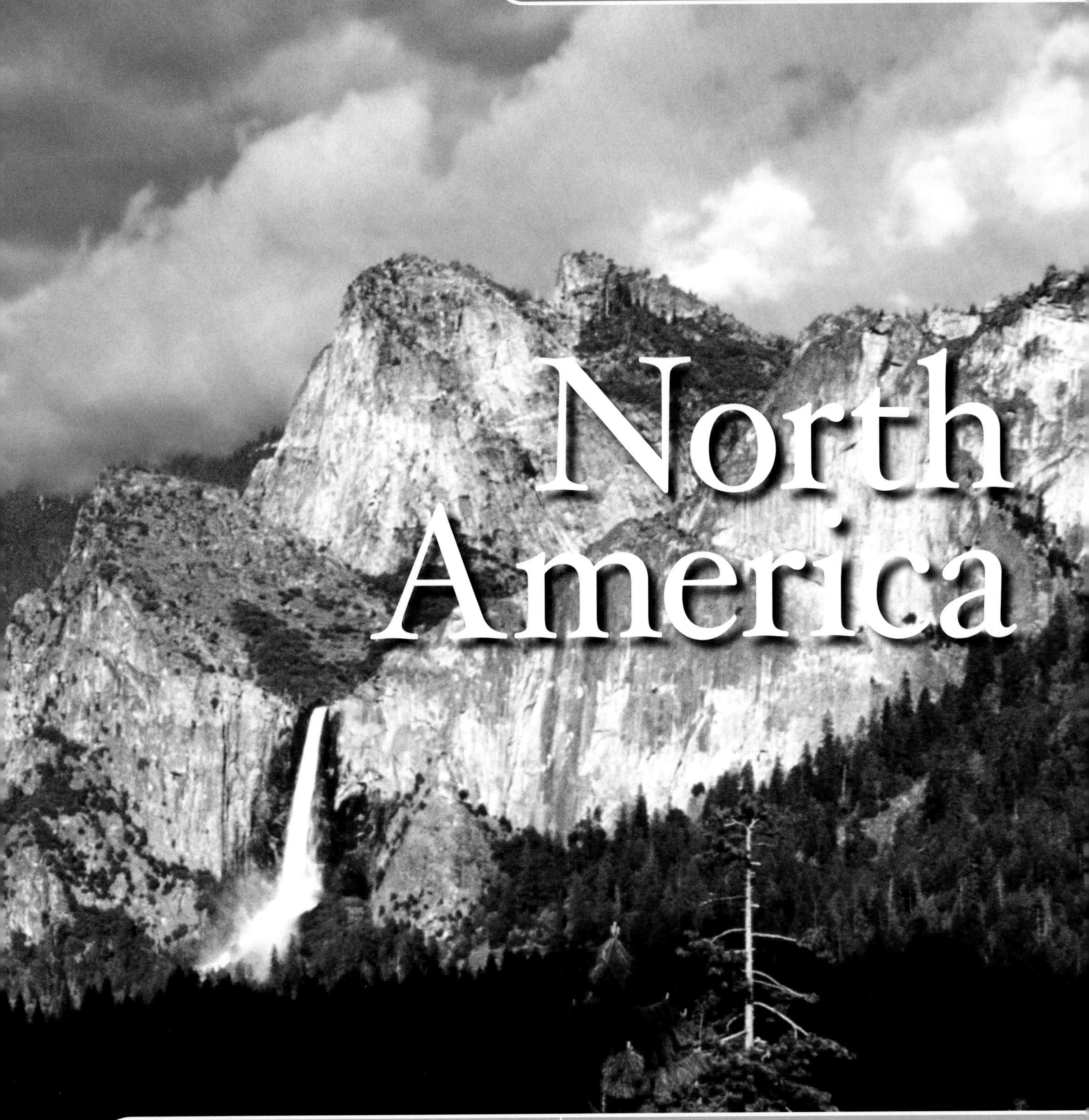

PHYSICAL

Land area
9,449,000 sq mi (24,474,000 sq km)

Highest point
Mount McKinley (Denali), Alaska
20,320 ft (6,194 m)

Lowest point
Death Valley, California
-282 ft (-86 m)

Longest river
Mississippi-Missouri, United States
3,710 mi (5,971 km)

Largest lake
Lake Superior, U.S.-Canada
31,700 sq mi (82,100 sq km)

POLITICAL

Population
523,082,000

Number of independent countries
23

Largest country
Canada
3,855,101 sq mi (9,984,670 sq km)

Smallest country
St. Kitts and Nevis
104 sq mi (269 sq km)

Most populous country
United States
Pop. 302,200,000

Least populous country
St. Kitts and Nevis
Pop. 47,000

THE CONTINENT: NORTH AMERICA

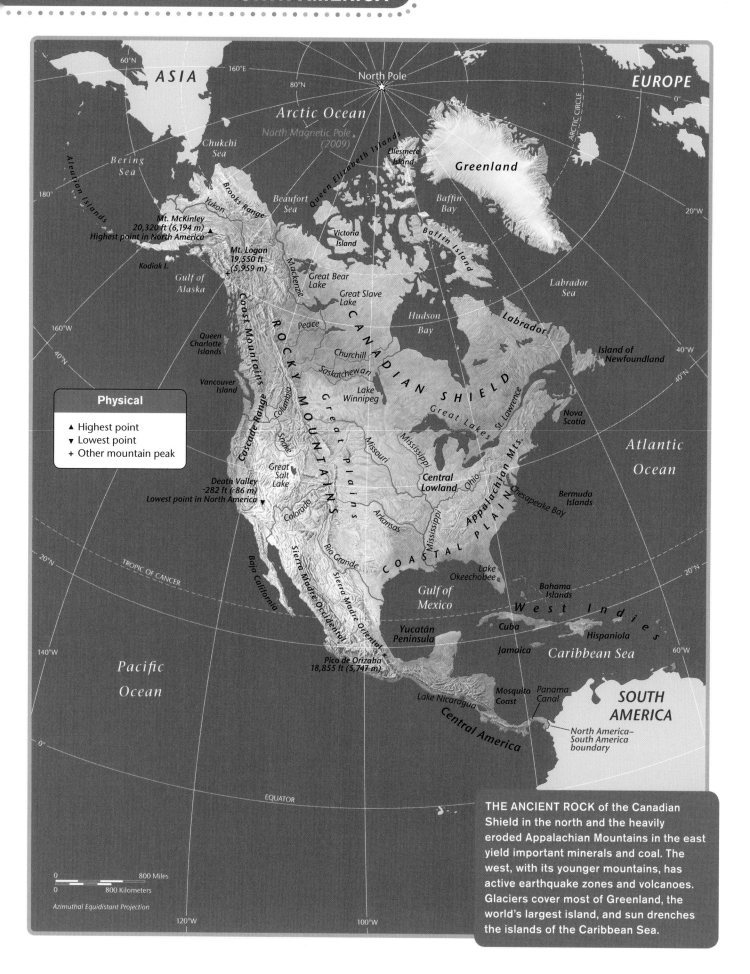

ASIA

EUROPE

North Pole

Arctic Ocean

North Magnetic Pole
(2009)

ARCTIC CIRCLE

0°

Chukchi
Sea

Bering
Sea

Queen Elizabeth Islands

Ellesmere
Island

Greenland

20°W

Aleutian Islands

Brooks Range

Beaufort
Sea

Baffin
Bay

180°

Yukon

Mt. McKinley
20,320 ft (6,194 m)
Highest point in North America

Mt. Logan
19,550 ft
(5,959 m)

Mackenzie

Victoria
Island

Baffin Island

Labrador
Sea

160°W

Kodiak I.

Gulf of
Alaska

Great Bear
Lake

Great Slave
Lake

Hudson
Bay

Labrador

40°W

Queen
Charlotte
Islands

Peace

C A N A D I A N   S H I E L D

Island of
Newfoundland

40°N

Vancouver
Island

Churchill

Saskatchewan

Coast Mountains

Lake
Winnipeg

Great Lakes

St. Lawrence

Nova
Scotia

Cascade Range

Columbia

Snake

R O C K Y   M O U N T A I N S

G r e a t   P l a i n s

Missouri

Mississippi

Central
Lowland

Ohio

Appalachian Mts.

Chesapeake Bay

Atlantic
Ocean

Physical

▲ Highest point
▼ Lowest point
+ Other mountain peak

Great
Salt
Lake

Death Valley
-282 ft (-86 m)
Lowest point in North America ▼

Colorado

Arkansas

Mississippi

COASTAL PLAIN

Bermuda
Islands

20°N

TROPIC OF CANCER

Baja California

Sierra Madre Occidental

Rio Grande

Sierra Madre Oriental

Lake
Okeechobee

Bahama
Islands

W e s t   I n d i e s

20°N

140°W

Pacific
Ocean

Gulf of
Mexico

Yucatán
Peninsula

Cuba

Jamaica

Hispaniola

Caribbean Sea

60°W

Pico de Orizaba
18,855 ft (5,747 m)

+

Lake Nicaragua

Mosquito
Coast

Panama
Canal

SOUTH
AMERICA

0°

Central America

North America–
South America
boundary

EQUATOR

0 _____ 800 Miles
0 _____ 800 Kilometers

Azimuthal Equidistant Projection

120°W

100°W

THE ANCIENT ROCK of the Canadian
Shield in the north and the heavily
eroded Appalachian Mountains in the east
yield important minerals and coal. The
west, with its younger mountains, has
active earthquake zones and volcanoes.
Glaciers cover most of Greenland, the
world's largest island, and sun drenches
the islands of the Caribbean Sea.

THE CONTINENT: NORTH AMERICA

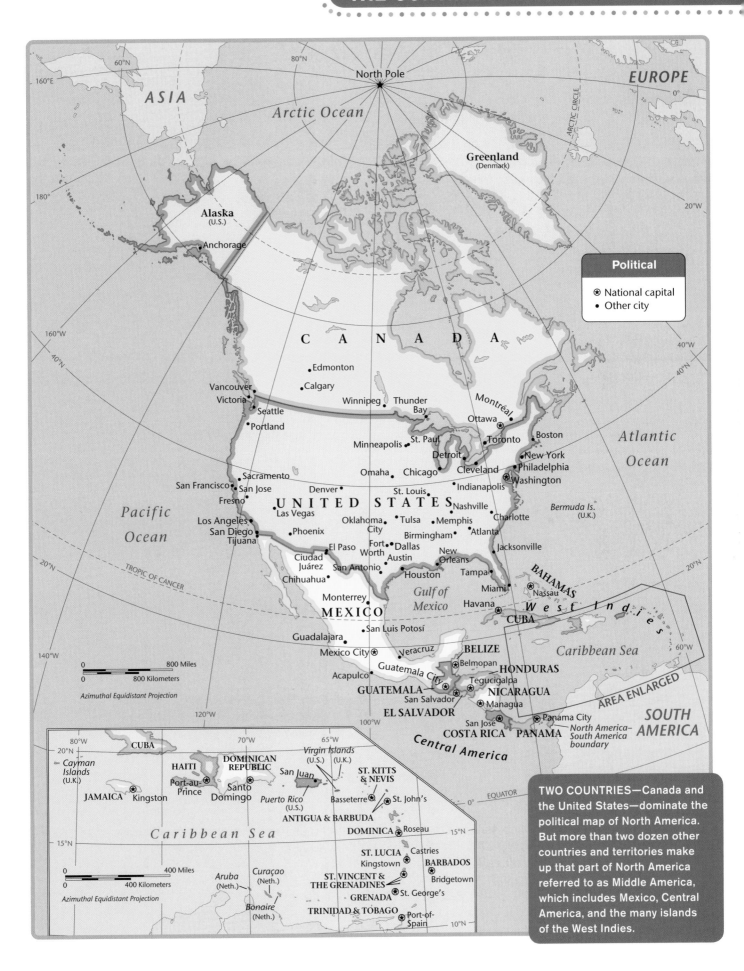

North Pole

ASIA

Arctic Ocean

EUROPE

Greenland
(Denmark)

Alaska
(U.S.)

Anchorage

ARCTIC CIRCLE

Political

⊗ National capital
• Other city

C A N A D A

Edmonton

Calgary

Vancouver
Victoria
Seattle
Portland

Winnipeg · Thunder
Bay

Montréal

Ottawa ⊗
Toronto · Boston

Minneapolis · St. Paul
Detroit · Cleveland · New York
Omaha · Chicago · Philadelphia
Denver · St. Louis · Indianapolis · Washington ⊗

Sacramento
San Francisco · San Jose
Fresno

U N I T E D   S T A T E S

Nashville
Las Vegas

Bermuda Is.
(U.K.)

Los Angeles
San Diego
Tijuana

Oklahoma · Tulsa · Memphis
City · Birmingham · Atlanta
Phoenix

Charlotte

Pacific

Ocean

El Paso · Fort · Dallas
Worth · Austin · New
Ciudad · San Antonio · Orleans
Juárez
Chihuahua

Jacksonville

Houston
Tampa

Gulf of
Mexico

Miami

BAHAMAS
⊗ Nassau

Monterrey

Havana
⊗

West Indies

MEXICO

CUBA

· San Luis Potosí

Guadalajara
Mexico City ⊗ · Veracruz
Acapulco

Caribbean Sea

BELIZE
⊗ Belmopan

HONDURAS

Guatemala City ⊗ · Tegucigalpa ⊗
GUATEMALA · **NICARAGUA**
San Salvador ⊗
EL SALVADOR · Managua ⊗

Central America

San José ⊗
COSTA RICA

Panama City ⊗
PANAMA · *North America–*
South America
boundary

AREA ENLARGED

SOUTH
AMERICA

Atlantic

Ocean

TROPIC OF CANCER

Inset map (Caribbean):

CUBA

Cayman
Islands
(U.K.)

HAITI

DOMINICAN
REPUBLIC

Virgin Islands
(U.S.) (U.K.)

ST. KITTS
& NEVIS

JAMAICA · Kingston ⊗

Port-au-
Prince ⊗
Santo
Domingo ⊗

San Juan
Puerto Rico
(U.S.)

Basseterre ⊗ · St. John's ⊗

ANTIGUA & BARBUDA

C a r i b b e a n   S e a

DOMINICA ⊗ Roseau

ST. LUCIA · Castries ⊗
Kingstown ⊗

BARBADOS
⊗ Bridgetown

Aruba
(Neth.)

Curaçao
(Neth.)

ST. VINCENT &
THE GRENADINES
GRENADA ⊗ St. George's

Bonaire
(Neth.)

TRINIDAD & TOBAGO

⊗ Port-of-
Spain

EQUATOR

0 — 800 Miles
0 — 800 Kilometers
Azimuthal Equidistant Projection

0 — 400 Miles
0 — 400 Kilometers
Azimuthal Equidistant Projection

TWO COUNTRIES—Canada and
the United States—dominate the
political map of North America.
But more than two dozen other
countries and territories make
up that part of North America
referred to as Middle America,
which includes Mexico, Central
America, and the many islands
of the West Indies.

THE CONTINENT: NORTH AMERICA

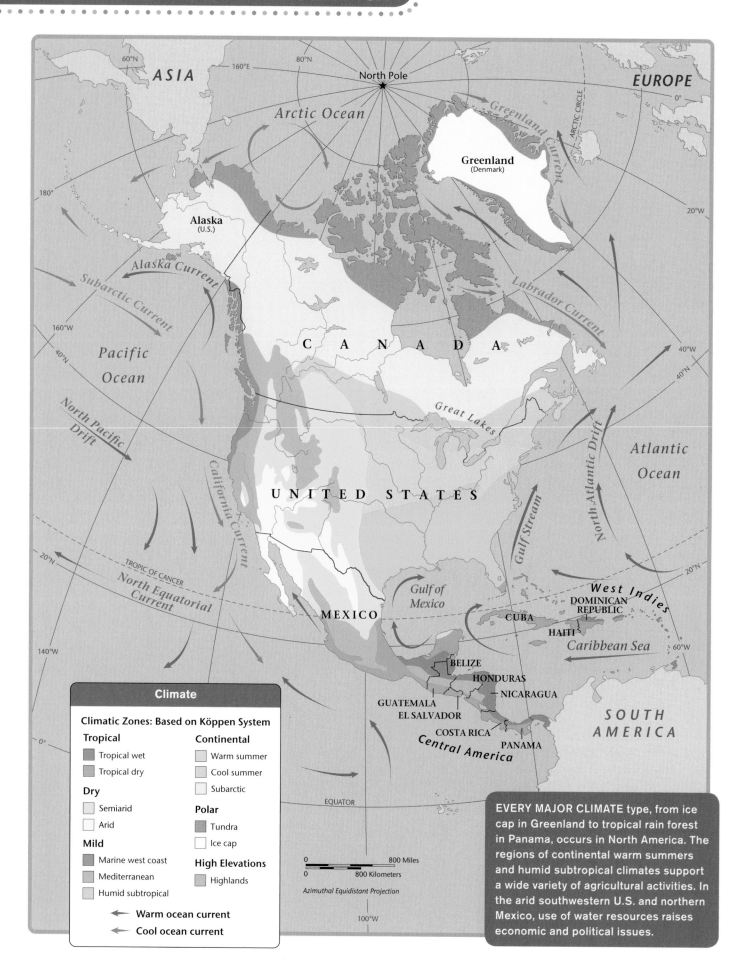

Climate

Climatic Zones: Based on Köppen System

Tropical
- Tropical wet
- Tropical dry

Dry
- Semiarid
- Arid

Mild
- Marine west coast
- Mediterranean
- Humid subtropical

Continental
- Warm summer
- Cool summer
- Subarctic

Polar
- Tundra
- Ice cap

High Elevations
- Highlands

← Warm ocean current
← Cool ocean current

0 — 800 Miles
0 — 800 Kilometers

Azimuthal Equidistant Projection

EVERY MAJOR CLIMATE type, from ice cap in Greenland to tropical rain forest in Panama, occurs in North America. The regions of continental warm summers and humid subtropical climates support a wide variety of agricultural activities. In the arid southwestern U.S. and northern Mexico, use of water resources raises economic and political issues.

THE CONTINENT: NORTH AMERICA

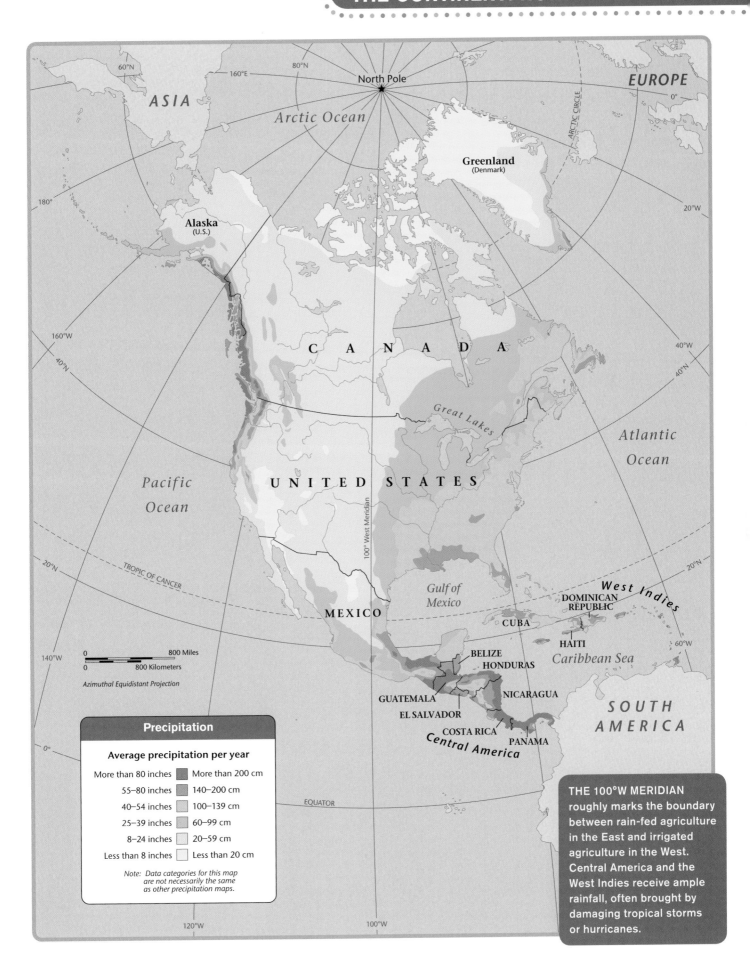

ASIA

Arctic Ocean

North Pole

160°E

80°N

60°N

EUROPE

0°

Greenland
(Denmark)

ARCTIC CIRCLE

20°W

180°

Alaska
(U.S.)

C A N A D A

40°N

40°W

40°N

160°W

40°N

Great Lakes

Atlantic
Ocean

Pacific
Ocean

U N I T E D   S T A T E S

100° West Meridian

20°N

TROPIC OF CANCER

20°N

Gulf of
Mexico

West Indies

DOMINICAN
REPUBLIC

MEXICO

CUBA

140°W

800 Miles

800 Kilometers

Azimuthal Equidistant Projection

HAITI

BELIZE

HONDURAS

Caribbean Sea

60°W

GUATEMALA

NICARAGUA

SOUTH
AMERICA

EL SALVADOR

COSTA RICA

PANAMA

Central America

0°

Precipitation

Average precipitation per year

More than 80 inches	More than 200 cm
55–80 inches	140–200 cm
40–54 inches	100–139 cm
25–39 inches	60–99 cm
8–24 inches	20–59 cm
Less than 8 inches	Less than 20 cm

Note: Data categories for this map are not necessarily the same as other precipitation maps.

EQUATOR

120°W

100°W

THE 100°W MERIDIAN
roughly marks the boundary
between rain-fed agriculture
in the East and irrigated
agriculture in the West.
Central America and the
West Indies receive ample
rainfall, often brought by
damaging tropical storms
or hurricanes.

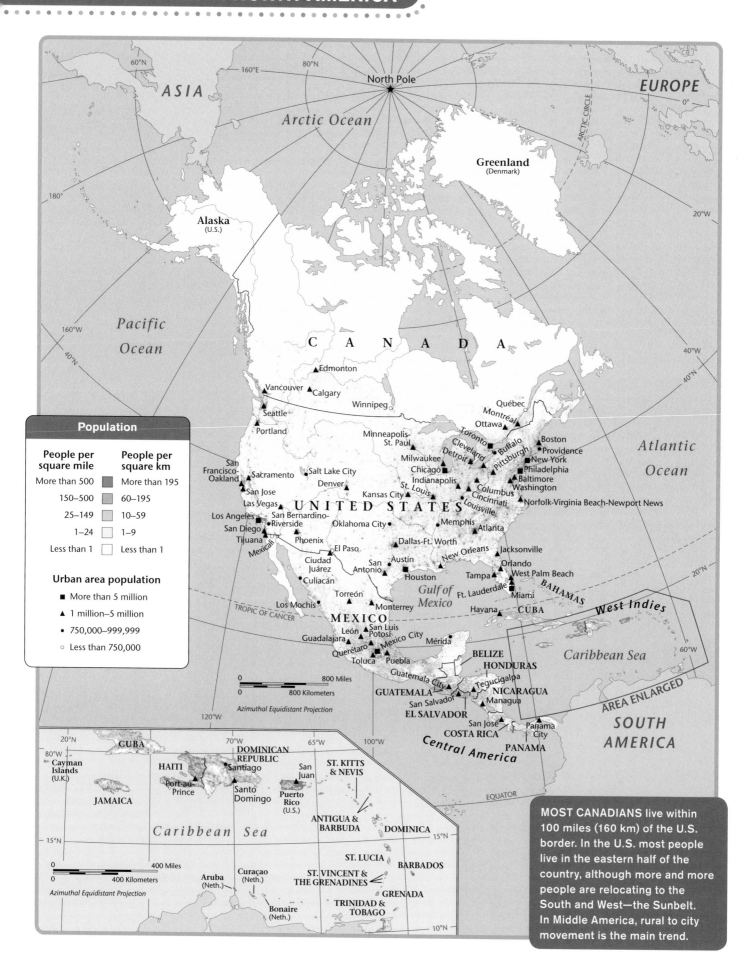

ASIA

EUROPE

Arctic Ocean

North Pole

Greenland
(Denmark)

Pacific
Ocean

Alaska
(U.S.)

C A N A D A

Atlantic
Ocean

Edmonton

Vancouver
Calgary

Winnipeg

Seattle

Québec
Montréal
Ottawa

Portland

Minneapolis-
St. Paul

Toronto
Cleveland
Buffalo
Boston
Providence

San
Francisco-
Oakland

Milwaukee
Detroit
Pittsburgh
New York

Sacramento

Salt Lake City

Chicago

Philadelphia
Baltimore
Washington

San Jose

Denver

Indianapolis
Columbus
Cincinnati

Las Vegas

Kansas City

St. Louis

U N I T E D   S T A T E S

Louisville

Norfolk-Virginia Beach-Newport News

Los Angeles
San Bernardino-
Riverside

Oklahoma City

Memphis
Atlanta

San Diego

Tijuana

Phoenix

Dallas-Ft. Worth

Jacksonville

Mexicali

El Paso

Austin

New Orleans

Orlando
West Palm Beach

Ciudad
Juárez

San
Antonio

Houston

Tampa

Ft. Lauderdale
Miami

Culiacán

Gulf of
Mexico

BAHAMAS

TROPIC OF CANCER

Los Mochis

Torreón

Monterrey

Havana
CUBA

West Indies

MEXICO

León
San Luis
Potosí

Guadalajara

Mérida

Caribbean Sea

Querétaro
Mexico City

Toluca
Puebla

BELIZE

AREA ENLARGED

Guatemala City
HONDURAS
Tegucigalpa

SOUTH
AMERICA

GUATEMALA
San Salvador
NICARAGUA
Managua

EL SALVADOR

San José
COSTA RICA
PANAMA

Panama
City

Central America

PANAMA

EQUATOR

Population

People per square mile | People per square km

More than 500 | More than 195

150–500 | 60–195

25–149 | 10–59

1–24 | 1–9

Less than 1 | Less than 1

Urban area population

■ More than 5 million

▲ 1 million–5 million

● 750,000–999,999

○ Less than 750,000

0   800 Miles
0   800 Kilometers

Azimuthal Equidistant Projection

Caribbean Sea inset

CUBA

Cayman
Islands
(U.K.)

DOMINICAN
REPUBLIC

HAITI
Santiago

San
Juan

ST. KITTS
& NEVIS

Port-au-
Prince

Santo
Domingo

Puerto
Rico
(U.S.)

JAMAICA

ANTIGUA &
BARBUDA

DOMINICA

Caribbean   Sea

ST. LUCIA

BARBADOS

0   400 Miles
0   400 Kilometers

Azimuthal Equidistant Projection

Aruba
(Neth.)

Curaçao
(Neth.)

ST. VINCENT &
THE GRENADINES

GRENADA

TRINIDAD &
TOBAGO

Bonaire
(Neth.)

MOST CANADIANS live within 100 miles (160 km) of the U.S. border. In the U.S. most people live in the eastern half of the country, although more and more people are relocating to the South and West—the Sunbelt. In Middle America, rural to city movement is the main trend.

THE CONTINENT: NORTH AMERICA

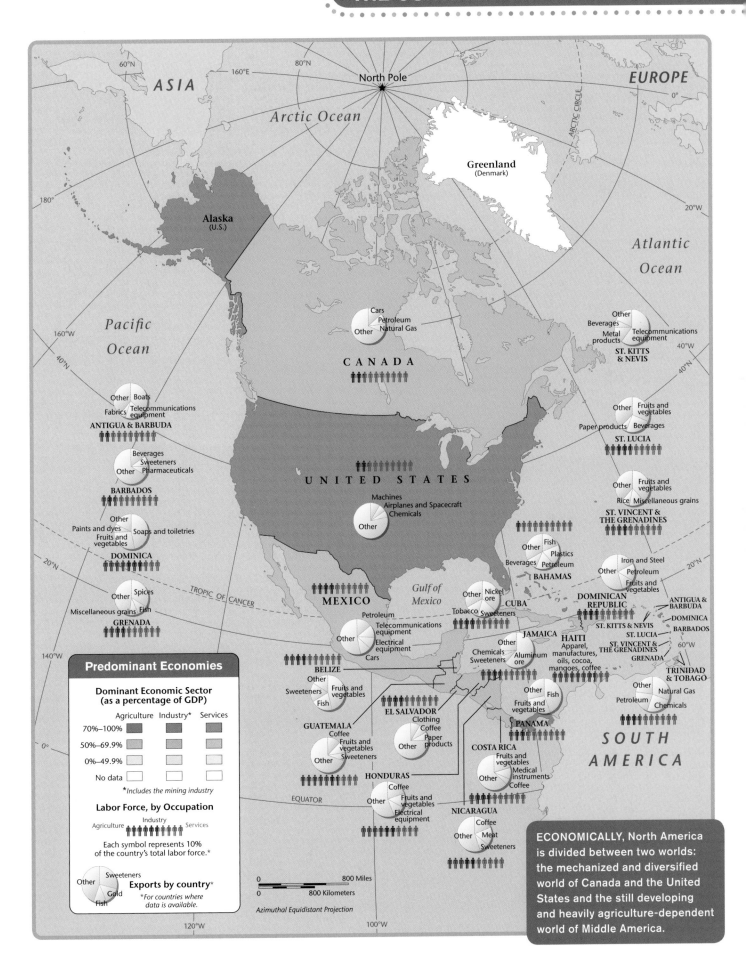

ASIA

Arctic Ocean

North Pole

EUROPE

Greenland
(Denmark)

Alaska
(U.S.)

Atlantic
Ocean

Pacific
Ocean

CANADA
Cars
Petroleum
Natural Gas
Other

Other
Beverages
Metal
products
Telecommunications
equipment
**ST. KITTS
& NEVIS**

Other
Boats
Fabrics
Telecommunications
equipment
ANTIGUA & BARBUDA

Other
Fruits and
vegetables
Paper products
Beverages
ST. LUCIA

Beverages
Sweeteners
Other
Pharmaceuticals
BARBADOS

UNITED STATES

Other
Fruits and
vegetables
Rice
Miscellaneous grains
**ST. VINCENT &
THE GRENADINES**

Machines
Airplanes and Spacecraft
Chemicals
Other

Other
Paints and dyes
Fruits and
vegetables
Soaps and toiletries
DOMINICA

Other
Fish
Beverages
Plastics
Petroleum
BAHAMAS

Other
Iron and Steel
Petroleum
Fruits and
vegetables
**DOMINICAN
REPUBLIC**

ANTIGUA &
BARBUDA

Other
Spices
Miscellaneous grains
Fish
GRENADA

TROPIC OF CANCER

MEXICO

Other
Nickel
ore
Tobacco
Sweeteners
CUBA

ST. KITTS & NEVIS

DOMINICA

BARBADOS

ST. LUCIA

ST. VINCENT &
THE GRENADINES

Gulf of
Mexico

Other
Aluminum
ore
Chemicals
Sweeteners
JAMAICA

HAITI
Apparel,
manufactures,
oils, cocoa,
mangoes, coffee

GRENADA

**TRINIDAD
& TOBAGO**

Other
Natural Gas
Petroleum
Chemicals

Petroleum
Telecommunications
equipment
Electrical
equipment
Other
Cars

BELIZE
Other
Sweeteners
Fruits and
vegetables
Fish

Other
Fruits and
vegetables
Fish

Clothing
Coffee
Paper
products
Other
EL SALVADOR

SOUTH
AMERICA

GUATEMALA
Coffee
Fruits and
vegetables
Sweeteners
Other

PANAMA

COSTA RICA
Fruits and
vegetables
Medical
instruments
Coffee
Other

HONDURAS
Coffee
Fruits and
vegetables
Electrical
equipment
Other

NICARAGUA
Coffee
Meat
Sweeteners
Other

EQUATOR

Predominant Economies

Dominant Economic Sector
(as a percentage of GDP)

	Agriculture	Industry*	Services
70%–100%			
50%–69.9%			
0%–49.9%			
No data			

*Includes the mining industry

Labor Force, by Occupation

Agriculture   Industry   Services

Each symbol represents 10%
of the country's total labor force.*

Other
Sweeteners
Gold
Fish

Exports by country*

*For countries where
data is available.

0   800 Miles
0   800 Kilometers

Azimuthal Equidistant Projection

ECONOMICALLY, North America
is divided between two worlds:
the mechanized and diversified
world of Canada and the United
States and the still developing
and heavily agriculture-dependent
world of Middle America.

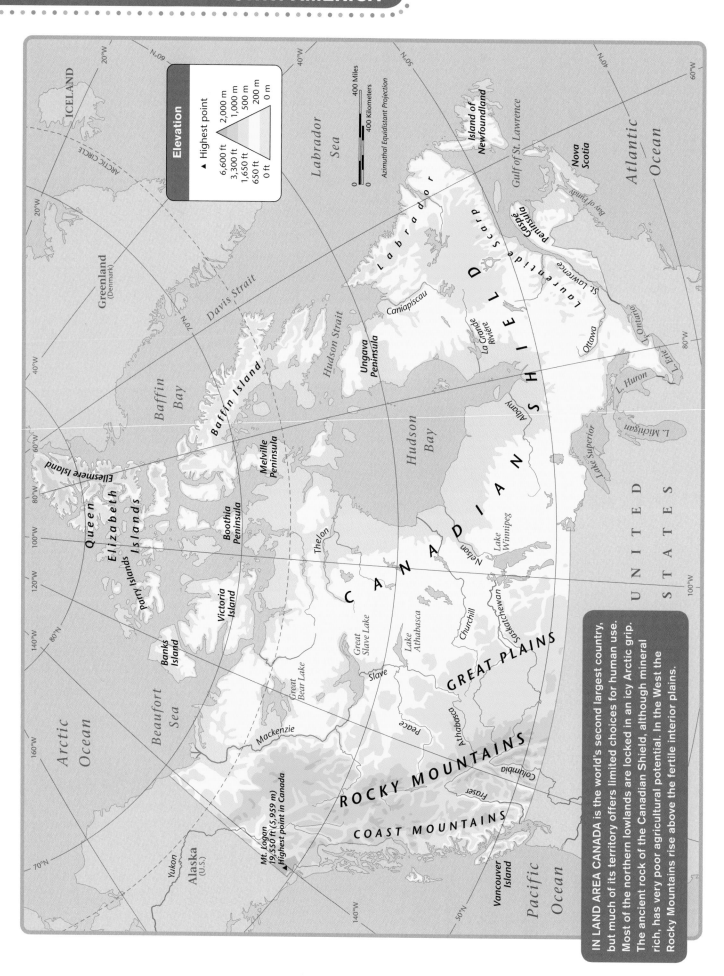

Elevation

▲ Highest point

6,600 ft	2,000 m
3,300 ft	1,000 m
1,650 ft	500 m
650 ft	200 m
0 ft	0 m

400 Miles
400 Kilometers
Azimuthal Equidistant Projection

ICELAND

Greenland
(Denmark)

ARCTIC CIRCLE

Labrador
Sea

Island of
Newfoundland

Gulf of St. Lawrence

Nova
Scotia

Gaspé
Peninsula

Bay of Fundy

Laurentide Scarp

St. Lawrence

Atlantic
Ocean

Davis Strait

Baffin
Bay

Baffin Island

Labrador

Caniapiscau

La Grande
Rivière

Ottawa

L. Ontario

L. Erie

Hudson Strait

Ungava
Peninsula

Albany

L. Huron

Lake Superior

L. Michigan

Ellesmere Island

Melville
Peninsula

Boothia
Peninsula

C A N A D I A N   S H I E L D

Hudson
Bay

Lake
Superior

Queen
Elizabeth
Islands

Parry Islands

Victoria
Island

Thelon

Nelson

Lake
Winnipeg

U N I T E D

S T A T E S

Banks
Island

Great
Slave Lake

Lake
Athabasca

Churchill

Saskatchewan

G R E A T   P L A I N S

Beaufort
Sea

Great
Bear Lake

Slave

Athabasca

Peace

Mackenzie

Columbia

Fraser

Arctic
Ocean

R O C K Y   M O U N T A I N S

Mt. Logan
19,550 ft (5,959 m)
Highest point in Canada
▲

C O A S T   M O U N T A I N S

Yukon

Alaska
(U.S.)

Vancouver
Island

Pacific
Ocean

IN LAND AREA CANADA is the world's second largest country, but much of its territory offers limited choices for human use. Most of the northern lowlands are locked in an icy Arctic grip. The ancient rock of the Canadian Shield, although mineral rich, has very poor agricultural potential. In the West the Rocky Mountains rise above the fertile interior plains.

THE CONTINENT: NORTH AMERICA

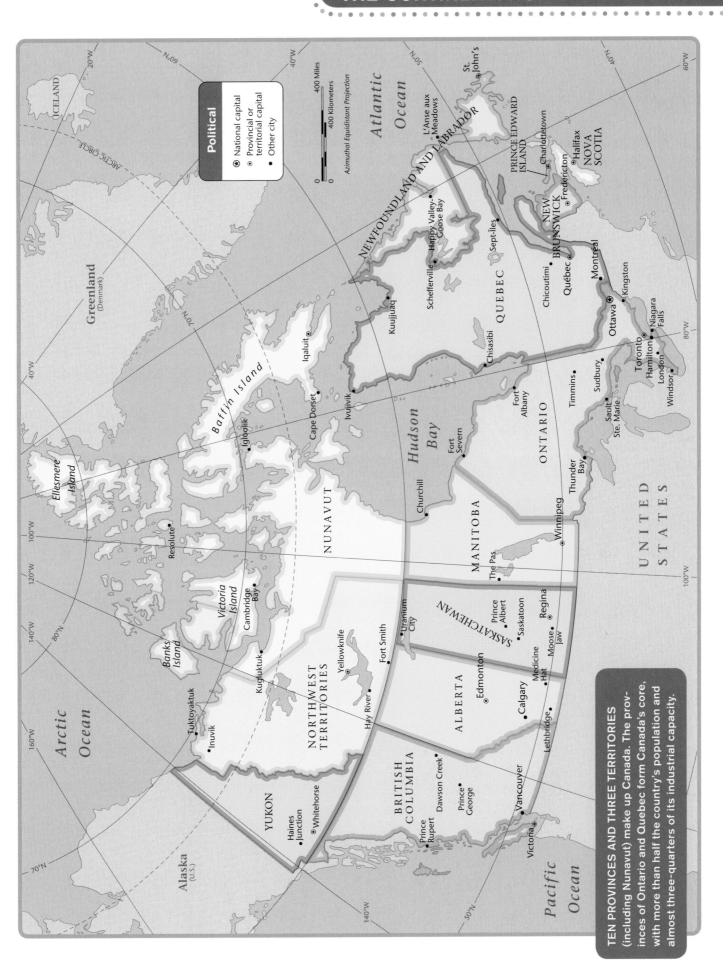

Political
- ⊛ National capital
- ⊙ Provincial or territorial capital
- • Other city

400 Miles
400 Kilometers

Azimuthal Equidistant Projection

ICELAND

ARCTIC CIRCLE

Greenland
(Denmark)

Atlantic Ocean

St. John's

L'Anse aux Meadows

NEWFOUNDLAND AND LABRADOR

PRINCE EDWARD ISLAND

Charlottetown

Halifax
NOVA SCOTIA

Happy Valley-Goose Bay

Fredericton

NEW BRUNSWICK

Scheffervile

Sept-Îles

Chicoutimi

Montréal

Kuujjuaq

QUEBEC

Québec

Kingston

Baffin Island

Iqaluit

Chisasibi

Ottawa

Niagara Falls

Toronto

Hamilton

London

Windsor

Ivujivik

Cape Dorset

Hudson Bay

Fort Albany

ONTARIO

Sudbury

Timmins

Sault Ste. Marie

Igloolik

Fort Severn

Thunder Bay

Ellesmere Island

NUNAVUT

Churchill

MANITOBA

Resolute

Winnipeg

The Pas

UNITED STATES

Victoria Island

Cambridge Bay

Uranium City

Prince Albert

Saskatoon

Regina

SASKATCHEWAN

Banks Island

Kugluktuk

Yellowknife

Fort Smith

Edmonton

Medicine Hat

Moose Jaw

Tuktoyaktuk

NORTHWEST TERRITORIES

Hay River

ALBERTA

Calgary

Inuvik

Lethbridge

Arctic Ocean

Dawson Creek

BRITISH COLUMBIA

Prince George

Vancouver

YUKON

Haines Junction

Whitehorse

Prince Rupert

Victoria

Alaska
(U.S.)

Pacific Ocean

TEN PROVINCES AND THREE TERRITORIES (including Nunavut) make up Canada. The provinces of Ontario and Quebec form Canada's core, with more than half the country's population and almost three-quarters of its industrial capacity.

THE CONTINENT: NORTH AMERICA

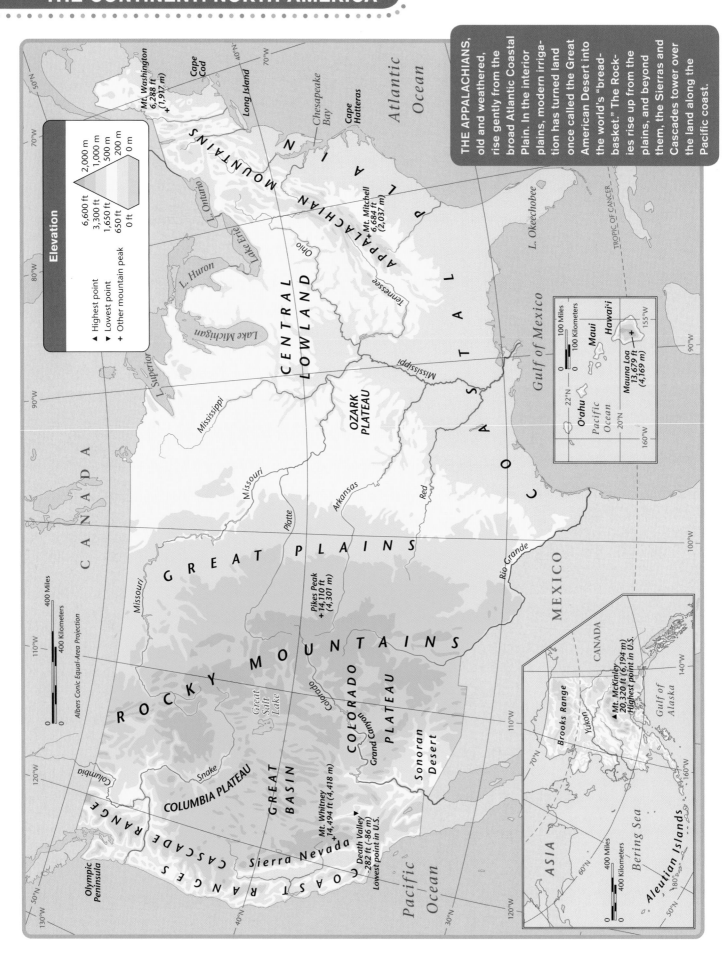

THE APPALACHIANS, old and weathered, rise gently from the broad Atlantic Coastal Plain. In the interior plains, modern irrigation has turned land once called the Great American Desert into the world's "breadbasket." The Rockies rise up from the plains, and beyond them, the Sierras and Cascades tower over the land along the Pacific coast.

Elevation

2,000 m	6,600 ft
1,000 m	3,300 ft
500 m	1,650 ft
200 m	650 ft
0 m	0 ft

▲ Highest point
▼ Lowest point
+ Other mountain peak

Mt. Washington
6,288 ft
(1,917 m)
+

Cape Cod

Long Island

Chesapeake Bay

Cape Hatteras

Atlantic Ocean

COASTAL PLAIN

APPALACHIAN MOUNTAINS

+ Mt. Mitchell
6,684 ft
(2,037 m)

L. Ontario

Lake Erie

L. Huron

Lake Michigan

L. Superior

Ohio

Tennessee

CENTRAL LOWLAND

Mississippi

CANADA

Mississippi

Missouri

Arkansas

Red

OZARK PLATEAU

L. Okeechobee

TROPIC OF CANCER

Gulf of Mexico

COASTAL PLAIN

G R E A T   P L A I N S

Platte

Pikes Peak
+ 14,110 ft
(4,301 m)

Rio Grande

MEXICO

R O C K Y   M O U N T A I N S

Missouri

Great Salt Lake

Colorado

COLORADO PLATEAU

Grand Canyon

Sonoran Desert

COLUMBIA PLATEAU

Snake

Columbia

GREAT BASIN

Mt. Whitney
+ 14,494 ft (4,418 m)

▼ Death Valley
-282 ft (-86 m)
Lowest point in U.S.

Sierra Nevada

CASCADE RANGE

COAST RANGES

Olympic Peninsula

Pacific Ocean

400 Miles
400 Kilometers
Albers Conic Equal-Area Projection

Hawai'i

Maui

O'ahu

Mauna Loa
13,679 ft
(4,169 m)
+

Pacific Ocean

100 Miles
100 Kilometers

22°N
20°N
160°W
155°W

ASIA

CANADA

Brooks Range

Yukon

▲ Mt. McKinley
20,320 ft (6,194 m)
Highest point in U.S.

Gulf of Alaska

Bering Sea

Aleutian Islands

400 Miles
400 Kilometers

50°N
60°N
70°N
180°
160°W
140°W

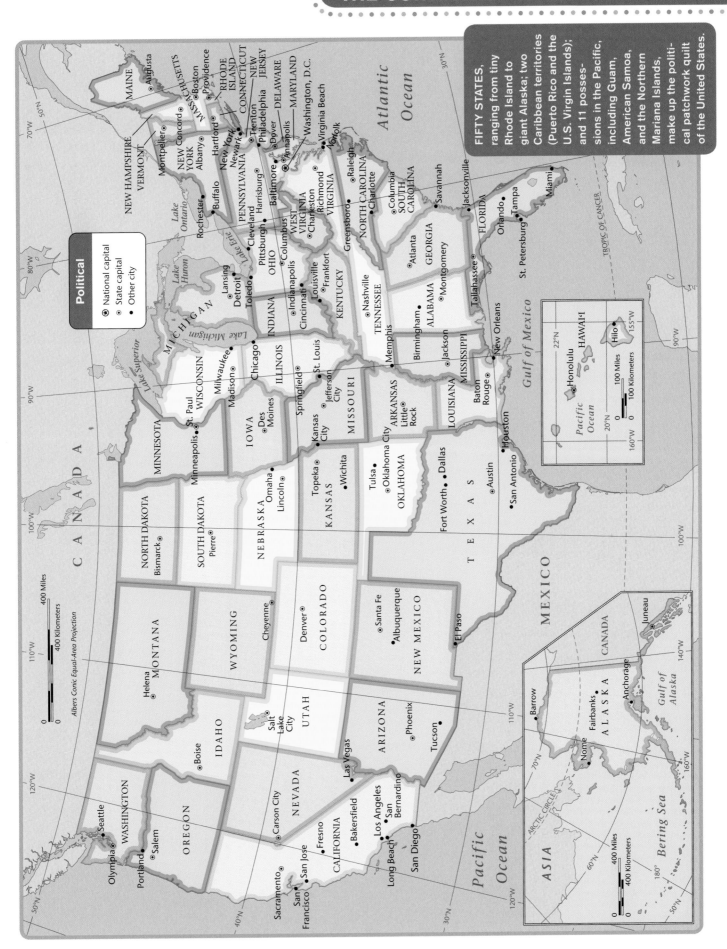

FIFTY STATES, ranging from tiny Rhode Island to giant Alaska; two Caribbean territories (Puerto Rico and the U.S. Virgin Islands); and 11 possessions in the Pacific, including Guam, American Samoa, and the Northern Mariana Islands, make up the political patchwork quilt of the United States.

Political
- ⊛ National capital
- ⊙ State capital
- • Other city

Albers Conic Equal-Area Projection

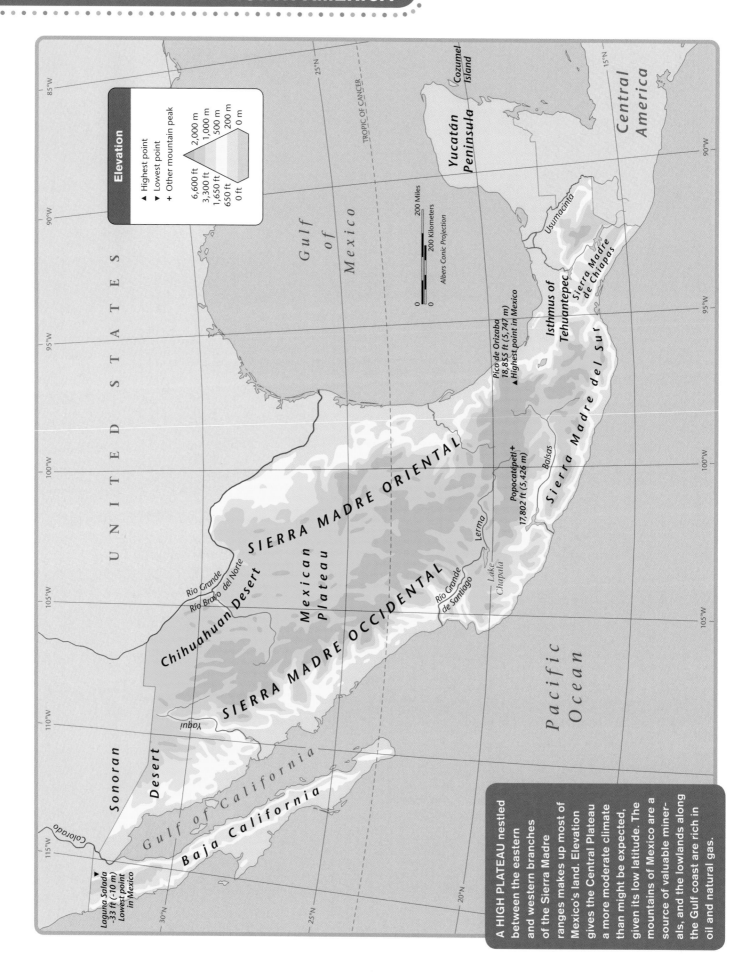

Elevation

▲ Highest point
▼ Lowest point
+ Other mountain peak

6,600 ft — 2,000 m
3,300 ft — 1,000 m
1,650 ft — 500 m
650 ft — 200 m
0 ft — 0 m

UNITED STATES

Gulf of Mexico

Yucatán Peninsula

Cozumel Island

Central America

200 Miles
200 Kilometers
Albers Conic Projection

Colorado

Sonoran Desert

Gulf of California

Baja California

Yaqui

SIERRA MADRE OCCIDENTAL

Río Grande
Río Bravo del Norte

Chihuahuan Desert

SIERRA MADRE ORIENTAL

Mexican Plateau

Río Grande de Santiago

Lerma

Lake Chapala

Popocatépetl +
17,802 ft (5,426 m)

Balsas

Pico de Orizaba
18,855 ft (5,747 m)
▲ Highest point in Mexico

Isthmus of Tehuantepec

Usumacinta

Sierra Madre de Chiapas

Sierra Madre del Sur

Pacific Ocean

Laguna Salada
-33 ft (-10 m)
Lowest point in Mexico

TROPIC OF CANCER

A HIGH PLATEAU nestled between the eastern and western branches of the Sierra Madre ranges makes up most of Mexico's land. Elevation gives the Central Plateau a more moderate climate than might be expected, given its low latitude. The mountains of Mexico are a source of valuable minerals, and the lowlands along the Gulf coast are rich in oil and natural gas.

THE CONTINENT: NORTH AMERICA

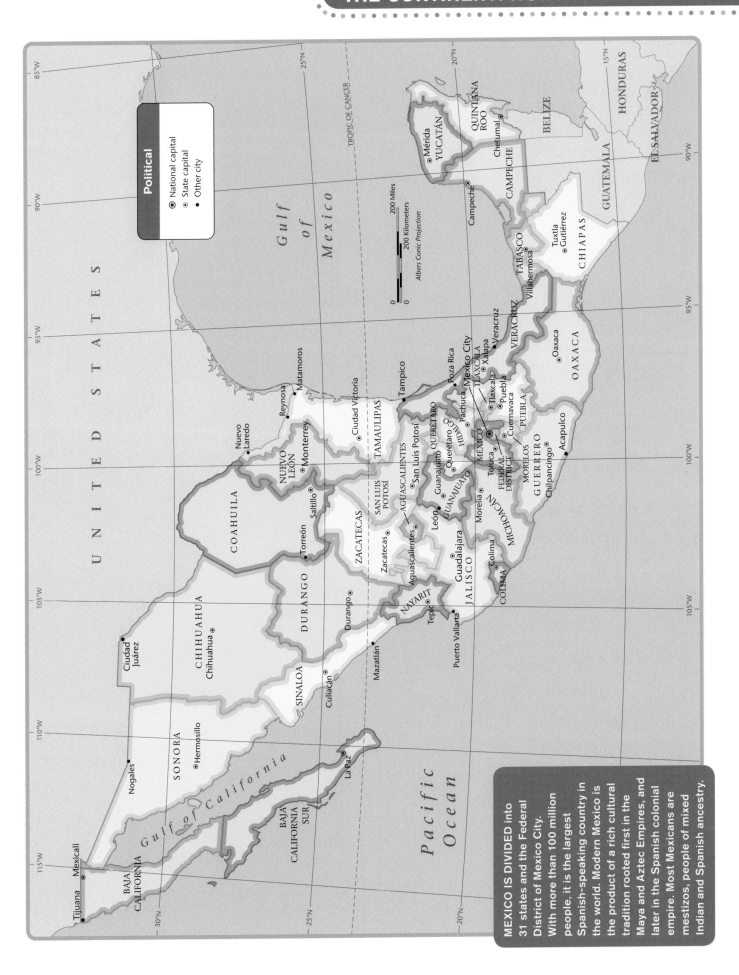

Political

⊛ National capital
⊙ State capital
• Other city

UNITED STATES

Gulf of Mexico

TROPIC OF CANCER

200 Miles
200 Kilometers
Albers Conic Projection

HONDURAS

BELIZE

QUINTANA ROO

Mérida
YUCATÁN

Chetumal

CAMPECHE

Campeche

TABASCO

Tuxtla
Gutiérrez

CHIAPAS

GUATEMALA

EL SALVADOR

Villahermosa

VERACRUZ

Veracruz

Xalapa

Oaxaca

OAXACA

Poza Rica

Mexico City

TLAXCALA

Tlaxcala

Puebla

PUEBLA

Pachuca

HIDALGO

Cuernavaca

MORELOS

Acapulco

GUERRERO

Chilpancingo

Tampico

Ciudad Victoria

TAMAULIPAS

Matamoros

Reynosa

Nuevo
Laredo

NUEVO
LEÓN

Monterrey

SAN LUIS
POTOSÍ

San Luis Potosí

QUERÉTARO

Querétaro

GUANAJUATO

Guanajuato

MÉXICO

Toluca

FEDERAL
DISTRICT

MICHOACÁN

Morelia

AGUASCALIENTES

Aguascalientes

ZACATECAS

Zacatecas

León

Guadalajara

JALISCO

Colima

COLIMA

COAHUILA

Saltillo

Torreón

DURANGO

Durango

CHIHUAHUA

Chihuahua

Ciudad
Juárez

SINALOA

Culiacán

Mazatlán

NAYARIT

Tepic

Puerto Vallarta

SONORA

Hermosillo

Nogales

Gulf of California

BAJA
CALIFORNIA
SUR

La Paz

Pacific Ocean

BAJA
CALIFORNIA

Mexicali

Tijuana

MEXICO IS DIVIDED into 31 states and the Federal District of Mexico City. With more than 100 million people, it is the largest Spanish-speaking country in the world. Modern Mexico is the product of a rich cultural tradition rooted first in the Maya and Aztec Empires, and later in the Spanish colonial empire. Most Mexicans are mestizos, people of mixed Indian and Spanish ancestry.

NATURAL HAZARDS: SELECTED STATISTICS

Hurricanes

This list names North America's eight most intense hurricanes (based on barometric pressure) since 1950. Average sea-level pressure is 1,013.25 millibars or 29.92 inches.

1968	Camille	909 mbr/26.84 in
2005	Katrina	920 mbr/27.17 in
1992	Andrew	922 mbr/27.23 in
1960	Donna	930 mbr/27.46 in
1961	Carla	931 mbr/27.49 in
1989	Hugo	934 mbr/27.58 in
2005	Rita	937 mbr/27.67 in
1954	Hazel	938 mbr/27.70 in

Tornadoes

The following states had the highest average annual number of tornadoes from 1953 to 2004.

Texas: 139

Oklahoma: 57

Florida: 55

Kansas: 55

Nebraska: 45

Iowa: 37

Earthquakes

This list shows the number of earthquakes in North America since 1900 that had a magnitude of 8.0 or greater on the Richter scale.

Alaska (U.S.): 6

Mexico: 4

British Columbia (Canada): 1

Dominican Republic: 1

Volcanoes

This list shows major volcanic eruptions in the U.S. since 1980.

Mount St. Helens (WA): 1980–1986

Kilauea (HI): 1983–ongoing

Mauna Loa (HI): 1984

Augustine (AK): 1986

Redoubt (AK): 1989–1990

Natural Hazards

The forces of nature inspire awe. They can also bring damage and destruction, especially when people locate homes and businesses in places that are at risk of experiencing violent storms, earthquakes, volcanoes, floods, wildfires, or other natural hazards. Tornadoes—violent, swirling storms with winds that can exceed 200 miles (300 km) per hour—strike the U.S. more than 800 times each year. Hurricanes, massive low-pressure storms that form over warm ocean waters, bring destructive winds and rain primarily to the Gulf of Mexico and the southeastern mainland. Melting spring snows and heavy rains trigger flooding; periods of drought make other regions vulnerable to wildfires. These and other hazards of nature are not limited to this continent. Natural hazards pose serious threats to lives and property wherever people live.

⇧ VOLCANOES. From deep inside Earth, molten rock, called magma, rises and breaks through the surface, sometimes quietly, but more often violently, shooting billowing ash clouds as shown here at Mount St. Helens, in Washington State.

⇩ WILDFIRES. Putting lives and property at great risk, wildfires destroy millions of acres of forest each year. At the same time, fires help renew ecosystems by removing debris and encouraging seedling growth.

⇨ FLOODS. Towns located along rivers are always at risk of floods. In 2008 residents of Clarksville, Missouri, had to resort to boats as rising waters of the Mississippi River flooded the town.

THE CONTINENT: NORTH AMERICA

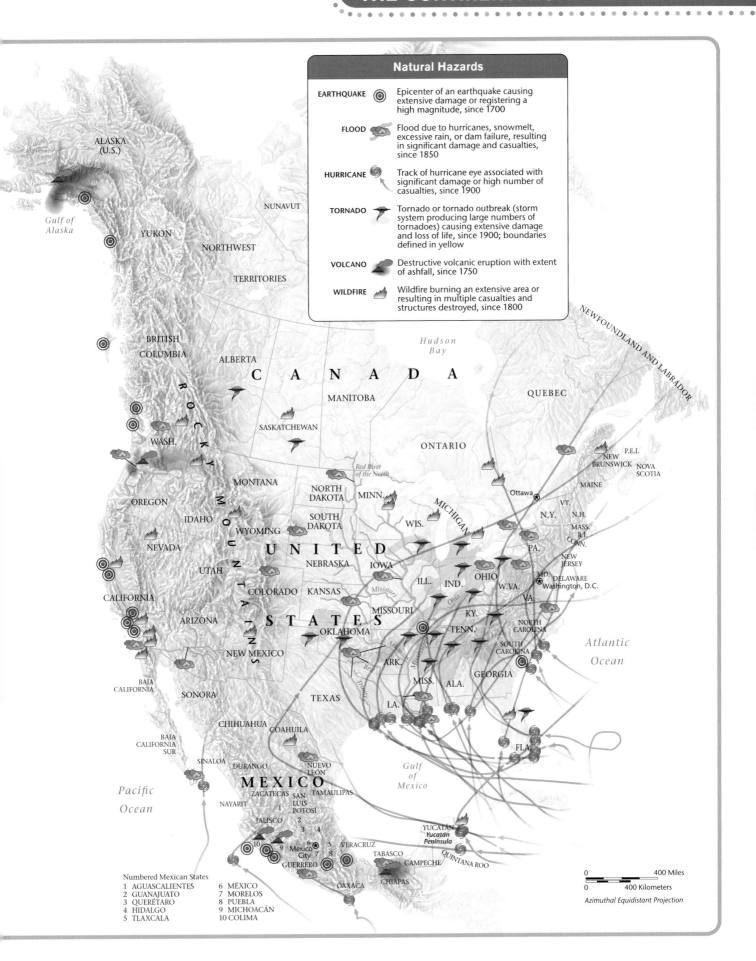

Natural Hazards

EARTHQUAKE — Epicenter of an earthquake causing extensive damage or registering a high magnitude, since 1700

FLOOD — Flood due to hurricanes, snowmelt, excessive rain, or dam failure, resulting in significant damage and casualties, since 1850

HURRICANE — Track of hurricane eye associated with significant damage or high number of casualties, since 1900

TORNADO — Tornado or tornado outbreak (storm system producing large numbers of tornadoes) causing extensive damage and loss of life, since 1900; boundaries defined in yellow

VOLCANO — Destructive volcanic eruption with extent of ashfall, since 1750

WILDFIRE — Wildfire burning an extensive area or resulting in multiple casualties and structures destroyed, since 1800

Numbered Mexican States
1 AGUASCALIENTES
2 GUANAJUATO
3 QUERÉTARO
4 HIDALGO
5 TLAXCALA
6 MÉXICO
7 MORELOS
8 PUEBLA
9 MICHOACÁN
10 COLIMA

0   400 Miles
0   400 Kilometers
Azimuthal Equidistant Projection

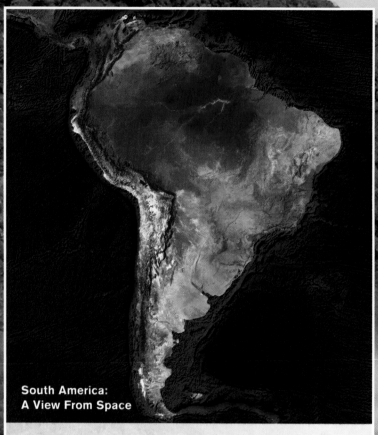

South America:
A View From Space

From the towering, snow-capped Andes in the west to the steamy rain forest of the Amazon Basin in the north, and from the fertile grasslands of the Pampas to the arid Atacama Desert along the Pacific coast, South America is a continent of extremes. North to south the continent extends from the tropical waters of the Caribbean Sea to the wind-blown islands of Tierra del Fuego. Its longest river, the Amazon, carries more water than any other river in the world.

A rainbow arches over Iguazu Falls, Argentina.

South America

PHYSICAL

Land area
6,880,000 sq mi
(17,819,000 sq km)

Highest point
Cerro Aconcagua,
Argentina
22,834 ft (6,960 m)

Lowest point
Laguna del Carbón,
Argentina
-344 ft (-105 m)

Longest river
Amazon
4,000 mi (6,437 km)

Largest lake
Lake Titicaca,
Bolivia-Peru
3,200 sq mi
(8,290 sq km)

POLITICAL

Population
381,045,000

**Number of
independent
countries**
12

Largest country
Brazil
3,300,169 sq mi (8,547,403 sq km)

Smallest country
Suriname
63,037 sq mi (163,265 sq km)

Most populous country
Brazil
Pop. 189,335,000

Least populous country
Suriname
Pop. 503,000

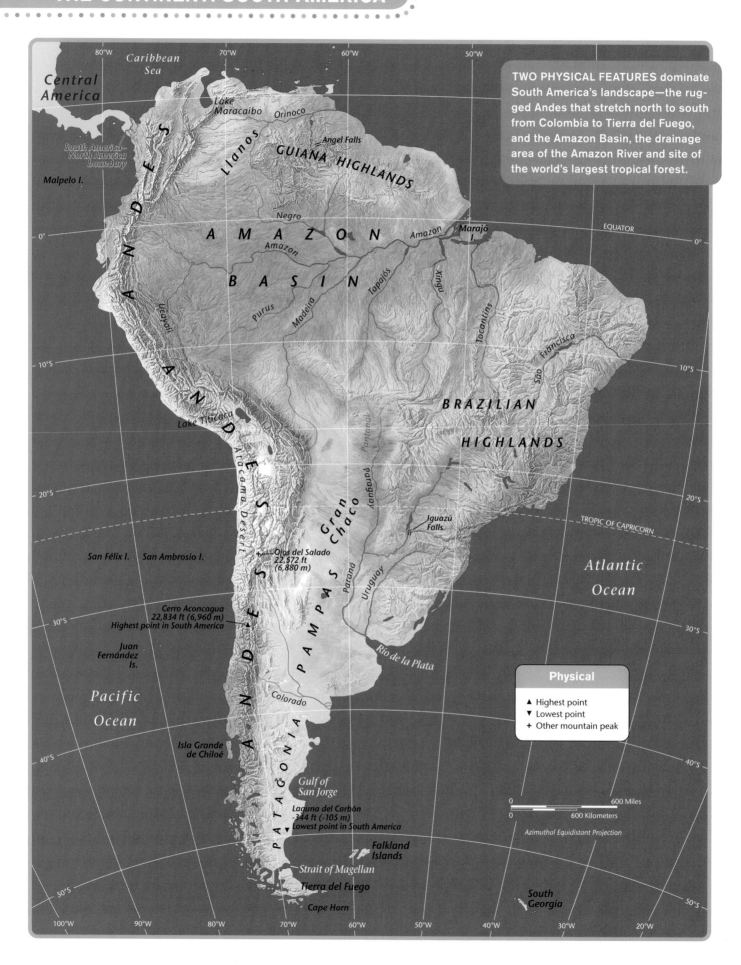

Central
America

Caribbean
Sea

80°W

70°W

60°W

50°W

Lake
Maracaibo

Orinoco

Llanos

Angel Falls

GUIANA HIGHLANDS

South America–
North America
boundary

Malpelo I.

A N D E S

Negro

A M A Z O N

Amazon

Marajó
I.

EQUATOR

0°

0°

Amazon

B A S I N

Ucayali

Purus

Madeira

Tapajós

Xingu

Tocantins

São Francisco

10°S

10°S

Lake Titicaca

BRAZILIAN

Atacama Desert

Pantanal

HIGHLANDS

20°S

Gran Chaco

Paraguay

Iguazú
Falls

TROPIC OF CAPRICORN

20°S

San Félix I.   San Ambrosio I.

A N D E S

Ojos del Salado
22,572 ft
(6,880 m)

Paraná

Uruguay

Atlantic

Ocean

Cerro Aconcagua
22,834 ft (6,960 m)
Highest point in South America

Juan
Fernández
Is.

P A M P A S

30°S

30°S

Pacific

Colorado

Río de la Plata

Ocean

A N D E S

Physical

▲ Highest point
▼ Lowest point
+ Other mountain peak

Isla Grande
de Chiloé

40°S

40°S

P A T A G O N I A

Gulf of
San Jorge

Laguna del Carbón
-344 ft (-105 m)
▼ Lowest point in South America

0   600 Miles
0   600 Kilometers

Azimuthal Equidistant Projection

Falkland
Islands

Strait of Magellan

Tierra del Fuego

South
Georgia

Cape Horn

50°S

50°S

100°W   90°W   80°W   70°W   60°W   50°W   40°W   30°W   20°W

TWO PHYSICAL FEATURES dominate South America's landscape—the rugged Andes that stretch north to south from Colombia to Tierra del Fuego, and the Amazon Basin, the drainage area of the Amazon River and site of the world's largest tropical forest.

THE CONTINENT: SOUTH AMERICA

TWELVE COUNTRIES and one French territory (French Guiana) make up South America. The continent was under mainly Spanish and Portuguese control from the 16th to the 19th century. Colonial influence is still evident in the use of Spanish and Portuguese languages and in the widespread presence of the Roman Catholic church.

Political
- ⊛ National capital
- • Other city

0   600 Miles
0   600 Kilometers

Azimuthal Equidistant Projection

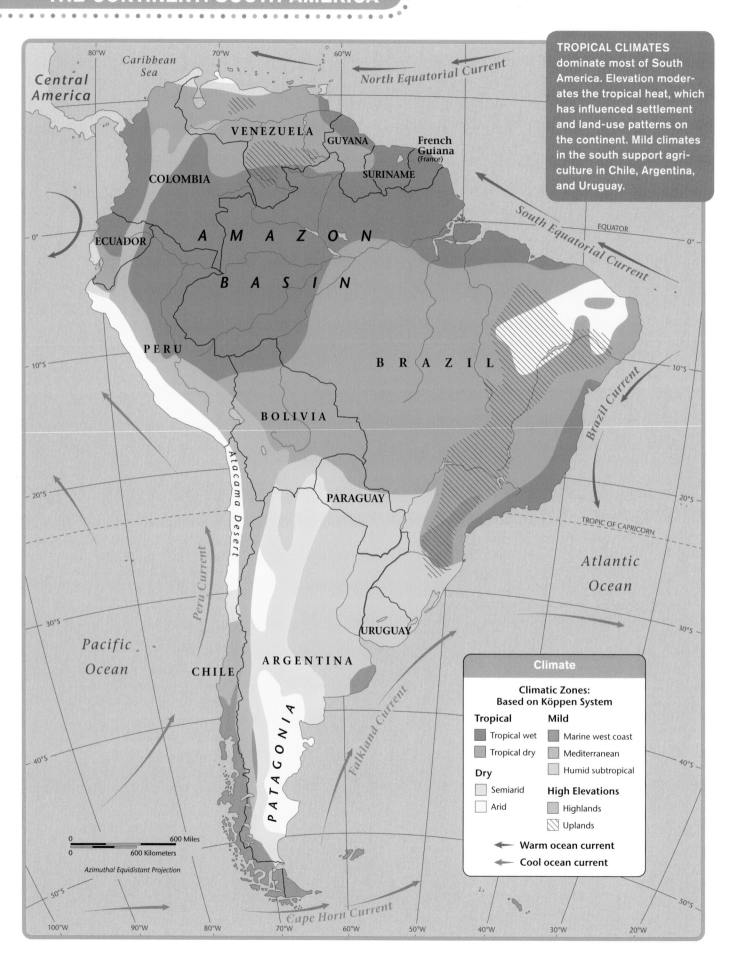

TROPICAL CLIMATES dominate most of South America. Elevation moderates the tropical heat, which has influenced settlement and land-use patterns on the continent. Mild climates in the south support agriculture in Chile, Argentina, and Uruguay.

Climate

Climatic Zones: Based on Köppen System

Tropical
- Tropical wet
- Tropical dry

Dry
- Semiarid
- Arid

Mild
- Marine west coast
- Mediterranean
- Humid subtropical

High Elevations
- Highlands
- Uplands

← Warm ocean current
← Cool ocean current

0   600 Miles
0   600 Kilometers
Azimuthal Equidistant Projection

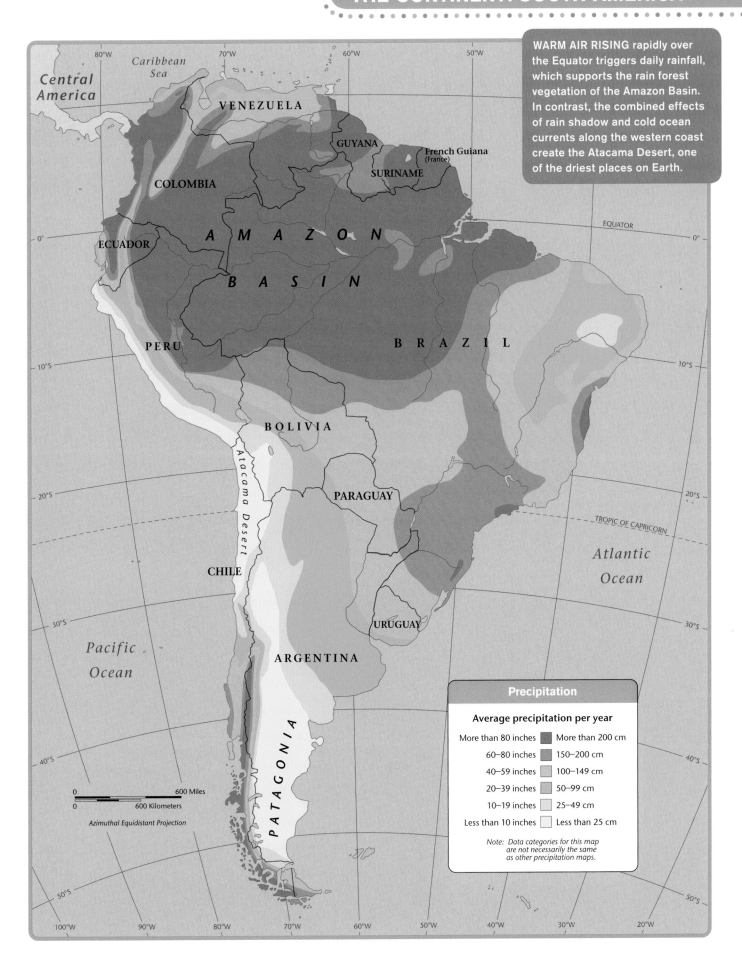

WARM AIR RISING rapidly over the Equator triggers daily rainfall, which supports the rain forest vegetation of the Amazon Basin. In contrast, the combined effects of rain shadow and cold ocean currents along the western coast create the Atacama Desert, one of the driest places on Earth.

Caribbean Sea

Central America

VENEZUELA

GUYANA

French Guiana (France)

SURINAME

COLOMBIA

A M A Z O N

EQUATOR

ECUADOR

B A S I N

PERU

B R A Z I L

BOLIVIA

Atacama Desert

PARAGUAY

TROPIC OF CAPRICORN

Atlantic Ocean

CHILE

URUGUAY

Pacific Ocean

ARGENTINA

P A T A G O N I A

0   600 Miles
0   600 Kilometers

Azimuthal Equidistant Projection

Precipitation

Average precipitation per year

More than 80 inches		More than 200 cm
60–80 inches		150–200 cm
40–59 inches		100–149 cm
20–39 inches		50–99 cm
10–19 inches		25–49 cm
Less than 10 inches		Less than 25 cm

Note: Data categories for this map are not necessarily the same as other precipitation maps.

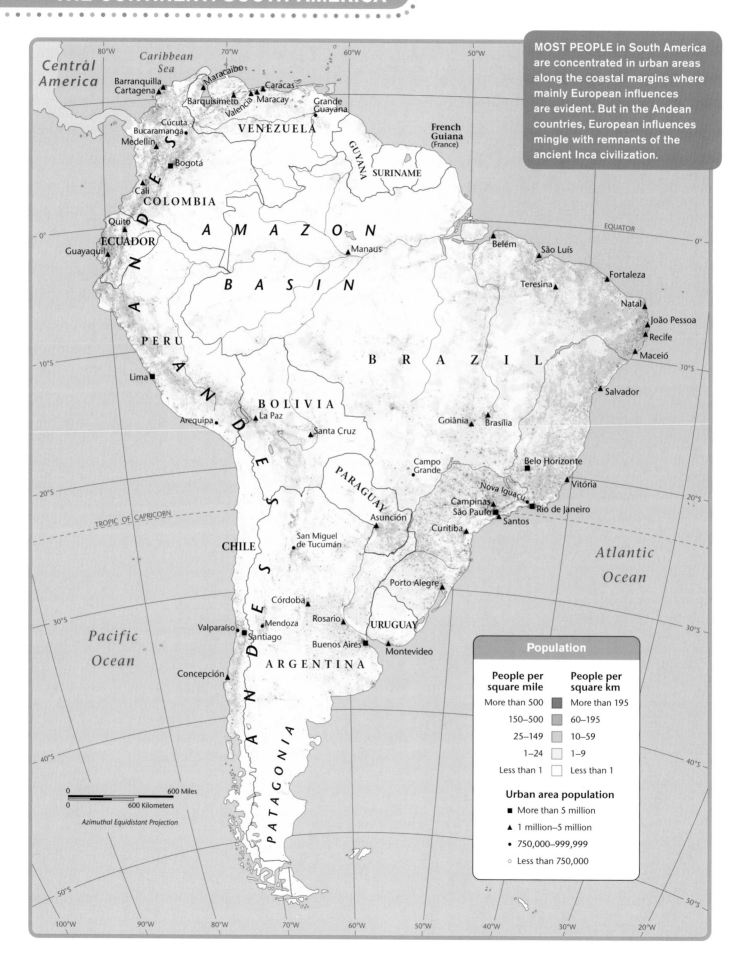

MOST PEOPLE in South America are concentrated in urban areas along the coastal margins where mainly European influences are evident. But in the Andean countries, European influences mingle with remnants of the ancient Inca civilization.

Population

People per square mile		People per square km
More than 500		More than 195
150–500		60–195
25–149		10–59
1–24		1–9
Less than 1		Less than 1

Urban area population

■ More than 5 million

▲ 1 million–5 million

● 750,000–999,999

○ Less than 750,000

Azimuthal Equidistant Projection

THE CONTINENT: SOUTH AMERICA

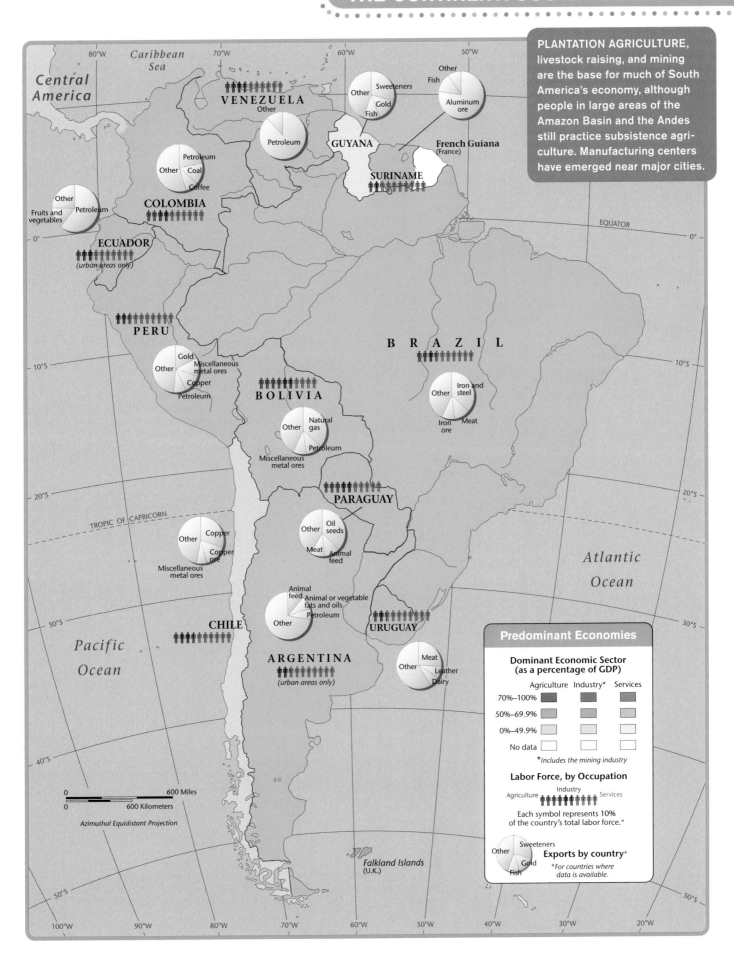

PLANTATION AGRICULTURE, livestock raising, and mining are the base for much of South America's economy, although people in large areas of the Amazon Basin and the Andes still practice subsistence agriculture. Manufacturing centers have emerged near major cities.

Caribbean Sea

Central America

VENEZUELA
Other
Petroleum

GUYANA
Other
Sweeteners
Gold
Fish

Other
Fish
Aluminum ore

French Guiana (France)

SURINAME

COLOMBIA
Petroleum
Other
Coal
Coffee

ECUADOR
Other
Fruits and vegetables
Petroleum
(urban areas only)

PERU

EQUATOR

0°

BRAZIL
Other
Iron and steel
Iron ore
Meat

Gold
Other
Miscellaneous metal ores
Copper
Petroleum

BOLIVIA
Other
Natural gas
Petroleum
Miscellaneous metal ores

PARAGUAY
Other
Oil seeds
Meat
Animal feed

CHILE
Other
Copper
Copper ore
Miscellaneous metal ores

ARGENTINA
Animal feed
Animal or vegetable fats and oils
Petroleum
Other
(urban areas only)

URUGUAY
Other
Meat
Leather
Dairy

Atlantic Ocean

Pacific Ocean

Falkland Islands (U.K.)

0 | 600 Miles
0 | 600 Kilometers
Azimuthal Equidistant Projection

Predominant Economies

Dominant Economic Sector
(as a percentage of GDP)

	Agriculture	Industry*	Services
70%–100%			
50%–69.9%			
0%–49.9%			
No data			

*Includes the mining industry

Labor Force, by Occupation

Agriculture — Industry — Services

Each symbol represents 10% of the country's total labor force.*

Exports by country*

Other
Sweeteners
Gold
Fish

*For countries where data is available.

Amazon Rain Forest

The Amazon rain forest, which covers approximately 2.7 million square miles (7 million sq km), is the world's largest tropical forest. Located mainly in Brazil, the Amazon rain forest accounts for more than 20 percent of all the world's tropical forests. Known in Brazil as the selva, the rain forest is a vast storehouse of biological diversity, filled with plants and animals both familiar and exotic. According to estimates, at least half of all species are found in tropical forests, but many of these species have not yet been identified.

Tropical forests contain many valuable resources, including cacao (chocolate), nuts, spices, rare hardwoods, and plant extracts used to make medicines. Some drugs used in treating cancer and heart disease come from plants found only in tropical forests. But human intervention—logging, mining, and clearing land for crops and grazing—has put tropical forests at great risk. In Brazil, roads cut into the rain forest have opened the way for settlers, who clear away the forest only to discover soil too poor in nutrients to sustain agriculture for more than a few years. Land usually is cleared by a method called slash-and-burn, which contributes to global warming by releasing great amounts of carbon dioxide into the atmosphere.

TROPICAL RAIN FORESTS: FACTS & FIGURES

- Tropical rain forests cover 6 percent of Earth's surface, but are home to half of Earth's species.

- Average monthly temperature is 68° to 82°F (20° to 28°C).

- Total annual rainfall averages 5 to 33 feet (1.5 to 10 m).

- Trees in tropical rain forests can grow up to 200 feet (60 m) in height.

- Most nutrients in tropical rain forests are stored in the vegetation rather than in the soil, which is very poor.

- Some of Earth's most valuable woods, such as teak, mahogany, rosewood, and sandalwood, grow in tropical rain forests.

- Up to 25 percent of all medicines include products originating in tropical rain forests.

- Tropical rain forests absorb carbon dioxide and release oxygen.

- Deforestation of tropical rain forests contributes to climate change.

- An estimated 100 acres (40 ha) of rain forest are lost every minute.

- Brazil loses 10.6 million acres (4.3 million ha) of tropical forests annually, but Nigeria, in Africa, has the highest rate of deforestation—more than 11 percent annually.

⇧ SLOW-MOVING, this three-toed sloth spends most of its life in the treetops. It is one of the many unusual species of animals that make their homes in the forests of the Amazon Basin.

⇩ DENSE CANOPY OF THE RAIN FOREST stands in sharp contrast to the silt-laden waters of one of the Amazon's many tributaries. Although seemingly endless, the forest in Brazil is decreasing in size at the rate of almost 15,000 acres (6,070 ha) per day.

⇩ SLASH-AND-BURN is a method used in the tropics for clearing land for farms. But the soil is poor in nutrients, and good yields are short-lived.

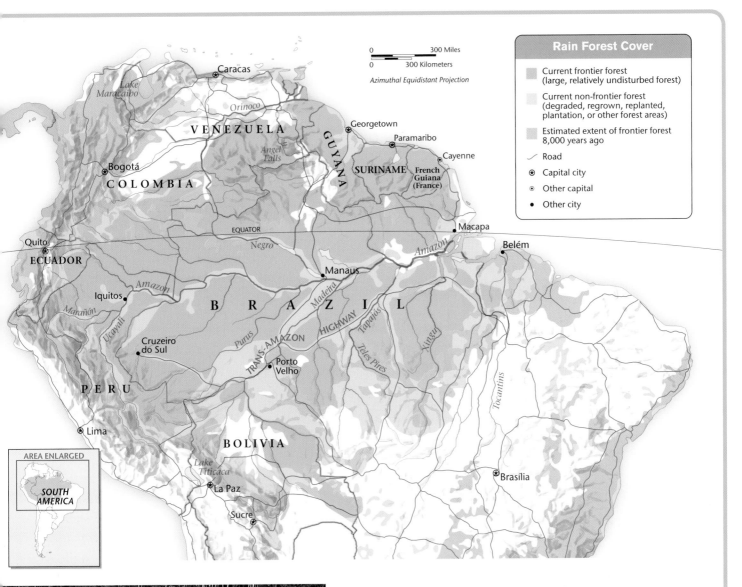

0 ——— 300 Miles
0 ——— 300 Kilometers
Azimuthal Equidistant Projection

Rain Forest Cover

Current frontier forest
(large, relatively undisturbed forest)

Current non-frontier forest
(degraded, regrown, replanted,
plantation, or other forest areas)

Estimated extent of frontier forest
8,000 years ago

⟋ Road

⊛ Capital city

⊙ Other capital

• Other city

Caracas
Lake Maracaibo
Orinoco
VENEZUELA
GUYANA
Georgetown
Paramaribo
Cayenne
SURINAME
French Guiana (France)
Bogotá
COLOMBIA
Angel Falls
EQUATOR
Macapa
Negro
Quito
ECUADOR
Amazon
Belém
Manaus
Iquitos
Amazon
Madeira
B R A Z I L
Marañón
Ucayali
Purus
TRANS-AMAZON HIGHWAY
Tapajos
Teles Pires
Xingu
Cruzeiro do Sul
Porto Velho
Tocantins
P E R U
BOLIVIA
Lima
Brasília
Lake Titicaca
La Paz
Sucre

AREA ENLARGED

SOUTH AMERICA

⟵ MINING OPERATIONS, such as this tin mine, remove forests to gain access to mineral deposits.

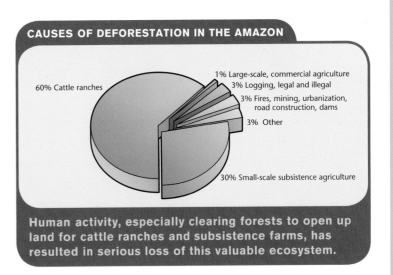

CAUSES OF DEFORESTATION IN THE AMAZON

60% Cattle ranches

1% Large-scale, commercial agriculture
3% Logging, legal and illegal
3% Fires, mining, urbanization, road construction, dams
3% Other

30% Small-scale subsistence agriculture

Human activity, especially clearing forests to open up land for cattle ranches and subsistence farms, has resulted in serious loss of this valuable ecosystem.

Europe:
A View From Space

Smaller than every other continent except Australia, Europe is a mosaic of islands and peninsulas. In fact, Europe itself is one big peninsula, jutting westward from the huge landmass of Asia and nearly touching Africa to the south. Europe's ragged coastline measures more than one and a half times the length of the Equator—38,279 miles (61,603 km) to be exact—giving 32 of its 46 countries direct access to the sea.

Hallstatt, Austria in the morning light

THE CONTINENT: EUROPE

Europe

PHYSICAL

Land area 3,841,000 sq mi (9,947,000 sq km)	**Lowest point** Caspian Sea -92 ft (-28 m)	**Largest lake entirely in Europe** Ladoga, Russia 6,853 sq mi (17,703 sq km)
Highest point El'brus, Russia 18,510 ft (5,642 m)	**Longest river** Volga, Russia 2,290 mi (3,685 m)	

POLITICAL

Population 732,552,000	**Largest country entirely in Europe** Ukraine 233,090 sq mi (603,700 sq km)	**Most populous country entirely in Europe** Germany Pop. 82,254,000
Number of independent countries 46	**Smallest country** Vatican City 0.2 sq mi (0.4 sq km)	**Least populous country** Vatican City Pop. 798

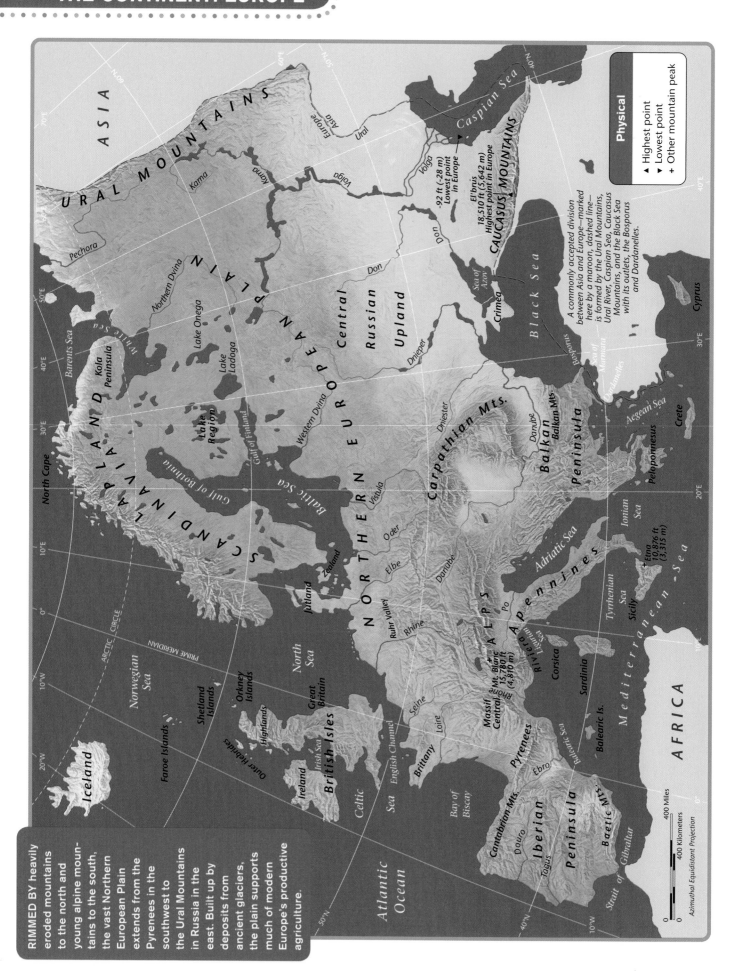

Physical
- ▲ Highest point
- ▼ Lowest point
- + Other mountain peak

A S I A

U R A L   M O U N T A I N S

Pechora

Kama

Kama

Europe
Asia
Ural

Volga

Don

Volga

-92 ft (-28 m)
Lowest point
in Europe

El'brus
18,510 ft (5,642 m)
Highest point in Europe
CAUCASUS MOUNTAINS

Caspian Sea

A commonly accepted division
between Asia and Europe—marked
here by a maroon, dashed line—
is formed by the Ural Mountains,
Ural River, Caspian Sea, Caucasus
Mountains, and the Black Sea
with its outlets, the Bosporus
and Dardanelles.

Cyprus

Sea of
Azov

Crimea

Black Sea

Bosporus

Sea of
Marmara

Dardanelles

Aegean Sea

Crete

Peloponnesus

Ionian
Sea

+ Etna
10,876 ft
(3,315 m)

Barents Sea

Northern Dvina

Lake Onega

Lake Ladoga

Kola Peninsula

White Sea

N O R T H E R N   E U R O P E A N   P L A I N

Central Russian Upland

Don

Dnieper

Dniester

Carpathian Mts.

Danube

Balkan Mts.

Balkan Peninsula

Adriatic Sea

Apennines

Tyrrhenian Sea

Sicily

Sardinia

Corsica

Mediterranean Sea

AFRICA

North Cape

S C A N D I N A V I A N   U P L A N D

Lake Region

Gulf of Finland

Gulf of Bothnia

Baltic Sea

Western Dvina

Vistula

Oder

Elbe

Danube

Rhine

A L P S

Mt. Blanc
15,780 ft
(4,810 m)

Massif Central

Rhône

Riviera

Po

Balearic Is.

Zealand

Jutland

Ruhr Valley

Iceland

Norwegian Sea

Faroe Islands

Shetland Islands

Orkney Islands

Highlands

Outer Hebrides

Great Britain

North Sea

Ireland

Inner Hebrides

British Isles

Celtic Sea

English Channel

Brittany

Seine

Loire

Bay of Biscay

Pyrenees

Cantabrian Mts.

Iberian Peninsula

Douro

Tagus

Ebro

Baetic Mts.

Balearic Sea

Strait of Gibraltar

Atlantic Ocean

ARCTIC CIRCLE

PRIME MERIDIAN

Azimuthal Equidistant Projection

0   400 Miles
0   400 Kilometers

RIMMED BY heavily
eroded mountains
to the north and
young alpine moun-
tains to the south,
the vast Northern
European Plain
extends from the
Pyrenees in the
southwest to
the Ural Mountains
in Russia in the
east. Built up by
deposits from
ancient glaciers,
the plain supports
much of modern
Europe's productive
agriculture.

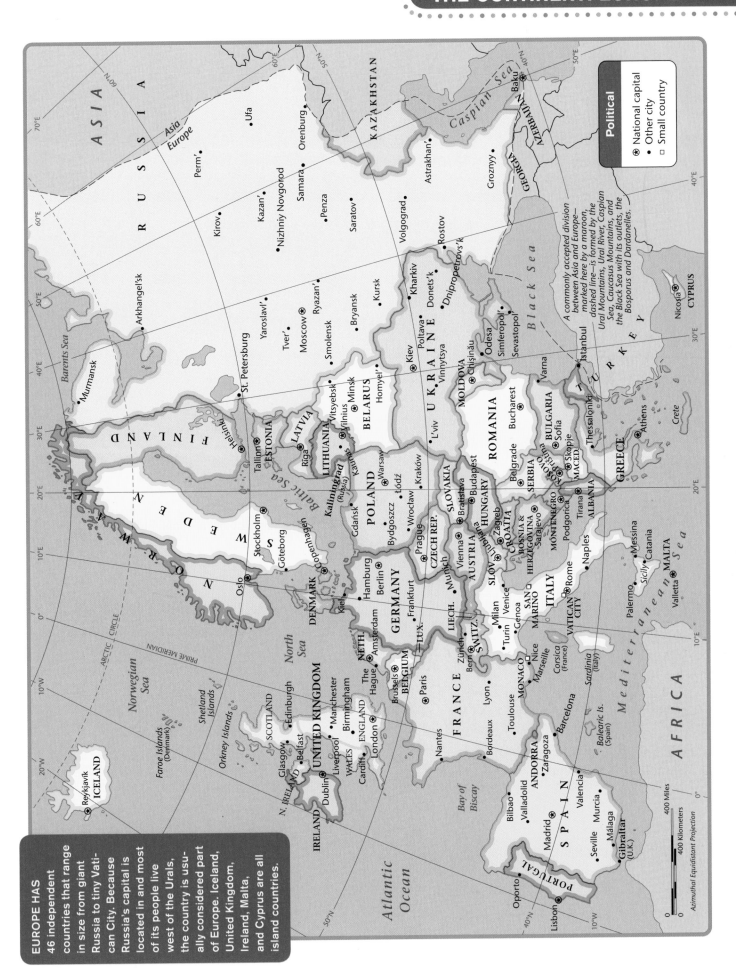

EUROPE HAS 46 independent countries that range in size from giant Russia to tiny Vatican City. Because Russia's capital is located in and most of its people live west of the Urals, the country is usually considered part of Europe. Iceland, United Kingdom, Ireland, Malta, and Cyprus are all island countries.

Political
- ⊛ National capital
- • Other city
- □ Small country

A commonly accepted division between Asia and Europe—marked here by a maroon, dashed line—is formed by the Ural Mountains, Ural River, Caspian Sea, Caucasus Mountains, and the Black Sea with its outlets, the Bosporus and Dardanelles.

ASIA

RUSSIA

KAZAKHSTAN

Asia / Europe

Ufa
Perm'
Orenburg
Kirov
Kazan'
Nizhniy Novgorod
Samara
Penza
Saratov
Astrakhan'
Volgograd
Grozny
Rostov
Arkhangel'sk
Yaroslavl'
Moscow ⊛
Ryazan'
Smolensk
Bryansk
Kursk
Kharkiv
Donets'k
Dnipropetrovs'k
Tver'
St. Petersburg
Murmansk
Helsinki ⊛

Barents Sea

Caspian Sea
Baku ⊛
AZERBAIJAN
GEORGIA

Black Sea

Poltava
Kiev ⊛
L'viv
UKRAINE
Vinnytsya
MOLDOVA
Chişinău ⊛
Odesa
Simferopol'
Sevastopol'
Istanbul
TURKEY
Nicosia ⊛
CYPRUS
Crete

FINLAND

ESTONIA
Tallinn ⊛
Riga ⊛
LATVIA
LITHUANIA
Vilnius ⊛
Vitsyebsk
Minsk ⊛
BELARUS
Homyel'
Kaliningrad (Russia)
Kaunas

Varna
Bucharest ⊛
ROMANIA
BULGARIA
Sofia ⊛
Skopje ⊛ MACED.
SERBIA
Belgrade ⊛
KOSOVO
Priština
MONTENEGRO
Podgorica ⊛
Tirana ⊛
ALBANIA
Thessaloniki
GREECE
Athens ⊛

SWEDEN
NORWAY
Stockholm ⊛
Göteborg
Oslo ⊛
Copenhagen ⊛
DENMARK
Kiel
Hamburg

Baltic Sea

POLAND
Warsaw ⊛
Łódź
Gdańsk
Bydgoszcz
Wrocław
Kraków
SLOVAKIA
Bratislava ⊛
CZECH REP.
Prague ⊛
Budapest ⊛
HUNGARY
Vienna ⊛
AUSTRIA
Zagreb ⊛
CROATIA
Ljubljana ⊛
SLOVENIA
BOSNIA & HERZEGOVINA
Sarajevo ⊛

Berlin ⊛
GERMANY
Frankfurt
Munich
LIECH.
Zürich
SWITZ.
Bern ⊛
Milan
Turin
Venice
Genoa
SAN MARINO
ITALY
Rome ⊛
VATICAN CITY
Naples
Palermo
Sicily
Catania
Messina
MALTA
Valletta ⊛

Mediterranean Sea

AFRICA

NETH.
Amsterdam ⊛
The Hague
BELGIUM
Brussels ⊛
LUX.
FRANCE
Paris ⊛
MONACO
Nice
Marseille
Corsica (France)
Sardinia (Italy)
Lyon
Toulouse
Bordeaux
Nantes
Bay of Biscay

Reykjavík ⊛
ICELAND

Faroe Islands (Denmark)
Shetland Islands
Orkney Islands
SCOTLAND
Glasgow
Edinburgh
Belfast
N. IRELAND
IRELAND
Dublin ⊛
Liverpool
Manchester
Birmingham
UNITED KINGDOM
ENGLAND
WALES
Cardiff
London ⊛

North Sea

Norwegian Sea

Atlantic Ocean

PORTUGAL
Oporto
Lisbon ⊛
SPAIN
Madrid ⊛
Valladolid
Bilbao
ANDORRA
Zaragoza
Barcelona
Valencia
Murcia
Seville
Málaga
Gibraltar (U.K.)
Balearic Is. (Spain)

ARCTIC CIRCLE
PRIME MERIDIAN

400 Miles
400 Kilometers
Azimuthal Equidistant Projection

THE CONTINENT: EUROPE

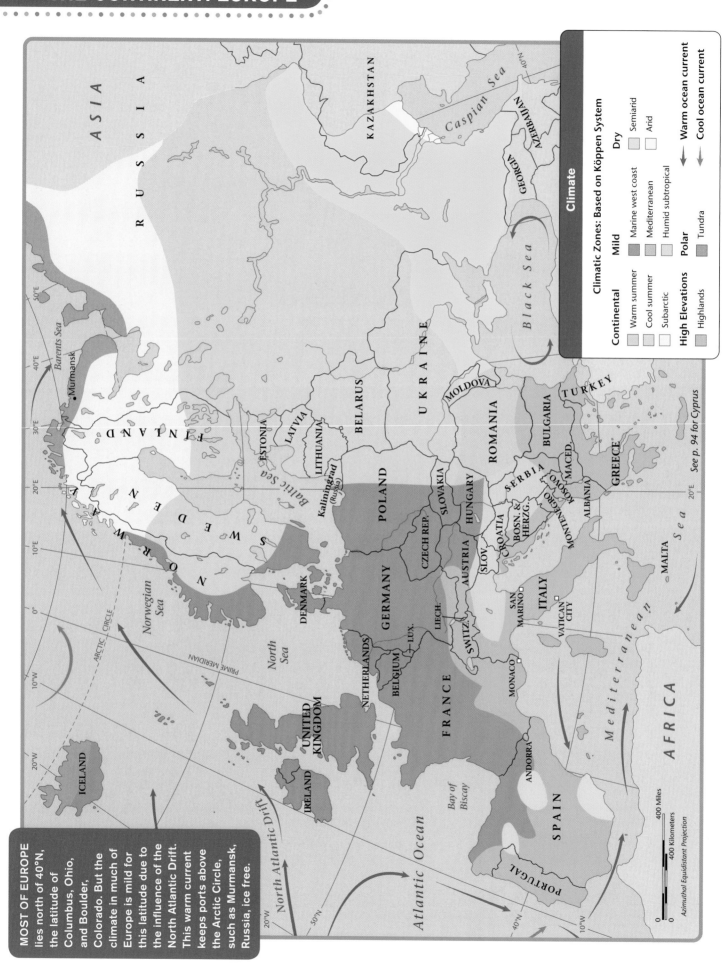

MOST OF EUROPE lies north of 40°N, the latitude of Columbus, Ohio, and Boulder, Colorado. But the climate in much of Europe is mild for this latitude due to the influence of the North Atlantic Drift. This warm current keeps ports above the Arctic Circle, such as Murmansk, Russia, ice free.

Climate

Climatic Zones: Based on Köppen System

Continental
- Warm summer
- Cool summer
- Subarctic

Mild
- Marine west coast
- Mediterranean
- Humid subtropical

Dry
- Semiarid
- Arid

Polar
- Tundra

High Elevations
- Highlands

→ Warm ocean current
→ Cool ocean current

See p. 94 for Cyprus

Azimuthal Equidistant Projection

400 Miles
400 Kilometers

THE CONTINENT: EUROPE

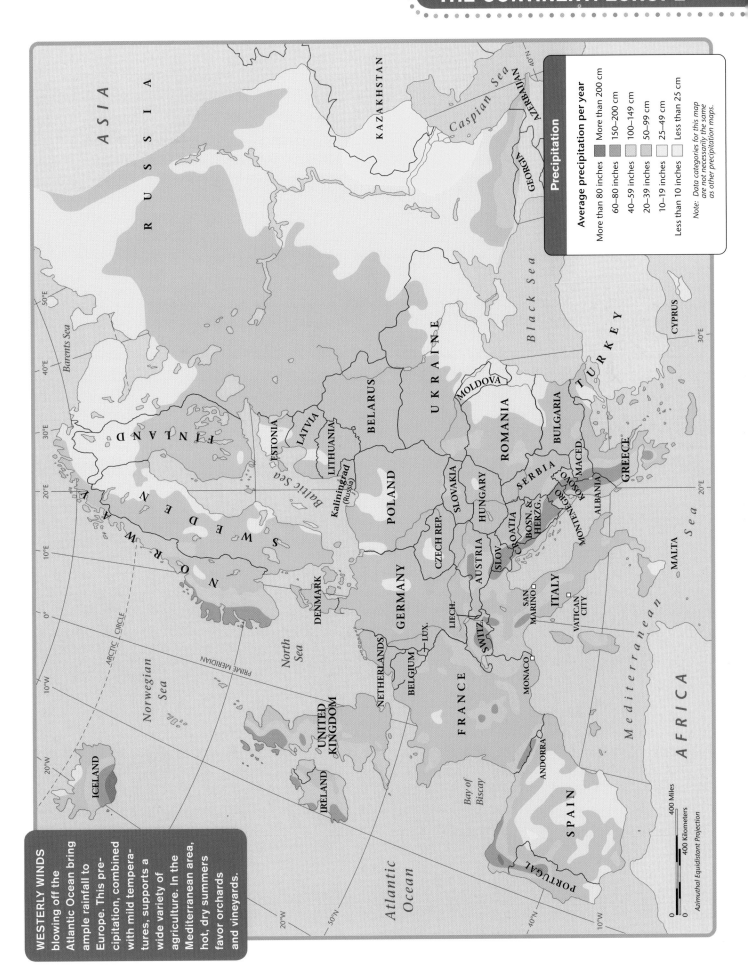

WESTERLY WINDS blowing off the Atlantic Ocean bring ample rainfall to Europe. This precipitation, combined with mild temperatures, supports a wide variety of agriculture. In the Mediterranean area, hot, dry summers favor orchards and vineyards.

Precipitation

Average precipitation per year

More than 80 inches	More than 200 cm
60–80 inches	150–200 cm
40–59 inches	100–149 cm
20–39 inches	50–99 cm
10–19 inches	25–49 cm
Less than 10 inches	Less than 25 cm

Note: Data categories for this map are not necessarily the same as other precipitation maps.

A S I A

R U S S I A

KAZAKHSTAN

Caspian Sea

AZERBAIJAN

GEORGIA

Black Sea

Barents Sea

F I N L A N D

ESTONIA

LATVIA

LITHUANIA

BELARUS

U K R A I N E

MOLDOVA

ROMANIA

BULGARIA

T U R K E Y

CYPRUS

N O R W A Y

S W E D E N

Baltic Sea

Kaliningrad (Russia)

POLAND

CZECH REP.

SLOVAKIA

HUNGARY

SERBIA

MACED.

GREECE

ALBANIA

KOSOVO

MONTENEGRO

BOSN. & HERZG.

CROATIA

SLOV.

AUSTRIA

DENMARK

NETHERLANDS

GERMANY

BELGIUM

LUX.

LIECH.

SWITZ.

SAN MARINO

ITALY

VATICAN CITY

MALTA

Mediterranean Sea

A F R I C A

MONACO

F R A N C E

ANDORRA

S P A I N

PORTUGAL

Bay of Biscay

UNITED KINGDOM

IRELAND

North Sea

Norwegian Sea

ICELAND

Atlantic Ocean

ARCTIC CIRCLE

PRIME MERIDIAN

50°E

40°E

30°E

20°E

10°E

0°

10°W

20°W

40°N

30°E

20°E

10°W

40°N

50°N

400 Miles

400 Kilometers

Azimuthal Equidistant Projection

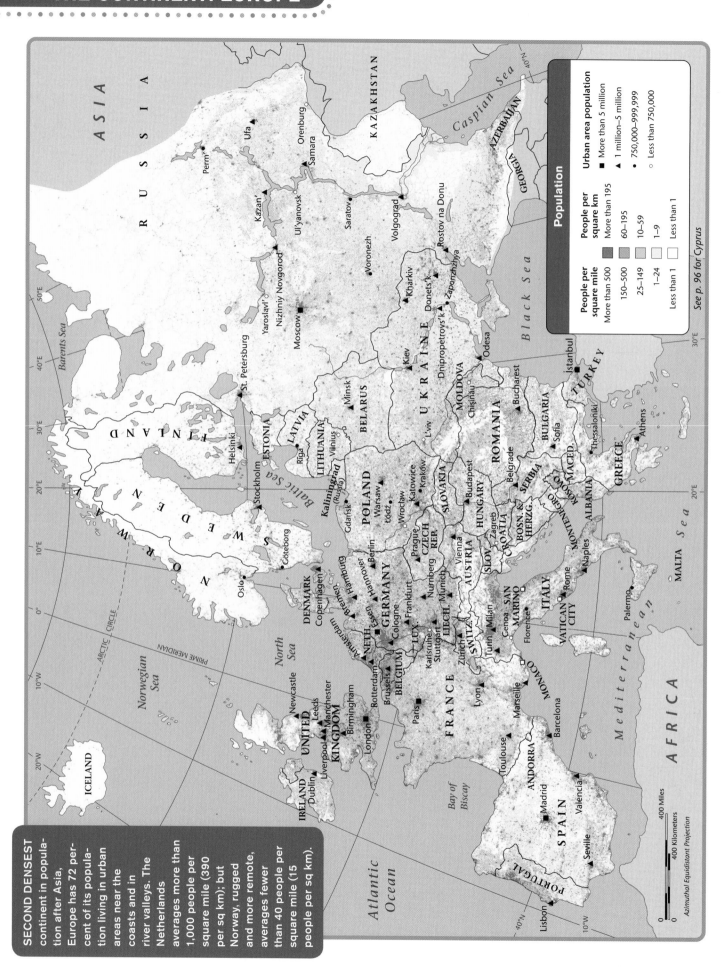

SECOND DENSEST continent in population after Asia, Europe has 72 percent of its population living in urban areas near the coasts and in river valleys. The Netherlands averages more than 1,000 people per square mile (390 per sq km); but Norway, rugged and more remote, averages fewer than 40 people per square mile (15 people per sq km).

Population

People per square mile | **People per square km**
More than 500 | More than 195
150–500 | 60–195
25–149 | 10–59
1–24 | 1–9
Less than 1 | Less than 1

Urban area population
■ More than 5 million
▲ 1 million–5 million
● 750,000–999,999
○ Less than 750,000

See p. 96 for Cyprus

Azimuthal Equidistant Projection

400 Miles
400 Kilometers

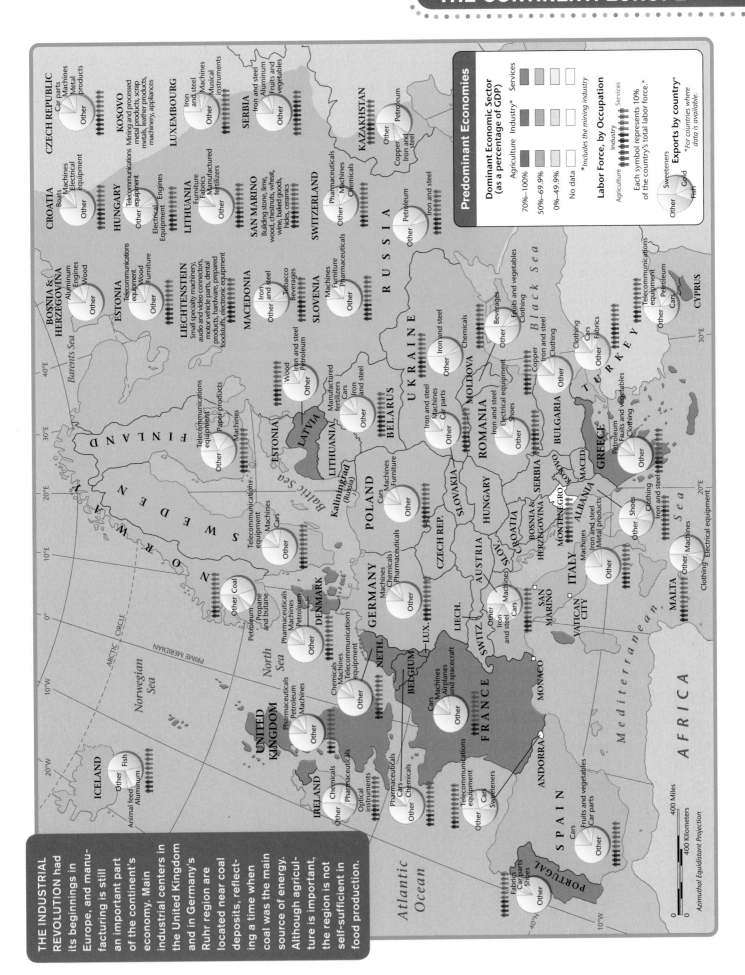

THE INDUSTRIAL REVOLUTION had its beginnings in Europe, and manufacturing is still an important part of the continent's economy. Main industrial centers in the United Kingdom and in Germany's Ruhr region are located near coal deposits, reflecting a time when coal was the main source of energy. Although agriculture is important, the region is not self-sufficient in food production.

Predominant Economies

Dominant Economic Sector (as a percentage of GDP)

Agriculture | Industry* | Services

70%—100%
50%—69.9%
0%—49.9%
No data

*Includes the mining industry

Labor Force, by Occupation

Agriculture | Industry | Services

Each symbol represents 10% of the country's total labor force.*

Exports by country*

*For countries where data is available.

European Union

In the years following World War II, the countries of Europe looked for ways to restore political stability to the continent while rebuilding their war-ravaged economies. The first step toward the European Union was taken in 1950 when France proposed creating common institutions to jointly govern coal and steel production in Europe. In 1951 France, West Germany, Italy, Belgium, Netherlands, and Luxembourg created the European Coal and Steel Community with the goal of bringing former adversaries together. In 1957 the Treaty of Rome established the European Economic Community (EEC), which removed trade barriers among member countries. In 1965 that organization joined with other countries of Europe to form the European Community (EC).

The Maastricht Treaty, signed in 1992 and effective in 1993, established today's European Union (EU) and paved the way for a common foreign policy and a single European currency—the euro. The euro now circulates in 12 member countries and will expand to others as strict economic and financial standards are met. The treaty also established the groundwork for the open flow of people, products, and services among member countries. In 1995 three more countries joined the EU, bringing the membership to 15. But in May 2004, the EU almost doubled in size with the admission of 10 countries to membership: Estonia, Latvia, Lithuania, Poland, Czech Republic, Slovakia, Hungary, Cyprus, Slovenia, and Malta. In 2007 the addition of Bulgaria and Romania raised membership to 27 countries. Three additional countries—Croatia, the former Yugoslav Republic of Macedonia, and Turkey—have applied for membership.

⇧ EUROPEAN UNION LEADERS hold a press conference at European Council headquarters in Brussels, Belgium. The Council, made up of ministers from member states, is the main decision-making body of the European Union. It passes laws, sets economic policies, and enters into international agreements between the European Union and non-EU countries.

THE CONTINENT: EUROPE

ASIA

ICELAND

Norwegian Sea

Faroe Islands (Denmark)

Shetland Islands

Orkney Islands

Atlantic Ocean

North Sea

UNITED KINGDOM
1973

IRELAND
1973

NETHERLANDS
1957

BELGIUM
1957

LUXEMBOURG
1957

Bay of Biscay

FRANCE
1957

SWITZ.

LIECH.

DENMARK
1973

1995

GERMANY
(WEST) (EAST)
1957   1990

Baltic Sea

N O R W A Y

S W E D E N

1995

FINLAND
1995

ESTONIA
2004

LATVIA
2004

LITHUANIA
2004

Kaliningrad (Russia)

BELARUS

RUSSIA

KAZAKHSTAN

POLAND
2004

CZECH REP.
2004

SLOVAKIA
2004

AUSTRIA
1995

HUNGARY
2004

SLOVENIA
2004

CROATIA

BOSN. &
HERZG.

SERBIA

MONT.

KOS.

MACED.

UKRAINE

MOLDOVA

ROMANIA
2007

BULGARIA
2007

Black Sea

Europe / Asia

GEORGIA

PORTUGAL
1986

S P A I N
1986

ANDORRA

MONACO

Corsica (France)

SAN MARINO

VATICAN CITY

ITALY
1957

ALBANIA

Sardinia (Italy)

Balearic Is. (Spain)

Gibraltar (U.K.)

Mediterranean Sea

Sicily

MALTA
2004

GREECE
1981

Crete

T U R K E Y

A S I A

CYPRUS
2004

A F R I C A

Europe / Asia / Africa

European Union

	Member country
	Newly admitted country
	Candidate country
	Other European country
1957	Year of admission

0   400 Miles
0   400 Kilometers
Azimuthal Equidistant Projection

EU IN THE GLOBAL ECONOMY

With a total population of almost 500 million, the European Union (EU) is a major player in the global economy. The EU leads all countries in total exports and is surpassed only by the United States in imports. More than one-fifth of the EU's exports go to the United States, while its leading import partners are China, the United States, and Russia. The EU's main exports include machinery, motor vehicles, airplanes, plastics, chemicals, and pharmaceuticals.

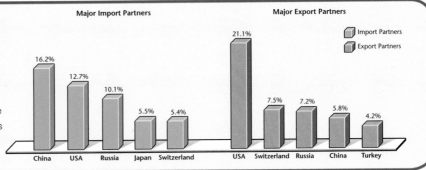

Major Import Partners

China 16.2%
USA 12.7%
Russia 10.1%
Japan 5.5%
Switzerland 5.4%

Major Export Partners

USA 21.1%
Switzerland 7.5%
Russia 7.2%
China 5.8%
Turkey 4.2%

Import Partners
Export Partners

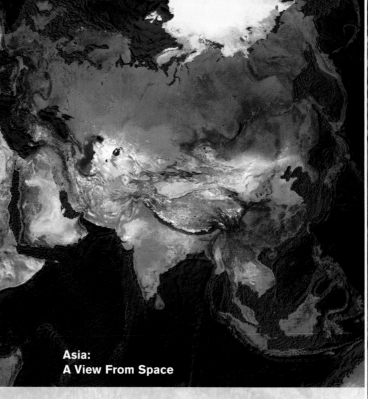

Asia:
A View From Space

From the frozen shores of the Arctic Ocean to the equatorial islands of Indonesia, Asia stretches across 90 degrees of latitude. From the Ural Mountains to the Pacific Ocean it covers more than 150 degrees of longitude. Here, three of history's great culture hearths emerged in the valleys of the Tigris and Euphrates, the Indus, and the Yellow (Huang) Rivers. Today, Asia is home to more than 60 percent of Earth's people and some of the world's fastest growing economies.

Terraced rice fields on Bali, Indonesia

THE CONTINENT: ASIA

Asia

PHYSICAL

Land area 17,208,000 sq mi (44,570,000 sq km)	**Lowest point** Dead Sea, Israel-Jordan -1,380 ft (-421 m)	**Largest lake entirely in Asia** Lake Baikal 12,200 sq mi (31,500 sq km)
Highest point Mount Everest, China-Nepal 29,035 ft (8,850 m)	**Longest river** Yangtze (Chang), China 3,964 mi (6,380 km)	

POLITICAL

Population 4,009,521,000	**Largest country entirely in Asia** China 3,705,405 sq mi (9,596,960 sq km)	**Most populous country** China Pop. 1,348,317,000
Number of independent countries 46 (excluding Russia)	**Smallest country** Maldives 115 sq mi (298 sq km)	**Least populous country** Maldives Pop. 304,000

THE CONTINENT: ASIA

ASIA'S PHYSICAL characteristics are impressive. It boasts the world's highest peak (Mount Everest), the deepest lake (Lake Baikal), and 30 percent of Earth's land area. Diversity also marks the Asian landscape, from the dry deserts of the Arabian Peninsula to the frozen tundra of Siberia to steamy rain forests in Borneo.

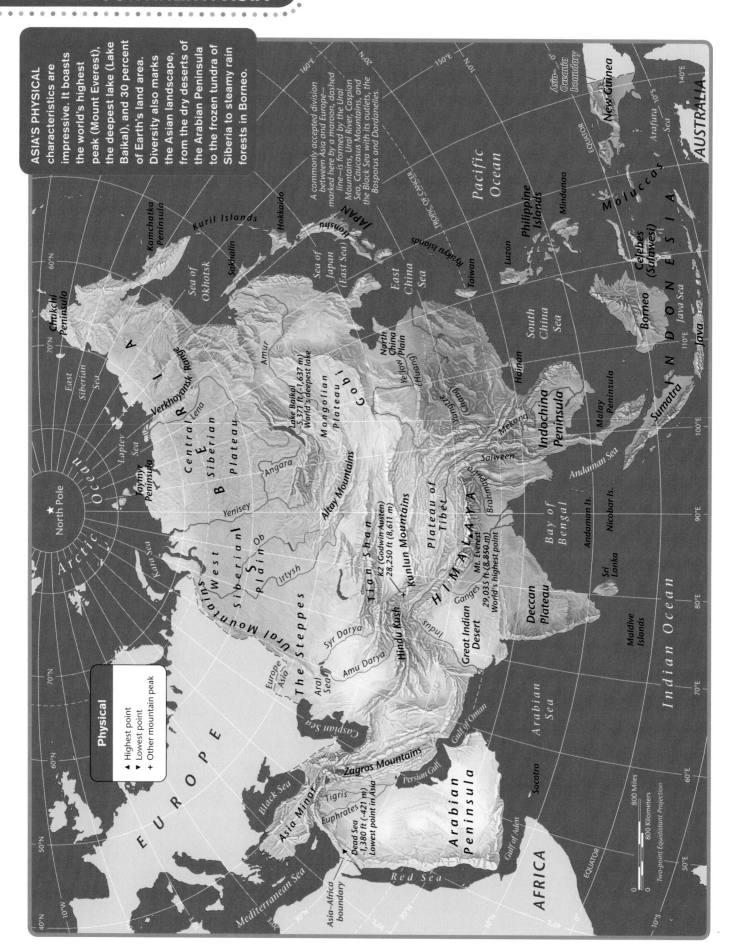

A commonly accepted division between Asia and Europe—marked here by a maroon, dashed line—is formed by the Ural Mountains, Ural River, Caspian Sea, Caucasus Mountains, and the Black Sea with its outlets, the Bosporus and Dardanelles.

Physical

◄ Highest point
▶ Lowest point
+ Other mountain peak

AUSTRALIA

New Guinea

Pacific Ocean

Moluccas

Philippine Islands

Mindanao

Celebes (Sulawesi)

I N D O N E S I A

Borneo

Sumatra

Java Sea

Java

Luzon

Taiwan

Hainan

South China Sea

East China Sea

Ryukyu Islands

JAPAN

Hokkaido

Honshu

Sea of Japan (East Sea)

Sakhalin

Kuril Islands

Sea of Okhotsk

Kamchatka Peninsula

Chukchi Peninsula

East Siberian Sea

S I B E R I A

Verkhoyansk Range

Central Siberian Plateau

Lena

Angara

Yenisey

Taymyr Peninsula

Laptev Sea

Kara Sea

North Pole

Arctic Ocean

West Siberian Plain

Ob

Irtysh

Ural Mountains

The Steppes

EUROPE

Black Sea

Asia Minor

Tigris

Euphrates

Zagros Mountains

Persian Gulf

Gulf of Oman

Arabian Sea

Arabian Peninsula

Socotra

Gulf of Aden

Red Sea

Mediterranean Sea

AFRICA

Asia-Africa boundary

▶ Dead Sea -1,380 ft (-421 m) Lowest point in Asia

Europe / Asia

Aral Sea

Caspian Sea

Syr Darya

Amu Darya

Hindu Kush

Tian Shan

+ K2 (Godwin Austen) 28,250 ft (8,611 m)

Kunlun Mountains

Plateau of Tibet

H I M A L A Y A

Indus

◄ Mt. Everest 29,035 ft (8,850 m) World's highest point

Ganges

Great Indian Desert

Deccan Plateau

Sri Lanka

Maldive Islands

Bay of Bengal

Andaman Is.

Nicobar Is.

Andaman Sea

Indian Ocean

Brahmaputra

Salween

Mekong

Yangtze (Chang)

Indochina Peninsula

Malay Peninsula

Yellow (Huang)

North China Plain

Gobi

Mongolian Plateau

Altay Mountains

Lake Baikal -5,371 ft (-1,637 m) World's deepest lake

Amur

EQUATOR

TROPIC OF CANCER

800 Miles
800 Kilometers
Two-point Equidistant Projection

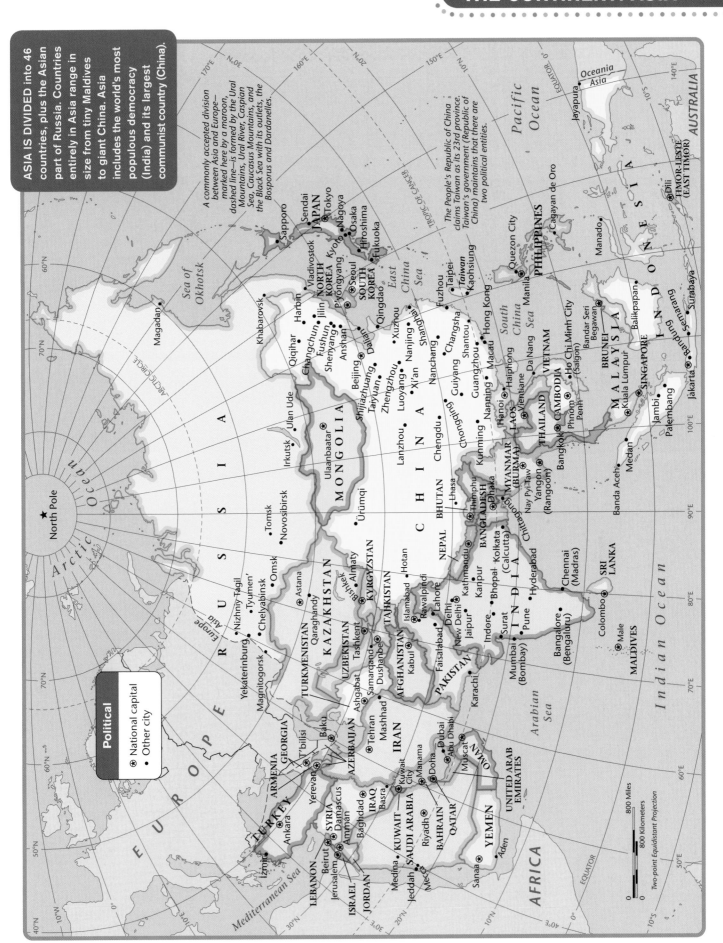

ASIA IS DIVIDED into 46 countries, plus the Asian part of Russia. Countries entirely in Asia range in size from tiny Maldives to giant China. Asia includes the world's most populous democracy (India) and its largest communist country (China).

A commonly accepted division between Asia and Europe—marked here by a maroon, dashed line—is formed by the Ural Mountains, Ural River, Caspian Sea, Caucasus Mountains, and the Black Sea with its outlets, the Bosporus and Dardanelles.

The People's Republic of China claims Taiwan as its 23rd province. Taiwan's government (Republic of China) maintains that there are two political entities.

Political

⊛ National capital
• Other city

800 Miles
800 Kilometers

Two-point Equidistant Projection

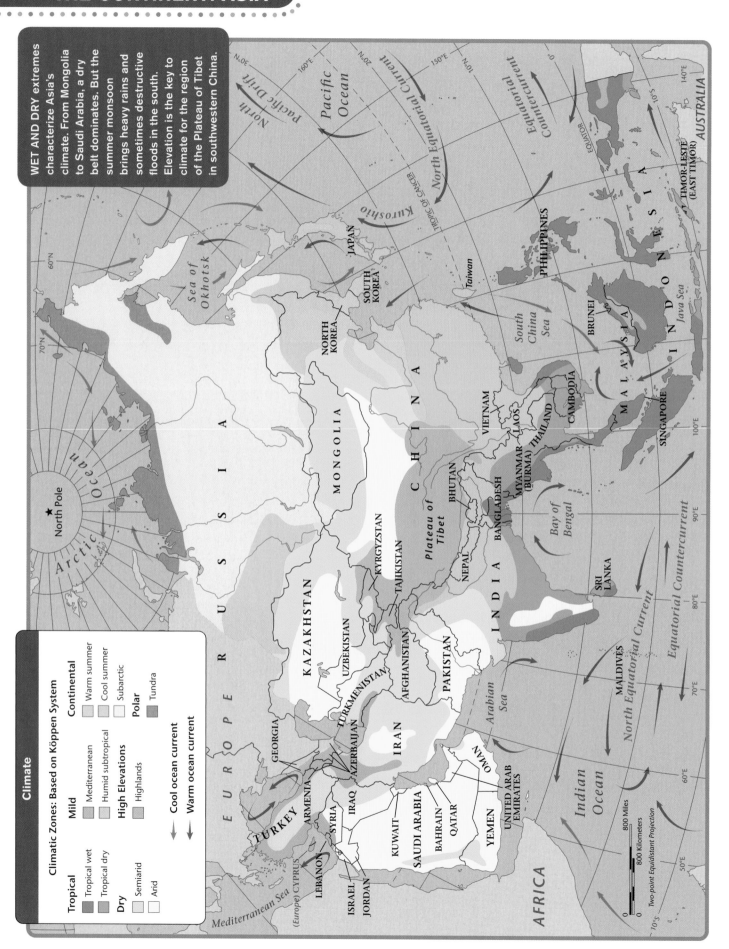

WET AND DRY extremes characterize Asia's climate. From Mongolia to Saudi Arabia, a dry belt dominates. But the summer monsoon brings heavy rains and sometimes destructive floods in the south. Elevation is the key to climate for the region of the Plateau of Tibet in southwestern China.

Climate

Climatic Zones: Based on Köppen System

Tropical
- Tropical wet
- Tropical dry

Dry
- Semiarid
- Arid

Mild
- Mediterranean
- Humid subtropical

High Elevations
- Highlands

Continental
- Warm summer
- Cool summer
- Subarctic

Polar
- Tundra

→ Cool ocean current
→ Warm ocean current

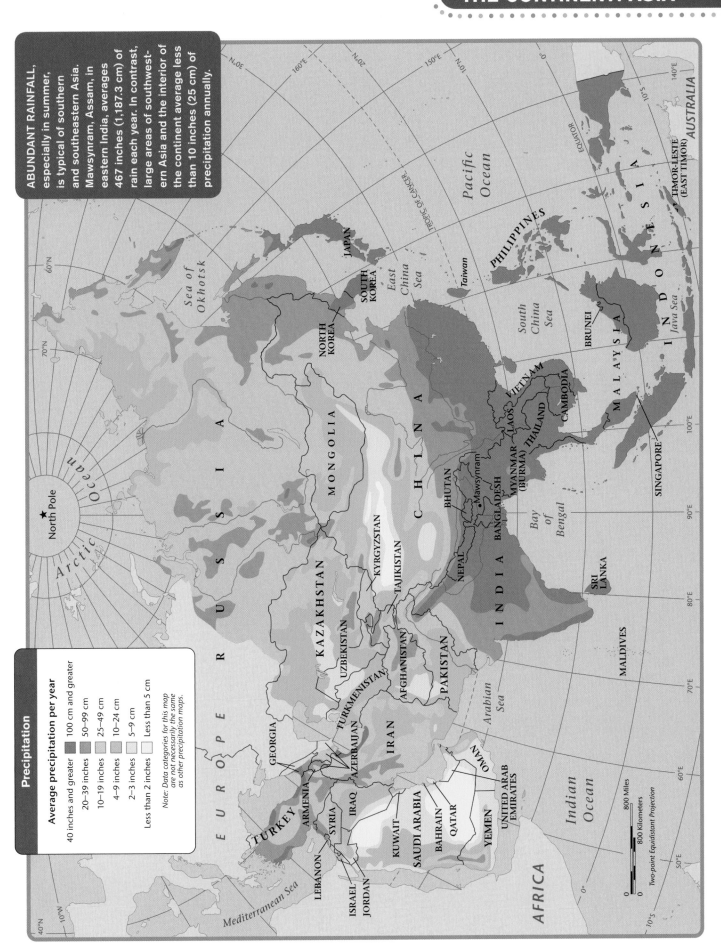

ABUNDANT RAINFALL, especially in summer, is typical of southern and southeastern Asia. Mawsynram, Assam, in eastern India, averages 467 inches (1,187.3 cm) of rain each year. In contrast, large areas of southwestern Asia and the interior of the continent average less than 10 inches (25 cm) of precipitation annually.

Precipitation

Average precipitation per year

40 inches and greater — 100 cm and greater
20–39 inches — 50–99 cm
10–19 inches — 25–49 cm
4–9 inches — 10–24 cm
2–3 inches — 5–9 cm
Less than 2 inches — Less than 5 cm

Note: Data categories for this map are not necessarily the same as other precipitation maps.

THE CONTINENT: ASIA

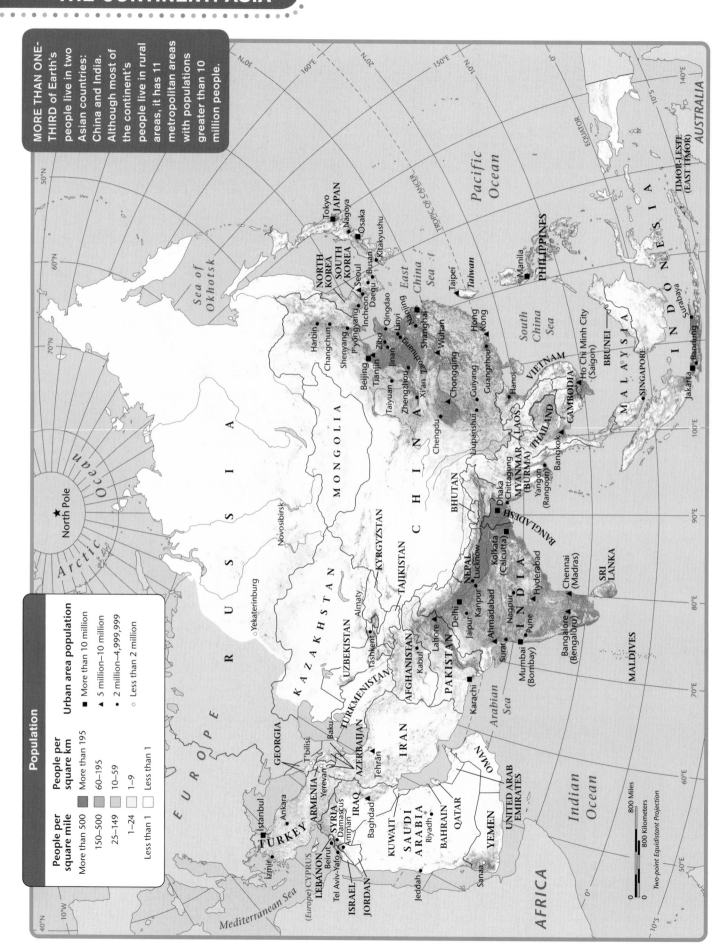

MORE THAN ONE-THIRD of Earth's people live in two Asian countries: China and India. Although most of the continent's people live in rural areas, it has 11 metropolitan areas with populations greater than 10 million people.

Population

People per square mile	People per square km
More than 500	More than 195
150–500	60–195
25–149	10–59
1–24	1–9
Less than 1	Less than 1

Urban area population
- ■ More than 10 million
- ▲ 5 million–10 million
- ● 2 million–4,999,999
- ○ Less than 2 million

NOMADIC HERDING, farming, and other subsistence activities define the economic lifestyle of the majority of Asia's people. But Asia also includes some of the world's industrial giants, such as Japan and South Korea.

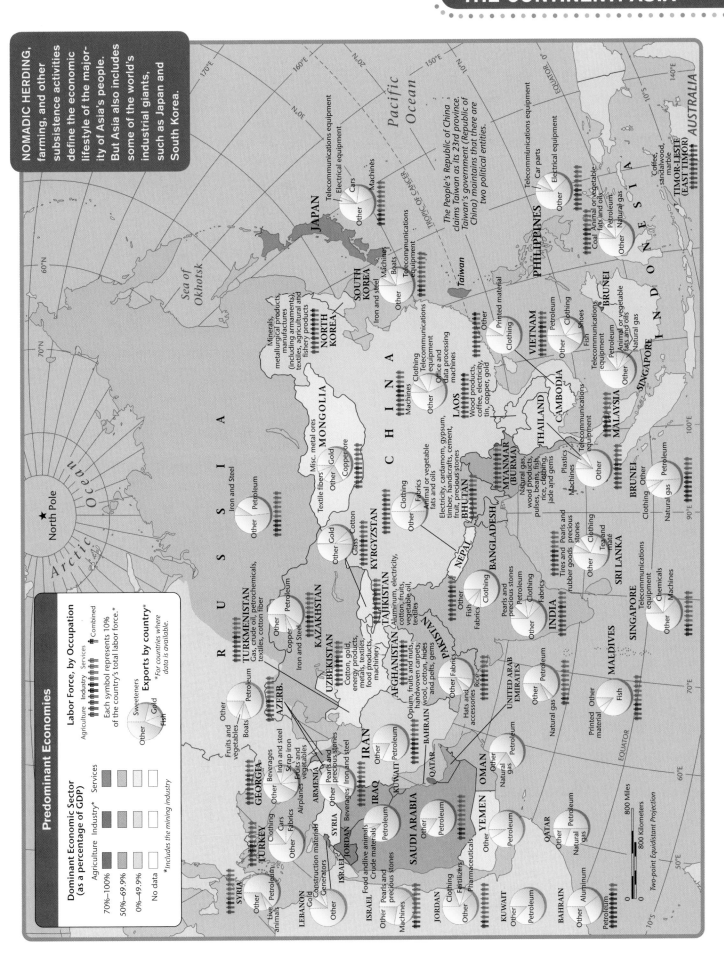

Predominant Economies

Dominant Economic Sector
(as a percentage of GDP)

Agriculture Industry* Services

70%–100%
50%–69.9%
0%–49.9%
No data

*Includes the mining industry

Labor Force, by Occupation

Agriculture Industry Services Combined

Each symbol represents 10% of the country's total labor force.*

Exports by country*

Sweeteners
Gold
Other
Fish

*For countries where data is available.

The People's Republic of China claims Taiwan as its 23rd province. Taiwan's government (Republic of China) maintains that there are two political entities.

GLOBAL CONTAINER PORTS: FACTS & FIGURES

Largest World Container Ports
(by volume – million tons)

Shanghai	443.0 MT
Singapore	423.3 FT
Rotterdam	376.6 MT
Ningbo	272.4 MT
Tianjin	245.1 MT
Guangzhou	241.7 MT
Hong Kong	230.1 MT
Busan	217.2 RT
South Louisiana	192.5 MT

MT=Metric Ton; FT=Freight Ton; RT=Revenue Ton

Leading U.S. Container Trade Partners
(exports by volume – metric tons)

China	19,950,429
Taiwan	8,204,783
Japan	7,980,335
South Korea	6,160,397
Hong Kong	3,704,075
Belgium	3,036,484
India	2,642,381
Indonesia	2,241,680
Brazil	2,191,802

Leading U.S. Container Trade Partners
(imports by volume – metric tons)

China	52,072,462
Brazil	5,320,929
Japan	5,234,186
South Korea	4,057,291
Taiwan	4,008,774
Germany	3,971,391
India	3,524,941
Thailand	3,318,148

Largest Container Shipping Companies
(by TEU capacity)*

A.P. Moller-Maersk Group	Denmark
Mediterranean Shipping Company S.A.	Italy
CMA CGM S.A.	France
Evergreen Marine Corp.	Taiwan
Hapag-Lloyd	Germany
China Shipping Container Lines	China
American President Lines Ltd.	U.S.A.
Hanjin-Senator	Korea/Germany
China Ocean Shipping Co.	China

*TEU is the standard unit for describing a ship's cargo carrying capacity, or a shipping terminal's cargo handling capacity.

East Asia Ports

Since the mid-20th century the world's economy has expanded to a truly global scale, made possible, in large part, by the growth of containerized shipping. The first container ship, a converted oil tanker, set sail from Newark, New Jersey, in 1956 carrying 58 containers. Today, more than 4,000 container vessels move manufactured goods cheaply and efficiently among ports around the world.

Container ships range in size up to 1,300 feet (396 m) long and 180 feet (55 m) wide—bigger than four football fields. The capacity of a container ship is measured in TEUs—a unit of measure equivalent to a 20-foot standard container. A large container vessel can carry more than 10,000 20-foot containers, each loaded with as much as 100 tons of cargo. Container ports are equipped with giant cranes, more than 400 feet (122 m) tall and weighing as much as 2,000 tons, that can move 30 to 40 containers on and off a ship each hour. With six of the world's busiest container ports, containerized shipping has played an important role in Asia's economic boom.

⇧ WAIGAOQIAO TERMINAL, Shanghai Port's largest container terminal, appears as a colorful mosaic when viewed from above. Shanghai leads all container ports in tonnage handled, moving more than 400 million tons of goods and material each year.

⇧ SHIPPING CONTAINERS are stacked high above trucks moving through the busy port of Busan, which opened in 2004, 280 miles (450 km) southeast of South Korea's capital, Seoul.

⇧ OLD MEETS NEW in the harbor of Ho Chi Minh City, Vietnam. Vendors sail their traditional sampan near a giant container vessel in this newly built Southeast Asian container port.

THE CONTINENT: ASIA

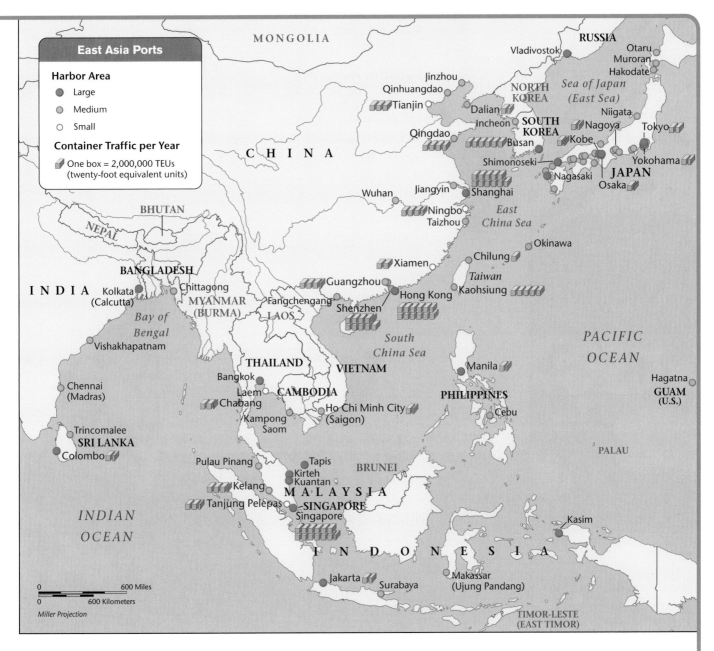

East Asia Ports

Harbor Area
- ⬤ Large
- ● Medium
- ○ Small

Container Traffic per Year
- ▨ One box = 2,000,000 TEUs (twenty-foot equivalent units)

MONGOLIA

RUSSIA
Vladivostok
Otaru
Muroran
Hakodate

Jinzhou
Qinhuangdao
Tianjin

NORTH
KOREA

Sea of Japan
(East Sea)

Niigata

Dalian
Incheon
SOUTH
KOREA
Nagoya
Tokyo

C H I N A

Qingdao
Busan
Kobe
Yokohama

Shimonoseki
JAPAN

Wuhan
Jiangyin
Shanghai
Nagasaki
Osaka

BHUTAN
NEPAL

Ningbo
Taizhou
East
China Sea

BANGLADESH
Chittagong

Xiamen

Okinawa
Chilung

I N D I A
Kolkata
(Calcutta)

MYANMAR
(BURMA)
LAOS

Fangchengang
Guangzhou
Shenzhen
Hong Kong

Taiwan
Kaohsiung

Bay of
Bengal

South
China Sea

PACIFIC
OCEAN

Vishakhapatnam

Chennai
(Madras)

THAILAND
Bangkok
Laem
Chabang

VIETNAM

CAMBODIA
Ho Chi Minh City
(Saigon)

Manila

PHILIPPINES
Cebu

Hagatna
GUAM
(U.S.)

Trincomalee
SRI LANKA
Colombo

Kampong
Saom

PALAU

Pulau Pinang
Kelang

Tapis
Kirteh
Kuantan

BRUNEI

INDIAN
OCEAN

Tanjung Pelepas
M A L A Y S I A
SINGAPORE
Singapore

Kasim

I N D O N E S I A

Jakarta
Surabaya

Makassar
(Ujung Pandang)

0   600 Miles
0   600 Kilometers
Miller Projection

TIMOR-LESTE
(EAST TIMOR)

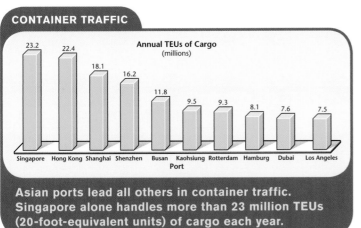

CONTAINER TRAFFIC

Annual TEUs of Cargo
(millions)

23.2	Singapore	
22.4	Hong Kong	
18.1	Shanghai	
16.2	Shenzhen	
11.8	Busan	
9.5	Kaohsiung	
9.3	Rotterdam	
8.1	Hamburg	
7.6	Dubai	
7.5	Los Angeles	

Port

Asian ports lead all others in container traffic. Singapore alone handles more than 23 million TEUs (20-foot-equivalent units) of cargo each year.

⇧ CONTAINER CRANES line this waterway in Hong Kong, one of the busiest international container ports in the world.

THE CONTINENT: AFRICA

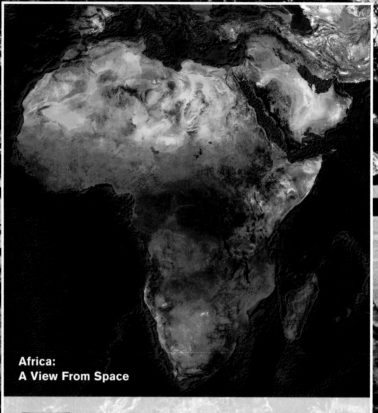

Africa:
A View From Space

From space, Africa appears divided into three regions: the north, dominated by the Sahara, the largest hot desert in the world; a central green band of rain forests and tropical grasslands; and more dry land to the south. Africa may actually be dividing: the Great Rift Valley, running from the Red Sea through the volcanic Afar Triangle to the southern lake district, may split apart the continent.

PHYSICAL

Land area 11,608,000 sq mi (30,065,000 sq km)	**Lowest point** Lake Assai, Djibouti -512 ft (-156 m)	**Largest lake** Victoria 26,800 sq mi (69,500 sq km)
Highest point Kilimanjaro, Tanzania 19,340 ft (5,895 m)	**Longest river** Nile 4,241 mi (6,825 km)	

POLITICAL

Population 943,758,000	**Largest country** Sudan 967,500 sq mi (2,505,813 sq km)	**Most populous country** Nigeria Pop. 144,430,000
Number of independent countries 53	**Smallest country** Seychelles 176 sq mi (455 sq km)	**Least populous country** Seychelles Pop. 86,000

THE CONTINENT: AFRICA

Africa

An Elephant and a calf take a walk in Amboseli National Park, Kenya.

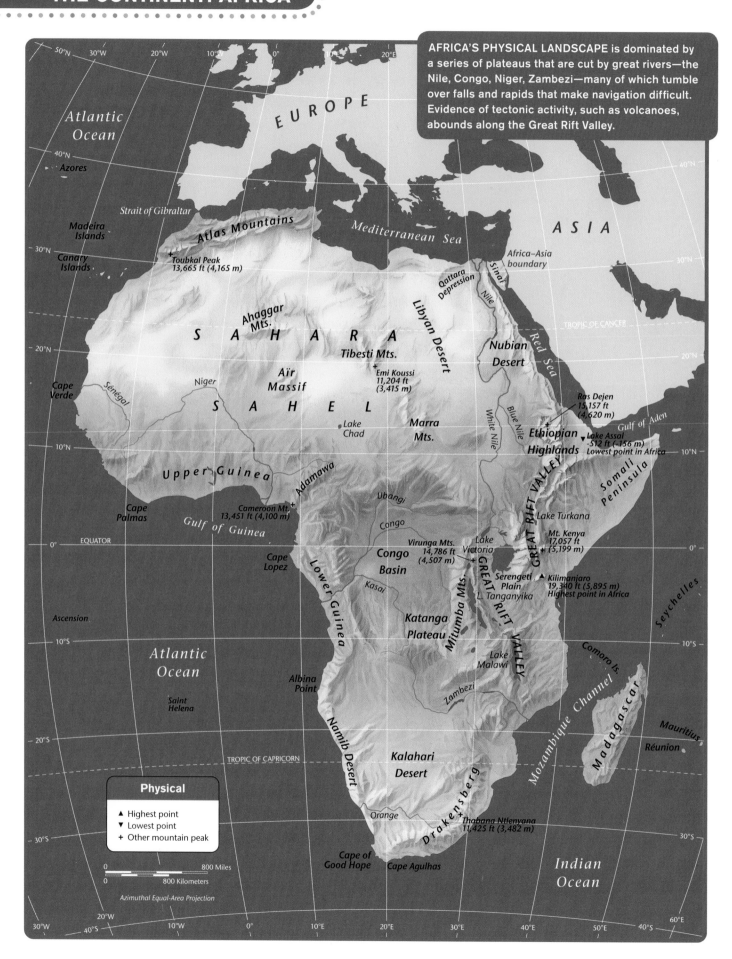

AFRICA'S PHYSICAL LANDSCAPE is dominated by a series of plateaus that are cut by great rivers—the Nile, Congo, Niger, Zambezi—many of which tumble over falls and rapids that make navigation difficult. Evidence of tectonic activity, such as volcanoes, abounds along the Great Rift Valley.

EUROPE

ASIA

Atlantic Ocean

Azores

Strait of Gibraltar

Madeira Islands

Canary Islands

Atlas Mountains

+ Toubkal Peak
13,665 ft (4,165 m)

Mediterranean Sea

Africa–Asia boundary

Sinai

Qattara Depression

Nile

Red Sea

TROPIC OF CANCER

Ahaggar Mts.

S A H A R A

Libyan Desert

Nubian Desert

Cape Verde

Senegal

Niger

Aïr Massif

S A H E L

Tibesti Mts.

+ Emi Koussi
11,204 ft
(3,415 m)

Lake Chad

Marra Mts.

White Nile

Blue Nile

Ethiopian Highlands

+ Ras Dejen
15,157 ft
(4,620 m)

Gulf of Aden

▼ Lake Assal
-512 ft (-156 m)
Lowest point in Africa

Upper Guinea

Adamawa

Somali Peninsula

Cape Palmas

Gulf of Guinea

Cameroon Mt.
13,451 ft (4,100 m)

Ubangi

Congo

Virunga Mts.
14,786 ft
(4,507 m)

Lake Victoria

Lake Turkana

Mt. Kenya
17,057 ft
(5,199 m)

G R E A T   R I F T   V A L L E Y

EQUATOR

Cape Lopez

Lower Guinea

Congo Basin

Kasai

Mitumba Mts.

Serengeti Plain

L. Tanganyika

▲ Kilimanjaro
19,340 ft (5,895 m)
Highest point in Africa

Seychelles

Ascension

Katanga Plateau

Lake Malawi

Comoro Is.

Atlantic Ocean

Saint Helena

Albina Point

Zambezi

Namib Desert

Mozambique Channel

Madagascar

Mauritius

Réunion

TROPIC OF CAPRICORN

Kalahari Desert

Drakensberg

Orange

+ Thabana Ntlenyana
11,425 ft (3,482 m)

Physical

▲ Highest point
▼ Lowest point
+ Other mountain peak

Cape of Good Hope

Cape Agulhas

Indian Ocean

0   800 Miles
0   800 Kilometers

Azimuthal Equal-Area Projection

THE CONTINENT: AFRICA

BOUNDARIES DRAWN by colonial powers at the 1884 Berlin Conference cut across culture and language divisions. These imposed borders contribute to much of the turmoil that has plagued African countries as they have moved from the colonial era to independence.

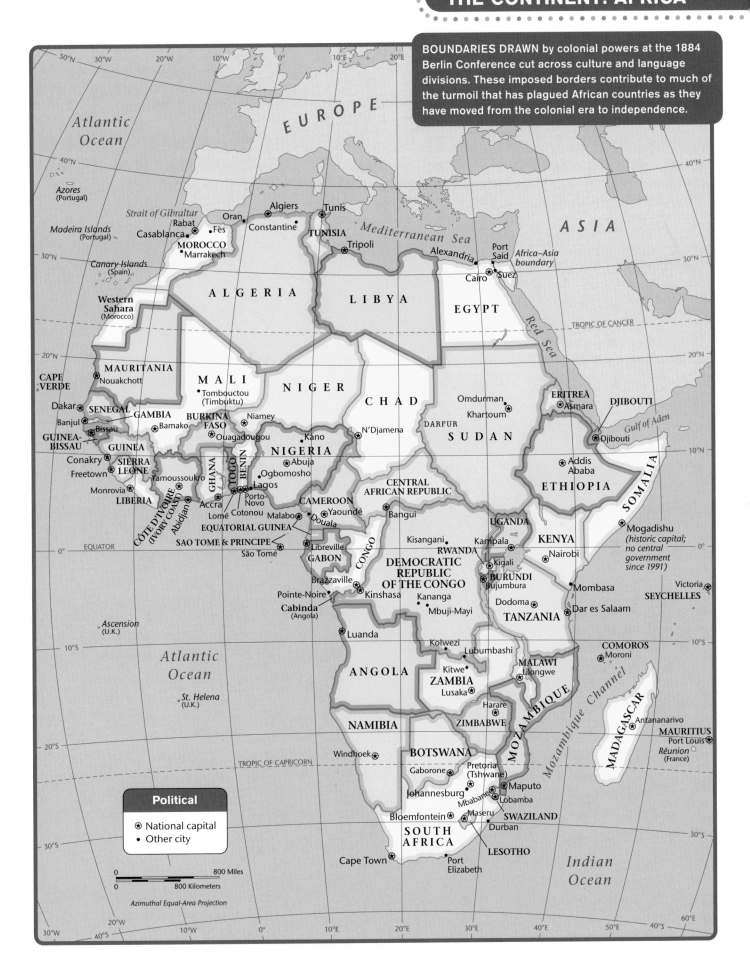

Political

⊛ National capital

• Other city

0   800 Miles

0   800 Kilometers

Azimuthal Equal-Area Projection

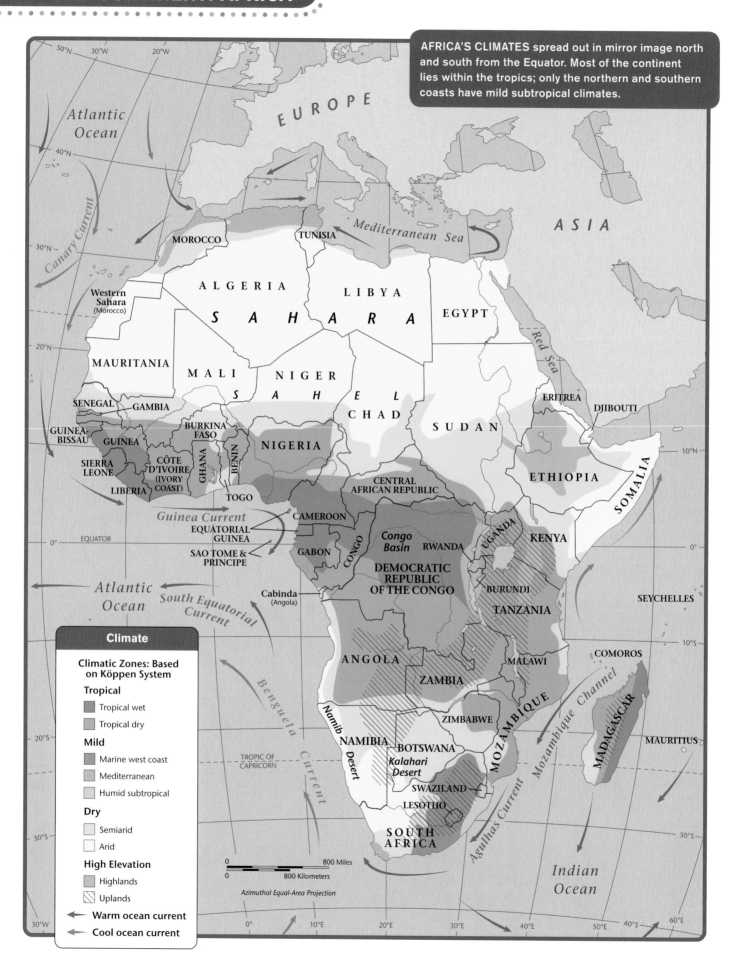

AFRICA'S CLIMATES spread out in mirror image north and south from the Equator. Most of the continent lies within the tropics; only the northern and southern coasts have mild subtropical climates.

EUROPE

Atlantic Ocean

Mediterranean Sea

ASIA

Canary Current

MOROCCO
TUNISIA
Western Sahara (Morocco)
ALGERIA
LIBYA
EGYPT
SAHARA
MAURITANIA
MALI
NIGER
SAHEL
CHAD
SUDAN
SENEGAL
GAMBIA
ERITREA
DJIBOUTI
GUINEA-BISSAU
BURKINA FASO
GUINEA
NIGERIA
SIERRA LEONE
CÔTE D'IVOIRE (IVORY COAST)
GHANA
BENIN
ETHIOPIA
LIBERIA
TOGO
CENTRAL AFRICAN REPUBLIC
SOMALIA
Guinea Current
CAMEROON
EQUATORIAL GUINEA
SAO TOME & PRINCIPE
GABON
CONGO
Congo Basin
RWANDA
UGANDA
KENYA
DEMOCRATIC REPUBLIC OF THE CONGO
BURUNDI
SEYCHELLES
EQUATOR
Atlantic Ocean
South Equatorial Current
Cabinda (Angola)
TANZANIA
COMOROS
Benguela Current
ANGOLA
MALAWI
ZAMBIA
MOZAMBIQUE
Mozambique Channel
MADAGASCAR
MAURITIUS
ZIMBABWE
Namib Desert
NAMIBIA
BOTSWANA
Kalahari Desert
TROPIC OF CAPRICORN
SWAZILAND
Agulhas Current
LESOTHO
SOUTH AFRICA
Indian Ocean

Red Sea

Climate

Climatic Zones: Based on Köppen System

Tropical
- Tropical wet
- Tropical dry

Mild
- Marine west coast
- Mediterranean
- Humid subtropical

Dry
- Semiarid
- Arid

High Elevation
- Highlands
- Uplands

→ Warm ocean current
→ Cool ocean current

0   800 Miles
0   800 Kilometers

Azimuthal Equal-Area Projection

THE CONTINENT: AFRICA

HEAVY RAINS near the Equator give way to the seasonal wet and dry patterns of the tall grass savanna that is home to Africa's big game animals. As rainfall decreases, short grass yields to desert—the Sahara in the north; the Kalahari and the Namib in the south.

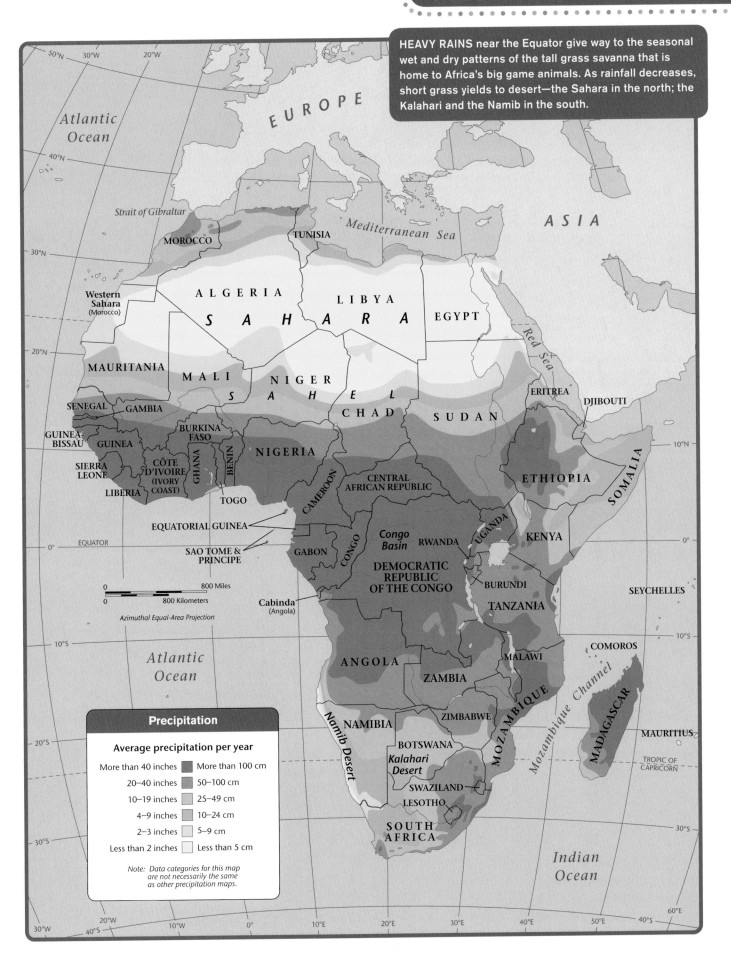

Precipitation

Average precipitation per year

More than 40 inches	More than 100 cm
20–40 inches	50–100 cm
10–19 inches	25–49 cm
4–9 inches	10–24 cm
2–3 inches	5–9 cm
Less than 2 inches	Less than 5 cm

Note: Data categories for this map are not necessarily the same as other precipitation maps.

800 Miles
800 Kilometers
Azimuthal Equal-Area Projection

THE CONTINENT: AFRICA

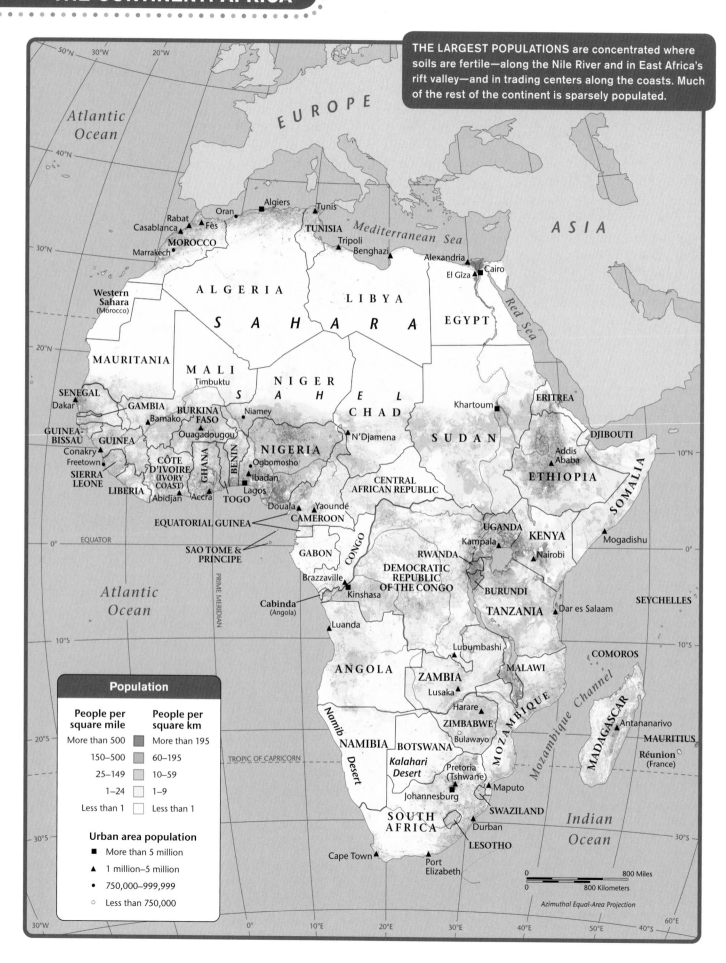

THE LARGEST POPULATIONS are concentrated where soils are fertile—along the Nile River and in East Africa's rift valley—and in trading centers along the coasts. Much of the rest of the continent is sparsely populated.

Atlantic Ocean

EUROPE

ASIA

Mediterranean Sea

Algiers
Oran
Rabat
Casablanca
Fès
MOROCCO
Marrakech

Tunis
TUNISIA
Tripoli
Benghazi

Alexandria
El Giza
Cairo

Red Sea

Western Sahara (Morocco)

ALGERIA

LIBYA

EGYPT

SAHARA

MAURITANIA

MALI

NIGER

CHAD

SAHEL

Khartoum

ERITREA

DJIBOUTI

SENEGAL
Dakar
GAMBIA
GUINEA-BISSAU
Conakry
Freetown
SIERRA LEONE
LIBERIA

Timbuktu
BURKINA FASO
Bamako
Ouagadougou
Niamey

NIGERIA
Ogbomosho
Ibadan
Lagos

N'Djamena

SUDAN

Addis Ababa
ETHIOPIA

SOMALIA

CÔTE D'IVOIRE (IVORY COAST)
Abidjan
GHANA
Accra
BENIN
TOGO

Douala
Yaoundé
CAMEROON

CENTRAL AFRICAN REPUBLIC

UGANDA
Kampala

KENYA
Nairobi
Mogadishu

EQUATORIAL GUINEA

SAO TOME & PRINCIPE

GABON
CONGO
Brazzaville
Kinshasa
Cabinda (Angola)

DEMOCRATIC REPUBLIC OF THE CONGO

RWANDA
BURUNDI
TANZANIA
Dar es Salaam

SEYCHELLES

EQUATOR

PRIME MERIDIAN

Atlantic Ocean

Luanda

Lubumbashi

ANGOLA

ZAMBIA
Lusaka

MALAWI

COMOROS

Namib Desert

NAMIBIA

BOTSWANA

Kalahari Desert

Harare
ZIMBABWE
Bulawayo

Pretoria (Tshwane)
Johannesburg

MOZAMBIQUE

Mozambique Channel

MADAGASCAR
Antananarivo
MAURITIUS
Réunion (France)

TROPIC OF CAPRICORN

SWAZILAND
Maputo
Durban
LESOTHO

SOUTH AFRICA

Cape Town
Port Elizabeth

Indian Ocean

Population

People per square mile

- More than 500
- 150–500
- 25–149
- 1–24
- Less than 1

People per square km

- More than 195
- 60–195
- 10–59
- 1–9
- Less than 1

Urban area population

- ■ More than 5 million
- ▲ 1 million–5 million
- • 750,000–999,999
- ○ Less than 750,000

0 — 800 Miles
0 — 800 Kilometers

Azimuthal Equal-Area Projection

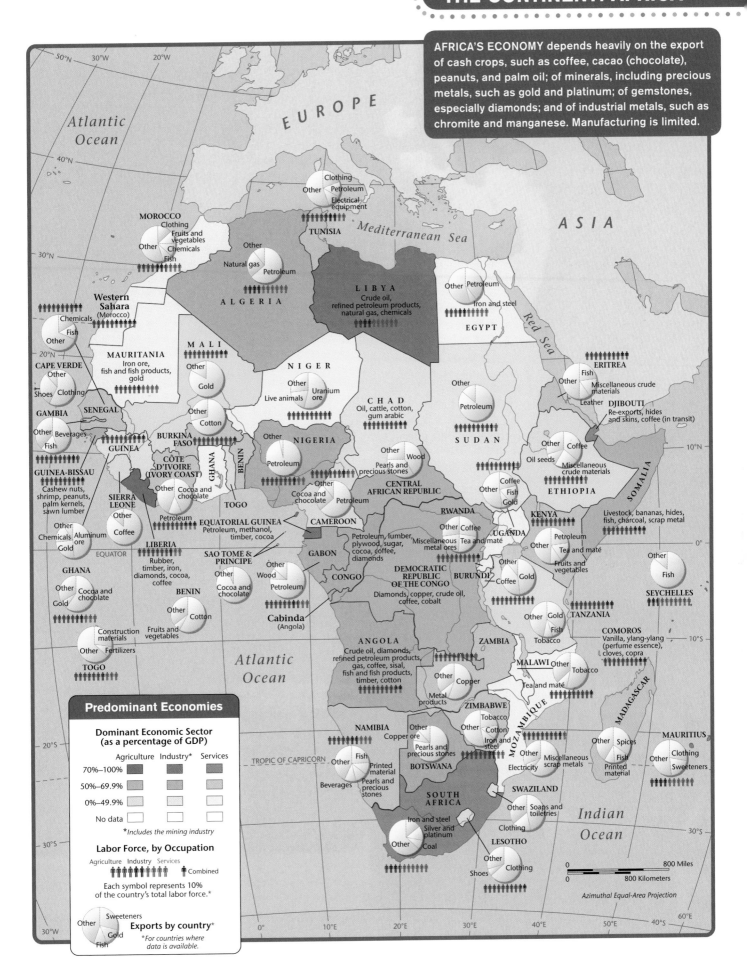

AFRICA'S ECONOMY depends heavily on the export of cash crops, such as coffee, cacao (chocolate), peanuts, and palm oil; of minerals, including precious metals, such as gold and platinum; of gemstones, especially diamonds; and of industrial metals, such as chromite and manganese. Manufacturing is limited.

EUROPE

ASIA

Atlantic Ocean

Mediterranean Sea

Red Sea

MOROCCO
Clothing, Fruits and vegetables, Chemicals, Fish, Other

TUNISIA
Clothing, Petroleum, Electrical equipment, Other

ALGERIA
Natural gas, Petroleum, Other

LIBYA
Crude oil, refined petroleum products, natural gas, chemicals

EGYPT
Petroleum, Iron and steel, Other

Western Sahara
(Morocco)

MAURITANIA
Iron ore, fish and fish products, gold
Chemicals, Fish, Other

MALI
Gold, Other

NIGER
Uranium ore, Live animals, Other

CHAD
Oil, cattle, cotton, gum arabic

SUDAN
Petroleum, Other

ERITREA
Fish, Miscellaneous crude materials, Leather, Other

DJIBOUTI
Re-exports, hides and skins, coffee (in transit)

CAPE VERDE
Shoes, Clothing, Other

GAMBIA
Beverages, Fish, Other

SENEGAL
Chemicals, Aluminum ore, Gold, Other

GUINEA

GUINEA-BISSAU
Cashew nuts, shrimp, peanuts, palm kernels, sawn lumber

BURKINA FASO
Cotton, Other

CÔTE D'IVOIRE (IVORY COAST)
Cocoa and chocolate, Other

GHANA

BENIN

TOGO
Construction materials, Fertilizers, Other

NIGERIA
Petroleum, Other

CENTRAL AFRICAN REPUBLIC
Wood, Pearls and precious stones, Other

ETHIOPIA
Coffee, Oil seeds, Miscellaneous crude materials, Other

SOMALIA
Livestock, bananas, hides, fish, charcoal, scrap metal

SIERRA LEONE
Coffee, Other

LIBERIA
Rubber, timber, iron, diamonds, cocoa, coffee

EQUATORIAL GUINEA
Petroleum, methanol, timber, cocoa

SAO TOME & PRINCIPE
Cocoa and chocolate, Other

CAMEROON
Petroleum, Cocoa and chocolate, Other

GABON
Wood, Petroleum, Other

CONGO

DEMOCRATIC REPUBLIC OF THE CONGO
Diamonds, copper, crude oil, coffee, cobalt
Petroleum, lumber, plywood, sugar, cocoa, coffee, diamonds
Miscellaneous metal ores

RWANDA
Coffee

UGANDA
Coffee, Tea and maté, Other

BURUNDI
Coffee, Gold, Other

KENYA
Tea and maté, Fruits and vegetables, Petroleum, Other

TANZANIA
Gold, Fish, Tobacco, Other

SEYCHELLES
Fish, Other

GHANA
Cocoa and chocolate, Gold, Other

BENIN
Cotton, Other

TOGO
Construction materials, Fertilizers, Other

Cabinda
(Angola)

ANGOLA
Crude oil, diamonds, refined petroleum products, gas, coffee, sisal, fish and fish products, timber, cotton

ZAMBIA
Copper, Metal products, Other

MALAWI
Tobacco, Tea and maté, Other

COMOROS
Vanilla, ylang-ylang (perfume essence), cloves, copra

MADAGASCAR
Spices, Fish, Printed material, Other

MAURITIUS
Clothing, Sweeteners, Other

ZIMBABWE
Tobacco, Cotton, Iron and steel, Other

MOZAMBIQUE
Electricity, Miscellaneous scrap metals, Other

NAMIBIA
Copper ore, Pearls and precious stones, Fish, Other

BOTSWANA
Printed material, Pearls and precious stones, Beverages, Other

SWAZILAND
Soaps and toiletries, Clothing, Other

SOUTH AFRICA
Iron and steel, Silver and platinum, Coal, Other

LESOTHO
Shoes, Clothing, Other

Atlantic Ocean

Indian Ocean

EQUATOR

TROPIC OF CAPRICORN

Predominant Economies

Dominant Economic Sector (as a percentage of GDP)

	Agriculture	Industry*	Services
70%–100%			
50%–69.9%			
0%–49.9%			
No data			

*Includes the mining industry

Labor Force, by Occupation

Agriculture Industry Services

Each symbol represents 10% of the country's total labor force.*

Exports by country*
Sweeteners, Gold, Fish, Other

*For countries where data is available.

0   800 Miles
0   800 Kilometers

Azimuthal Equal-Area Projection

PROTECTED AREAS: FACTS & FIGURES

Forest loss:
9.9 million acres
(4 million ha) each year

Main causes: logging, subsistence agriculture, fuelwood collection

Highest rate:
Nigeria: 11.1 percent each year

Greatest loss: Nigeria, Sudan

Threatened species:

Mammals	779
Birds	638
Reptiles	181
Fish	1,184
Plants	2,312

Selected species at risk:
African elephants, black rhinoceros, eastern chimpanzees, gazelles, hippopotamus, lemurs, mountain gorillas, mountain zebras

Protected areas in Africa:
More than 772,000 square miles (2 million sq km)

Land protected in Sub-Saharan Africa: 5.9 percent

Countries with highest percent of land protected:

Botswana	18.1%
Equatorial Guinea	16.8%
Tanzania	14.6%
Congo	14.1%

Protected Areas

Africa is home to many different animals. Some are familiar, such as giraffes and rhinoceros; others are rare. All are part of Earth's valuable storehouse of biodiversity, but many are at risk due to a variety of pressures. Natural changes, such as periodic drought, may put stress on both plant and animal populations, but human activity is the main threat. Africa's human population is growing on average at a rate of 2.4 percent each year. Converting land for agricultural use, hunting animals for food, and cutting trees for fuel, as well as expanding commercial logging and building roads have led to loss of natural habitat for many of Africa's animals. Some, such as the mountain gorilla, are even at risk of extinction.

To reverse this trend of biodiversity loss, many countries have created protected areas (see map at right), which include nature reserves, wilderness areas, and national parks. Protected areas allow animals to live in a natural environment. They also provide a source of income for African countries, many of which are very poor, as tourists come on photo safaris to view these unique animals.

⇧ ENDANGERED. A silverback mountain gorilla in Rwanda watches intently. Native to the Virunga Mountains of central Africa, only about 700 mountain gorillas remain in the wild.

⇐ STANDING TALL. At an average height of more than 18 feet (5.7 m), giraffes are the world's tallest mammal. This giraffe stands on the grassy plain of Kenya's Masai Mara.

BIODIVERSITY THREATENED

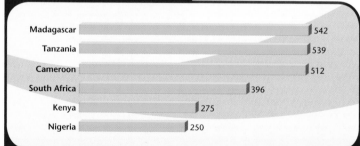

Country	Number
Madagascar	542
Tanzania	539
Cameroon	512
South Africa	396
Kenya	275
Nigeria	250

Madagascar, an island country off the southeast coast, leads all countries in Africa in numbers of species that are critically endangered, endangered, or vulnerable.

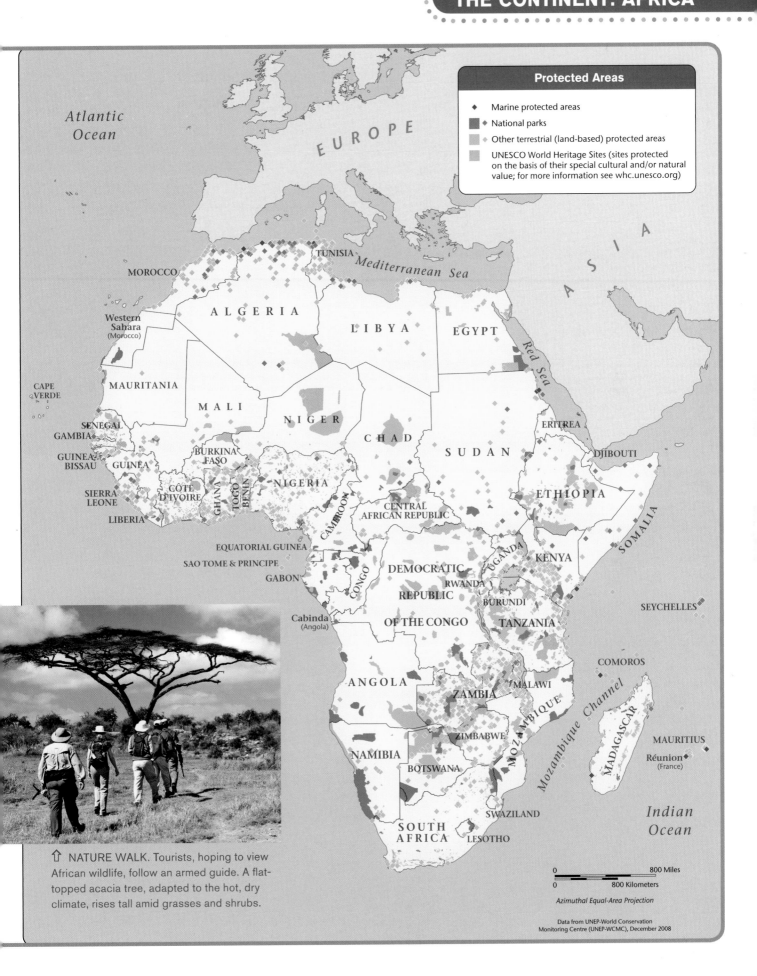

Protected Areas

- ◆ Marine protected areas
- ◆ National parks
- ◆ Other terrestrial (land-based) protected areas
- UNESCO World Heritage Sites (sites protected on the basis of their special cultural and/or natural value; for more information see whc.unesco.org)

Atlantic Ocean

EUROPE

ASIA

Mediterranean Sea

MOROCCO

TUNISIA

Western Sahara (Morocco)

ALGERIA

LIBYA

EGYPT

Red Sea

CAPE VERDE

MAURITANIA

MALI

NIGER

CHAD

SUDAN

ERITREA

DJIBOUTI

SENEGAL

GAMBIA

GUINEA-BISSAU

GUINEA

BURKINA FASO

NIGERIA

SIERRA LEONE

CÔTE D'IVOIRE

GHANA

TOGO

BENIN

ETHIOPIA

LIBERIA

CAMEROON

CENTRAL AFRICAN REPUBLIC

SOMALIA

EQUATORIAL GUINEA

SAO TOME & PRINCIPE

GABON

CONGO

DEMOCRATIC REPUBLIC OF THE CONGO

UGANDA

KENYA

RWANDA

BURUNDI

SEYCHELLES

Cabinda (Angola)

TANZANIA

ANGOLA

ZAMBIA

MALAWI

COMOROS

ZIMBABWE

MOZAMBIQUE

Mozambique Channel

MADAGASCAR

MAURITIUS

Réunion (France)

NAMIBIA

BOTSWANA

SWAZILAND

Indian Ocean

SOUTH AFRICA

LESOTHO

⇧ NATURE WALK. Tourists, hoping to view African wildlife, follow an armed guide. A flat-topped acacia tree, adapted to the hot, dry climate, rises tall amid grasses and shrubs.

0   800 Miles
0   800 Kilometers

Azimuthal Equal-Area Projection

Data from UNEP-World Conservation Monitoring Centre (UNEP-WCMC), December 2008

**Australia:
A View From Space**

Smallest of Earth's great landmasses, Australia is the only one that is both a continent and a country. It is part of the greater region of Oceania, which includes New Zealand, the eastern part of New Guinea, and hundreds of smaller islands scattered across the Pacific Ocean. Although Hawai'i is politically part of the United States, geographically and culturally it is part of Oceania.

Ayers Rock in the evening light, Uluru, Australia

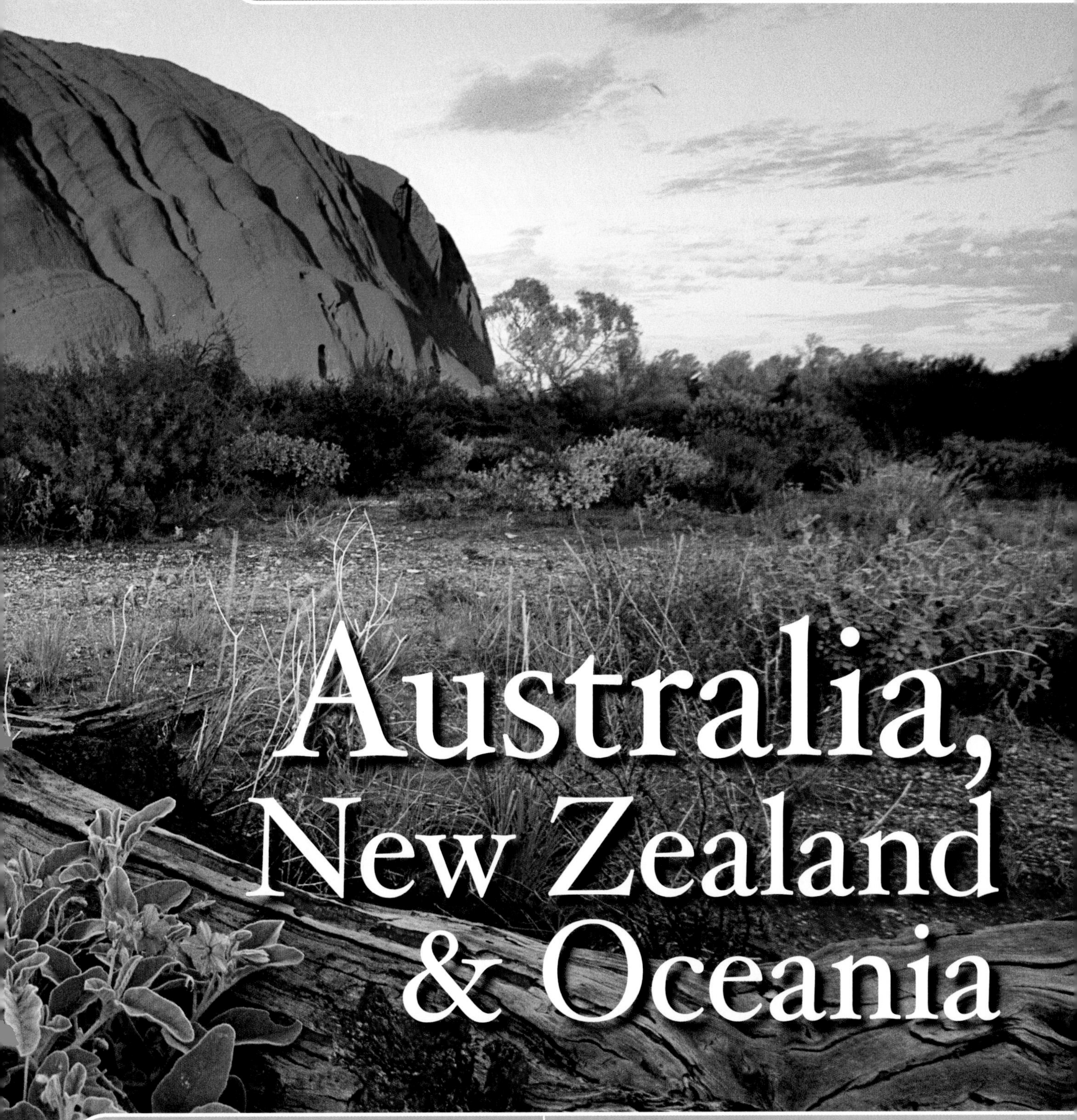

Australia, New Zealand & Oceania

PHYSICAL

Area and population totals are for the independent countries in the region only.

Land area
3,278,062 sq mi
(8,490,180 sq km)

Highest point
Mount Wilhelm,
Papua New Guinea
14,793 ft (4,509 m)

Lowest point
Lake Eyre, Australia
-52 ft (-16 m)

Longest river
Murray-Darling,
Australia
2,310 mi (3,718 km)

Largest lake
Lake Eyre, Australia
3,430 sq mi
(8,884 sq km)

POLITICAL

Population
34,569,000

Number of independent countries
14

Largest country
Australia
2,969,906 sq mi (7,692,024 sq km)

Smallest country
Nauru
8 sq mi (21 sq km)

Most populous country
Australia
Pop. 21,000,000

Least populous country
Tuvalu
Pop. 10,000

THE REGION: AUSTRALIA, NEW ZEALAND & OCEANIA

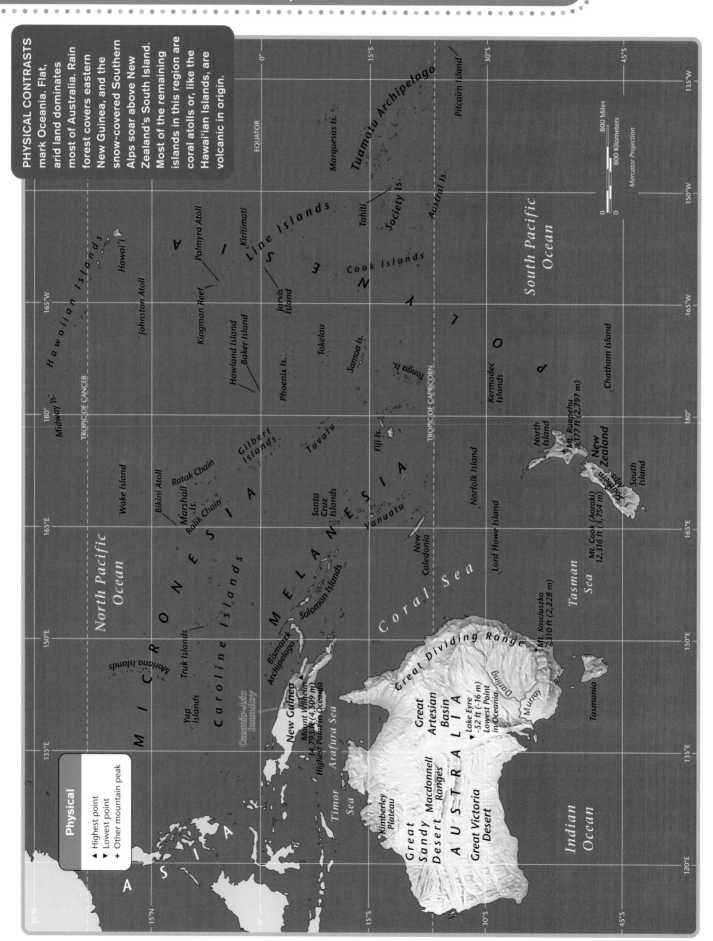

PHYSICAL CONTRASTS mark Oceania. Flat, arid land dominates most of Australia. Rain forest covers eastern New Guinea, and the snow-covered Southern Alps soar above New Zealand's South Island. Most of the remaining islands in this region are coral atolls or, like the Hawai'ian Islands, are volcanic in origin.

Physical
- ◄ Highest point
- ► Lowest point
- + Other mountain peak

800 Miles
800 Kilometers
Mercator Projection

Indian Ocean

Timor Sea
Arafura Sea

ASIA

New Guinea
Mount Wilhelm
14,793 ft (4,509 m)
Highest Point in Oceania

Oceania–Asia boundary

Yap Islands

Caroline Islands

MICRONESIA

Mariana Islands

Truk Islands

North Pacific Ocean

Wake Island

Bikini Atoll
Ratak Chain
Marshall Is.
Ralik Chain

Gilbert Islands

Tuvalu

MELANESIA

Bismarck Archipelago

Solomon Islands

Santa Cruz Islands

Vanuatu

New Caledonia

Coral Sea

AUSTRALIA

Great Sandy Desert

Kimberley Plateau

Macdonnell Ranges

Great Victoria Desert

Great Artesian Basin

Lake Eyre
-52 ft (-16 m)
Lowest Point in Oceania

Great Dividing Range

Darling

Murray

Mt. Kosciuszko
7310 ft (2,228 m)

Tasmania

Tasman Sea

Lord Howe Island

Norfolk Island

New Zealand

North Island

Mt. Ruapehu
9,177 ft (2,797 m)

Southern Alps

South Island

Mt. Cook (Aoraki)
12,316 ft (3,754 m)

Chatham Island

Fiji Is.

Tonga Is.

Kermadec Islands

Samoa Is.

Tokelau

Phoenix Is.

Howland Island
Baker Island

Johnston Atoll

Hawai'ian Islands

Hawai'i

Midway Is.

TROPIC OF CANCER

Kingman Reef

Palmyra Atoll

Kiritimati

Jarvis Island

Line Islands

POLYNESIA

Cook Islands

Tokelau

TROPIC OF CAPRICORN

Tahiti

Society Is.

Austral Is.

Marquesas Is.

Tuamotu Archipelago

Pitcairn Island

South Pacific Ocean

EQUATOR

0°

15°S

30°S

45°S

30°N

15°N

0°

15°S

30°S

45°S

135°E

150°E

165°E

180°

165°W

150°W

135°W

120°E

THE REGION: AUSTRALIA, NEW ZEALAND & OCEANIA

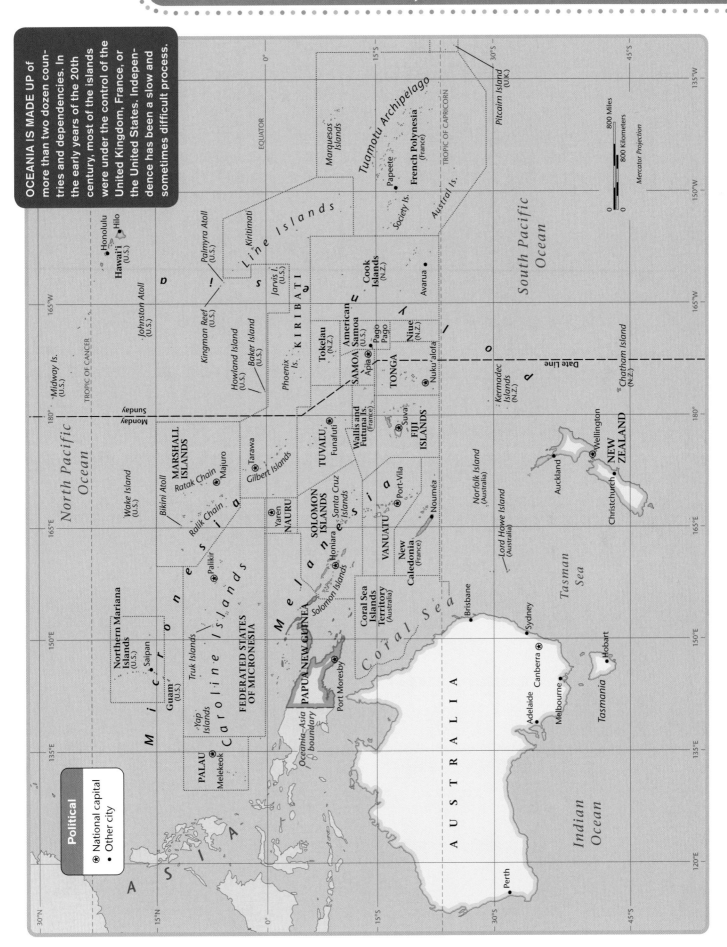

OCEANIA IS MADE UP of more than two dozen countries and dependencies. In the early years of the 20th century, most of the islands were under the control of the United Kingdom, France, or the United States. Independence has been a slow and sometimes difficult process.

Political
⊛ National capital
• Other city

800 Miles
800 Kilometers
Mercator Projection

North Pacific Ocean
South Pacific Ocean
Tasman Sea
Indian Ocean
Coral Sea

M i c r o n e s i a
Melanesia
P o l y n e s i a
Caroline Islands

EQUATOR
TROPIC OF CANCER
TROPIC OF CAPRICORN
Date Line
Monday / Sunday

Honolulu
Hilo
Hawai'i (U.S.)
Midway Is. (U.S.)
Johnston Atoll (U.S.)
Palmyra Atoll (U.S.)
Kingman Reef (U.S.)
Jarvis I. (U.S.)
Kiritimati
Line Islands
Howland Island (U.S.)
Baker Island (U.S.)
Phoenix Is.
KIRIBATI
Marquesas Islands
Tuamotu Archipelago
Papeete
French Polynesia (France)
Society Is.
Austral Is.
Pitcairn Island (U.K.)
Cook Islands (N.Z.)
Avarua
Niue (N.Z.)
Tokelau (N.Z.)
American Samoa (U.S.)
Pago Pago
SAMOA
Apia
TONGA
Nuku'alofa
Wake Island (U.S.)
MARSHALL ISLANDS
Ratak Chain
Majuro
Ralik Chain
Bikini Atoll
Tarawa
Gilbert Islands
TUVALU
Funafuti
Wallis and Futuna Is. (France)
Suva
FIJI ISLANDS
Kermadec Islands (N.Z.)
Chatham Island (N.Z.)
Wellington
NEW ZEALAND
Auckland
Christchurch
Northern Mariana Islands (U.S.)
Saipan
Guam (U.S.)
Truk Islands
Yap Islands
FEDERATED STATES OF MICRONESIA
Palikir
PALAU
Melekeok
Yaren
NAURU
SOLOMON ISLANDS
Santa Cruz Islands
Honiara
Solomon Islands
VANUATU
Port-Vila
New Caledonia (France)
Nouméa
Norfolk Island (Australia)
Lord Howe Island (Australia)
Oceania-Asia boundary
PAPUA NEW GUINEA
Port Moresby
Coral Sea Islands Territory (Australia)
ASIA
AUSTRALIA
Brisbane
Sydney
Canberra
Adelaide
Melbourne
Hobart
Tasmania
Perth

THE REGION: AUSTRALIA, NEW ZEALAND & OCEANIA

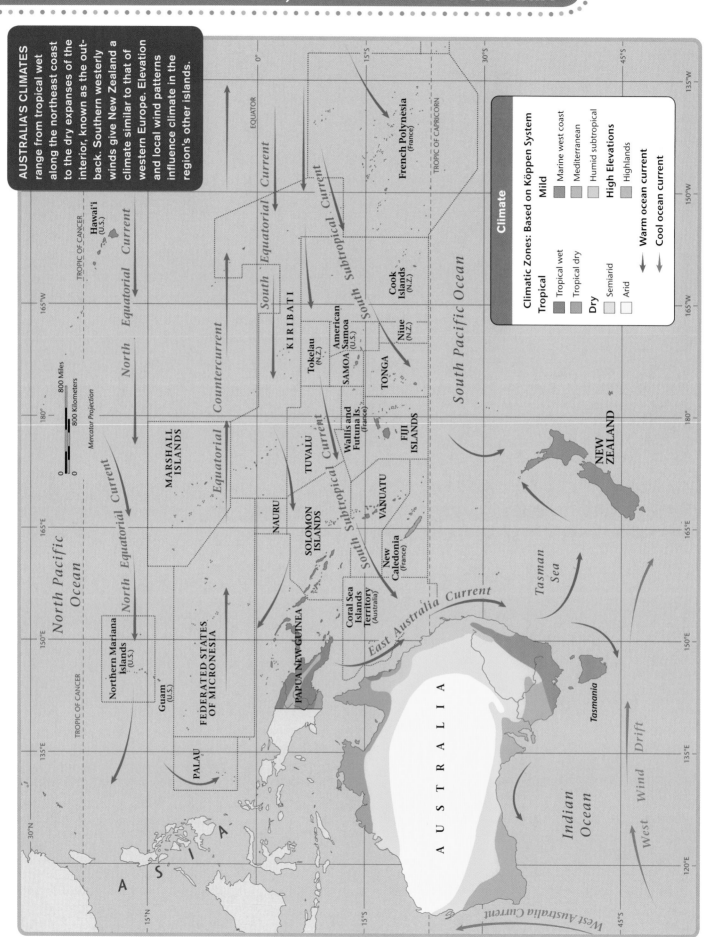

AUSTRALIA'S CLIMATES range from tropical wet along the northeast coast to the dry expanses of the interior, known as the out-back. Southern westerly winds give New Zealand a climate similar to that of western Europe. Elevation and local wind patterns influence climate in the region's other islands.

Climate

Climatic Zones: Based on Köppen System

Tropical
- Tropical wet
- Tropical dry

Dry
- Semiarid
- Arid

Mild
- Marine west coast
- Mediterranean
- Humid subtropical

High Elevations
- Highlands

→ Warm ocean current
→ Cool ocean current

Mercator Projection

800 Miles
800 Kilometers

TROPIC OF CANCER

EQUATOR

TROPIC OF CAPRICORN

North Pacific Ocean

South Pacific Ocean

Indian Ocean

Tasman Sea

North Equatorial Current

North Equatorial Current

Equatorial Countercurrent

South Equatorial Current

South Subtropical Current

South Subtropical Current

East Australia Current

West Wind Drift

West Australia Current

Hawai'i (U.S.)

Northern Mariana Islands (U.S.)

Guam (U.S.)

PALAU

FEDERATED STATES OF MICRONESIA

MARSHALL ISLANDS

NAURU

KIRIBATI

Tokelau (N.Z.)

American Samoa (U.S.)

SAMOA

TONGA

Niue (N.Z.)

Cook Islands (N.Z.)

French Polynesia (France)

TUVALU

Wallis and Futuna Is. (France)

FIJI ISLANDS

VANUATU

New Caledonia (France)

SOLOMON ISLANDS

PAPUA NEW GUINEA

Coral Sea Islands Territory (Australia)

AUSTRALIA

Tasmania

NEW ZEALAND

ASIA

THE REGION: AUSTRALIA, NEW ZEALAND & OCEANIA

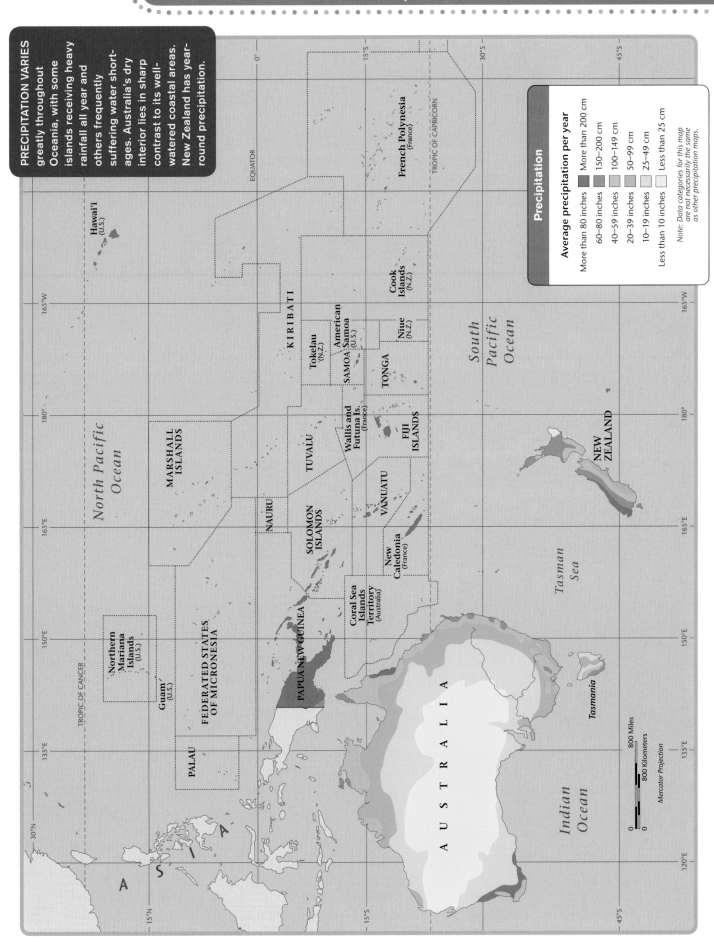

PRECIPITATION VARIES greatly throughout Oceania, with some islands receiving heavy rainfall all year and others frequently suffering water shortages. Australia's dry interior lies in sharp contrast to its well-watered coastal areas. New Zealand has year-round precipitation.

Precipitation

Average precipitation per year

	More than 200 cm
	150–200 cm
	100–149 cm
	50–99 cm
	25–49 cm
	Less than 25 cm

More than 80 inches
60–80 inches
40–59 inches
20–39 inches
10–19 inches
Less than 10 inches

Note: Data categories for this map are not necessarily the same as other precipitation maps.

Hawai'i (U.S.)

EQUATOR

French Polynesia (France)

TROPIC OF CAPRICORN

Cook Islands (N.Z.)

KIRIBATI

Tokelau (N.Z.)

American Samoa (U.S.)

SAMOA

Niue (N.Z.)

TONGA

South Pacific Ocean

North Pacific Ocean

MARSHALL ISLANDS

TUVALU

Wallis and Futuna Is. (France)

FIJI ISLANDS

NAURU

VANUATU

SOLOMON ISLANDS

New Caledonia (France)

NEW ZEALAND

Coral Sea Islands Territory (Australia)

PAPUA NEW GUINEA

Tasman Sea

TROPIC OF CANCER

Northern Mariana Islands (U.S.)

Guam (U.S.)

FEDERATED STATES OF MICRONESIA

PALAU

A S I A

Indian Ocean

A U S T R A L I A

Tasmania

800 Miles
800 Kilometers

Mercator Projection

THE REGION: AUSTRALIA, NEW ZEALAND & OCEANIA

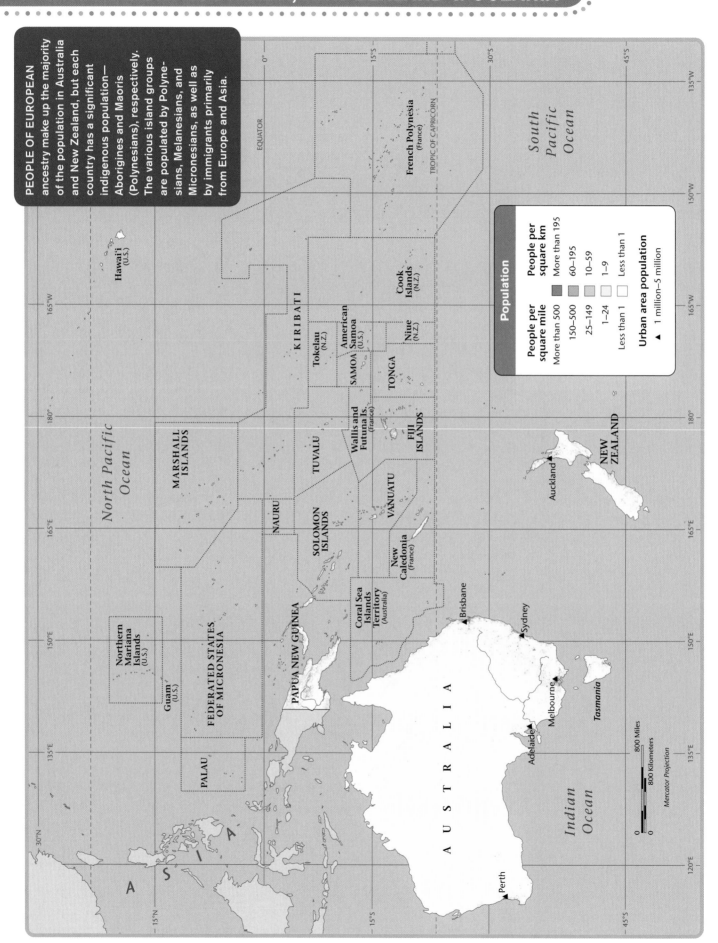

PEOPLE OF EUROPEAN ancestry make up the majority of the population in Australia and New Zealand, but each country has a significant indigenous population—Aborigines and Maoris (Polynesians), respectively. The various island groups are populated by Polynesians, Melanesians, and Micronesians, as well as by immigrants primarily from Europe and Asia.

Population

People per square mile	People per square km
More than 500	More than 195
150–500	60–195
25–149	10–59
1–24	1–9
Less than 1	Less than 1

Urban area population
▲ 1 million–5 million

Hawai'i (U.S.)

French Polynesia (France)

TROPIC OF CAPRICORN

South Pacific Ocean

EQUATOR

0°

15°S

30°S

45°S

KIRIBATI

Cook Islands (N.Z.)

Tokelau (N.Z.)

American Samoa (U.S.)

SAMOA

Niue (N.Z.)

TONGA

North Pacific Ocean

MARSHALL ISLANDS

Wallis and Futuna Is. (France)

FIJI ISLANDS

NAURU

TUVALU

VANUATU

SOLOMON ISLANDS

New Caledonia (France)

Northern Mariana Islands (U.S.)

Guam (U.S.)

FEDERATED STATES OF MICRONESIA

PALAU

PAPUA NEW GUINEA

Coral Sea Islands Territory (Australia)

Brisbane

Sydney

Melbourne

Adelaide

Tasmania

A U S T R A L I A

Perth

Indian Ocean

Auckland

NEW ZEALAND

180°

0°

15°N

30°N

15°S

30°S

45°S

120°E

135°E

150°E

165°E

180°

165°W

150°W

135°W

800 Miles
800 Kilometers
0
0

Mercator Projection

A S I A

THE REGION: AUSTRALIA, NEW ZEALAND & OCEANIA

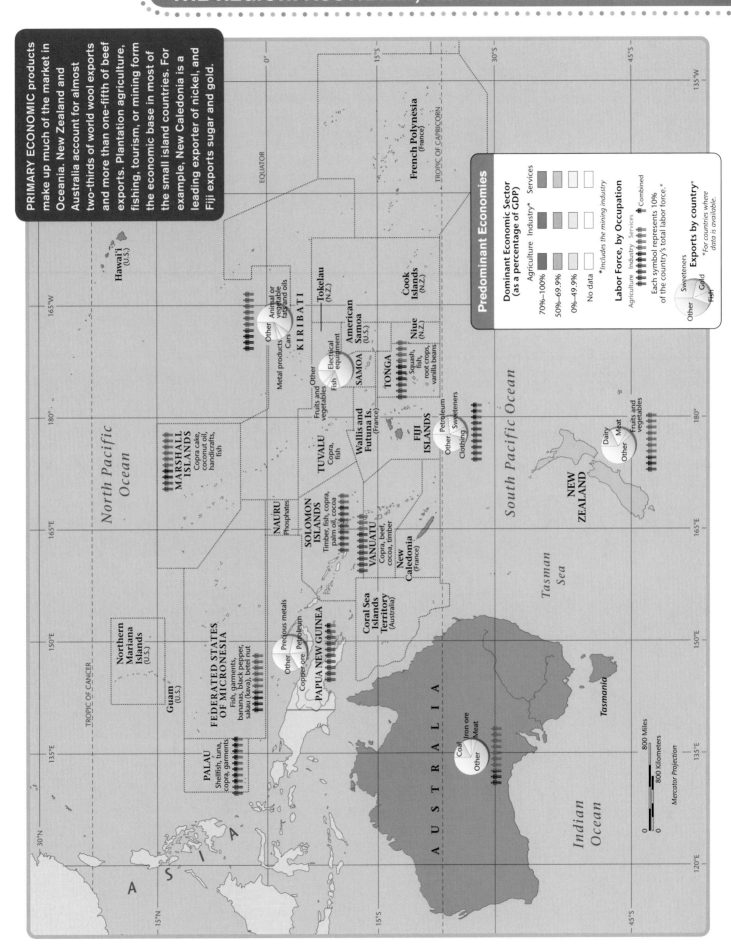

PRIMARY ECONOMIC products make up much of the market in Oceania. New Zealand and Australia account for almost two-thirds of world wool exports and more than one-fifth of beef exports. Plantation agriculture, fishing, tourism, or mining form the economic base in most of the small island countries. For example, New Caledonia is a leading exporter of nickel, and Fiji exports sugar and gold.

Predominant Economies

Dominant Economic Sector (as a percentage of GDP)

Agriculture   Industry*   Services

70%–100%
50%–69.9%
0%–49.9%
No data

*Includes the mining industry

Labor Force, by Occupation

Agriculture   Industry   Services   ▮ Combined

Each symbol represents 10% of the country's total labor force.*

Exports by country*

Sweeteners · Gold · Other · Fish

*For countries where data is available.

Map labels

Hawai'i (U.S.)

KIRIBATI — Tokelau (N.Z.)
Other · Animal or vegetable fats and oils · Cars · Metal products · Electrical equipment · Fish

Fruits and vegetables — SAMOA · American Samoa (U.S.)

Cook Islands (N.Z.)
Niue (N.Z.)

TONGA — Squash, fish, root crops, vanilla beans

MARSHALL ISLANDS
Copra cake, coconut oil, handicrafts, fish

North Pacific Ocean

NAURU — Phosphates

SOLOMON ISLANDS — Timber, fish, copra, palm oil, cocoa

TUVALU — Copra, fish

Wallis and Futuna Is. (France)

FIJI ISLANDS — Petroleum · Sweeteners · Clothing · Other

VANUATU — Copra, beef, cocoa, timber

New Caledonia (France)

South Pacific Ocean

NEW ZEALAND
Dairy · Meat · Other · Fruits and vegetables

Precious metals · Other · Petroleum · Copper ore

PAPUA NEW GUINEA

FEDERATED STATES OF MICRONESIA
Fish, garments, bananas, black pepper, sakau (kava), betel nut

Northern Mariana Islands (U.S.)

Guam (U.S.)

PALAU — Shellfish, tuna, copra, garments

Coral Sea Islands Territory (Australia)

TROPIC OF CANCER

A S I A

AUSTRALIA
Coal · Iron ore · Meat · Other

Tasmania

Indian Ocean

Tasman Sea

EQUATOR

TROPIC OF CAPRICORN

French Polynesia (France)

800 Miles
800 Kilometers
Mercator Projection

THE REGION: AUSTRALIA, NEW ZEALAND & OCEANIA

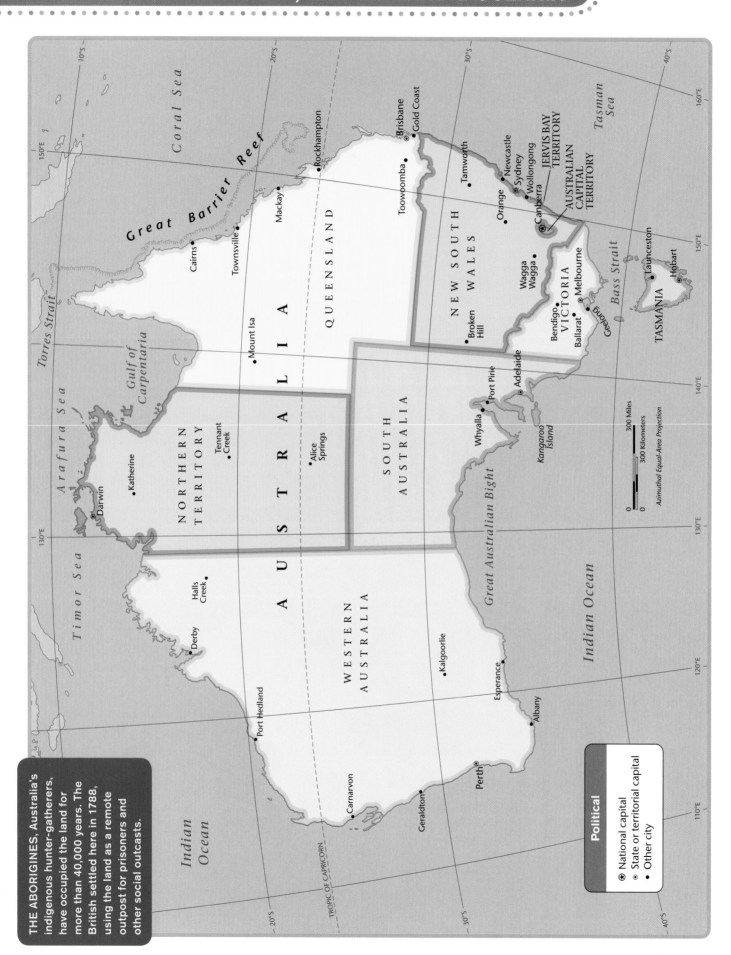

THE ABORIGINES, Australia's indigenous hunter-gatherers, have occupied the land for more than 40,000 years. The British settled here in 1788, using the land as a remote outpost for prisoners and other social outcasts.

Political

⊕ National capital
⊙ State or territorial capital
• Other city

Coral Sea

Great Barrier Reef

Tasman Sea

Bass Strait

Torres Strait

Gulf of Carpentaria

Arafura Sea

Timor Sea

Indian Ocean

Great Australian Bight

Indian Ocean

Brisbane
Gold Coast
Rockhampton
Toowoomba
Tamworth
Newcastle
Sydney
Wollongong
JERVIS BAY TERRITORY
Orange
Canberra
AUSTRALIAN CAPITAL TERRITORY
Mackay
QUEENSLAND
NEW SOUTH WALES
Cairns
Townsville
Wagga Wagga
Melbourne
Launceston
Hobart
Mount Isa
Broken Hill
Bendigo
VICTORIA
Ballarat
Geelong
TASMANIA
AUSTRALIA
SOUTH AUSTRALIA
Port Pirie
Adelaide
Whyalla
Kangaroo Island
Katherine
NORTHERN TERRITORY
Tennant Creek
Alice Springs
Darwin
Halls Creek
Derby
WESTERN AUSTRALIA
Kalgoorlie
Esperance
Albany
Port Hedland
Carnarvon
Geraldton
Perth

300 Miles
300 Kilometers
Azimuthal Equal-Area Projection

TROPIC OF CAPRICORN

10°S
20°S
30°S
40°S

110°E
120°E
130°E
140°E
150°E
160°E

THE REGION: AUSTRALIA, NEW ZEALAND & OCEANIA

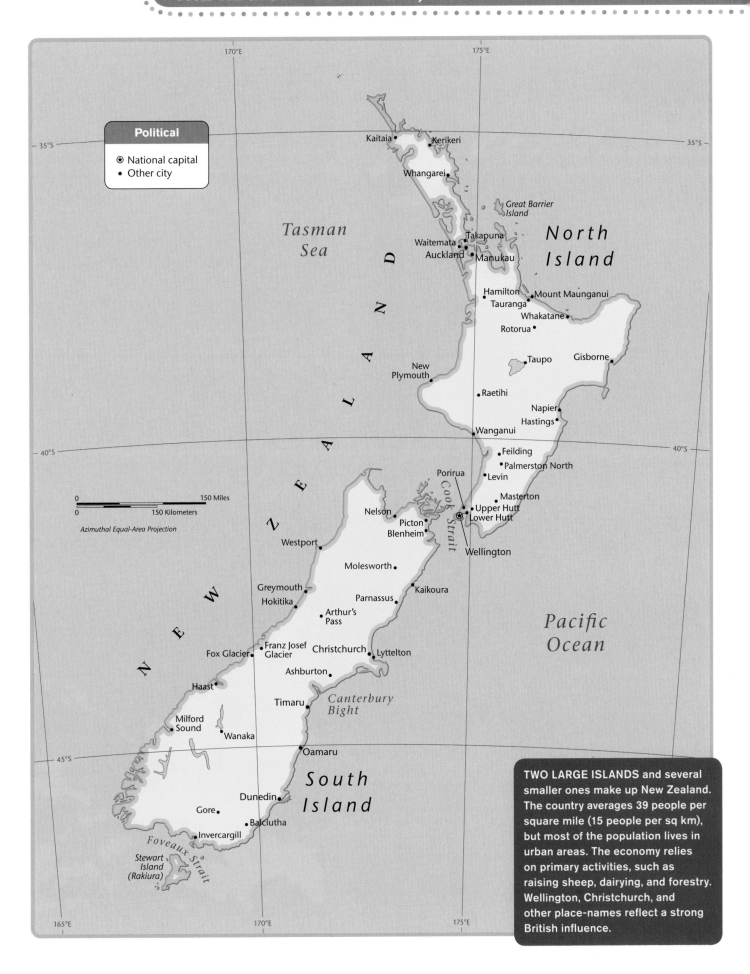

Political

⊗ National capital
• Other city

Tasman Sea

North Island

Kaitaia
Kerikeri
Whangarei

Great Barrier Island

Takapuna
Waitemata
Auckland
Manukau

Hamilton
Tauranga
Mount Maunganui
Whakatane
Rotorua

Taupo
Gisborne

New Plymouth

Raetihi

Napier
Hastings
Wanganui

Feilding
Palmerston North
Porirua
Levin
Masterton
Upper Hutt
Lower Hutt

Cook Strait

Nelson
Picton
Blenheim

Wellington

Westport

Molesworth

Greymouth
Hokitika
Parnassus
Kaikoura

Arthur's Pass

Franz Josef Glacier
Fox Glacier
Christchurch
Lyttelton

Ashburton

Haast

Timaru

Canterbury Bight

Milford Sound
Wanaka

Oamaru

Pacific Ocean

South Island

Dunedin

Gore

Balclutha

Invercargill

Foveaux Strait

Stewart Island (Rakiura)

150 Miles
150 Kilometers

Azimuthal Equal-Area Projection

NEW ZEALAND

TWO LARGE ISLANDS and several smaller ones make up New Zealand. The country averages 39 people per square mile (15 people per sq km), but most of the population lives in urban areas. The economy relies on primary activities, such as raising sheep, dairying, and forestry. Wellington, Christchurch, and other place-names reflect a strong British influence.

CORAL REEFS: SELECTED FACTS

Most coral reefs are between 5,000 and 10,000 years old, but some may have begun growing as much as 50 million years ago.

TYPES OF REEFS

FRINGING REEF – near coastlines of islands and continents

BARRIER REEF – parallel to a coastline but separated from it by deep lagoons

ATOLL – ring of coral surrounding protected lagoons

PATCH REEF – small, isolated reef growing up from a continental shelf

GROWING CONDITIONS

SUNLIGHT – corals grow in shallow water

CLEAR WATER – allows sunlight to penetrate

WARM WATER – between 70° and 85°F (21° and 29°C)

CLEAN WATER – pollution and sediments block sunlight and smother corals

SALT WATER – a certain balance in the ratio of salt to water is necessary

Great Barrier Reef

Stretching like intricate necklaces along the edges of landmasses in the warm ocean waters of the tropics, coral reefs form one of nature's most complex ecosystems. Corals are tiny marine animals that thrive in shallow coastal waters of the tropics. One type of coral, called a "hard coral," produces a limestone skeleton. When the tiny animal dies, its stone-like skeleton is left behind. The accumulation of millions of these skeletons over thousands of years has produced the large reef formations found in many coastal waters of the tropics.

⇧ ANEMONE FISH swim among the waving polyps of one of the reef's sea anemones. These fish are specially adapted to live safely among the venom-filled tentacles that can inject a paralyzing neurotoxin into unsuspecting prey when disturbed.

Most coral reefs are found between 30 degrees N and 30 degrees S latitude in waters with a temperature between 70 and 85 degrees Fahrenheit (21 and 29 degrees Celsius). It is estimated that Earth's coral reefs cover 110,000 square miles (284,300 sq km). Coral reefs are important because they form a habitat for marine animals such as fish, sea turtles, lobsters, and starfish. They also protect fragile coastlines from damaging ocean waves and may be a source of valuable medicines.

The world's largest coral reef, the Great Barrier Reef, lies off the northeast coast of Australia (see large map). This reef, which is made up of more than 400 different types of coral and is home to more than 1,500 species of fish, is a popular tourist destination. People visit to snorkel and dive along the reef and view the great diversity of marine life living among the corals.

⇨ BRILLIANTLY COLORED CORALS and the fish that live among them attract divers and snorkelers to the Great Barrier Reef every year.

CORAL COMMUNITIES

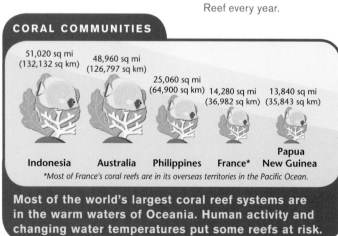

51,020 sq mi (132,132 sq km) — Indonesia

48,960 sq mi (126,797 sq km) — Australia

25,060 sq mi (64,900 sq km) — Philippines

14,280 sq mi (36,982 sq km) — France*

13,840 sq mi (35,843 sq km) — Papua New Guinea

Most of France's coral reefs are in its overseas territories in the Pacific Ocean.

Most of the world's largest coral reef systems are in the warm waters of Oceania. Human activity and changing water temperatures put some reefs at risk.

THE REGION: AUSTRALIA, NEW ZEALAND & OCEANIA

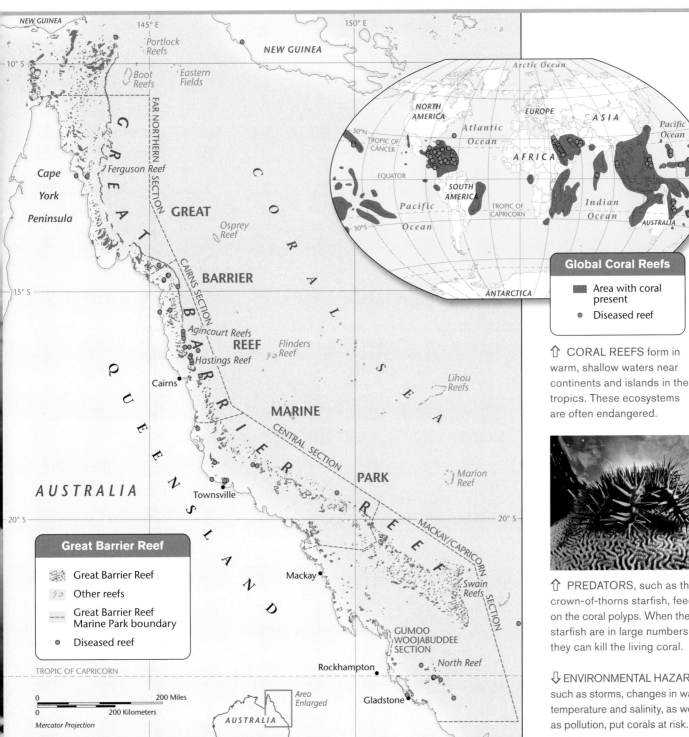

Great Barrier Reef

Great Barrier Reef

Other reefs

Great Barrier Reef
Marine Park boundary

Diseased reef

0   200 Miles

0   200 Kilometers

Mercator Projection

Area Enlarged

AUSTRALIA

Global Coral Reefs

Area with coral present

Diseased reef

⇧ CORAL REEFS form in warm, shallow waters near continents and islands in the tropics. These ecosystems are often endangered.

⇧ PREDATORS, such as this crown-of-thorns starfish, feed on the coral polyps. When these starfish are in large numbers, they can kill the living coral.

⇩ ENVIRONMENTAL HAZARDS, such as storms, changes in water temperature and salinity, as well as pollution, put corals at risk.

⇧ THE GREAT BARRIER REEF stretches along the northeast coast of Australia for 1,429 miles (2,300 km), from the tip of the Cape York Peninsula to just north of Brisbane in the state of Queensland. The reef is actually a collection of more than 3,000 individual reef systems and is home to many different species of fish, mollusks, rays, dolphins, reptiles, and birds. There are even giant clams more than 120 years old. In addition, the reef is habitat for several endangered species, including the dugong (sea cow) and the green sea turtle. UNESCO recognized the Great Barrier Reef as a World Heritage Site in 1981.

**Antarctica:
A View From Space**

About 180 million years ago Antarctica broke away from the ancient super-continent Gondwana. Slowly the continent drifted to its present location at the southernmost point on Earth. Approximately 98 percent of the continent lies under permanent ice sheets that are nearly 3 miles (5 km) thick in places. It is estimated that if all of Antarctica's ice was to melt, the global ocean level would rise more than 200 feet (60 m).

A humpback whale swims by an iceberg off the coast of Antarctica .

THE CONTINENT: ANTARCTICA

PHYSICAL			POLITICAL		
Land area 5,100,000 sq mi (13,209,000 sq km)	**Lowest point** Bentley Subglacial Trench -8,383 ft (-2,555 m)	**Average precipitation on the polar plateau** Less than 2 in (5 cm) per year	**Population** There are no indigenous inhabitants, but there are both permanent and summer-only staffed research stations.	**Number of independent countries** 0	**Number of countries operating year-round research stations** 19
Highest point Vinson Massif 16,067 ft (4,897 m)	**Coldest place** Annual average temperature Plateau Station -70°F (-56.7°C)			**Number of countries claiming land** 7	**Number of year-round research stations** 45

Antarctica

THE CONTINENT: ANTARCTICA

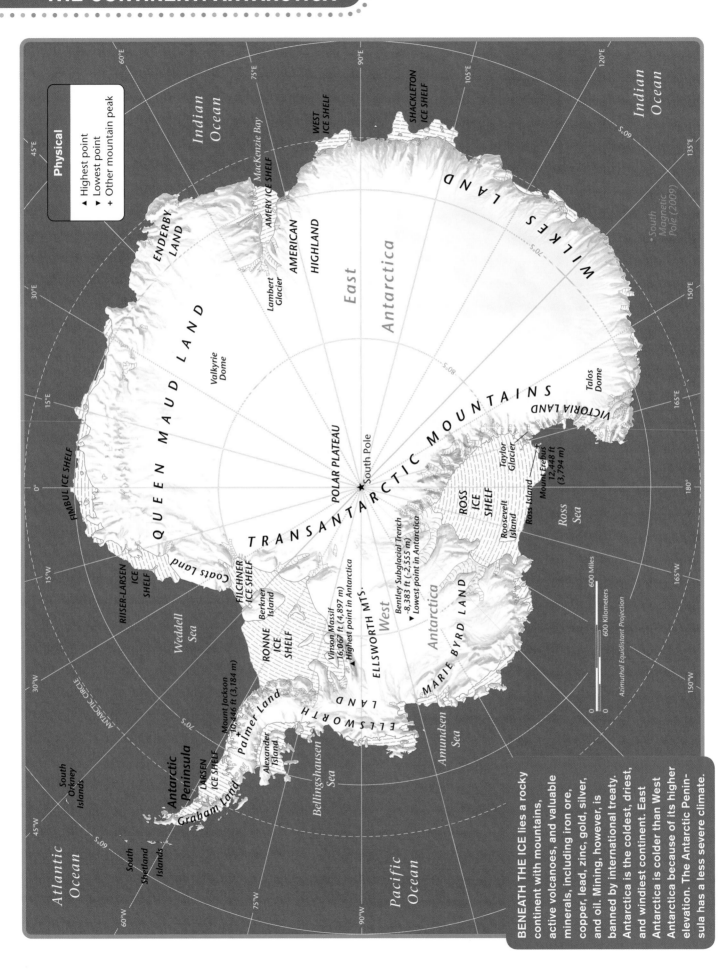

Physical

▲ Highest point
▼ Lowest point
+ Other mountain peak

Indian Ocean

Indian Ocean

60°E

45°E

30°E

15°E

75°E

90°E

105°E

120°E

135°E

150°E

165°E

180°

165°W

150°W

90°W

75°W

60°W

45°W

30°W

15°W

0°

Atlantic Ocean

Pacific Ocean

ENDERBY LAND

MacKenzie Bay

AMERY ICE SHELF

AMERICAN HIGHLAND

WEST ICE SHELF

SHACKLETON ICE SHELF

W I L K E S   L A N D

East Antarctica

South Magnetic Pole (2009)

Q U E E N   M A U D   L A N D

Lambert Glacier

Valkyrie Dome

POLAR PLATEAU

Talos Dome

VICTORIA LAND

FIMBUL ICE SHELF

RIISER-LARSEN ICE SHELF

Coats Land

FILCHNER ICE SHELF

Berkner Island

South Pole

T R A N S A N T A R C T I C   M O U N T A I N S

Taylor Glacier

Mount Erebus
12,448 ft
(3,794 m)

Ross Island

ROSS ICE SHELF

Roosevelt Island

Ross Sea

Weddell Sea

RONNE ICE SHELF

Vinson Massif
16,067 ft (4,897 m)
▲ Highest point in Antarctica

Bentley Subglacial Trench
-8,383 ft (-2,555 m)
▼ Lowest point in Antarctica

ELLSWORTH MTS.

West Antarctica

MARIE BYRD LAND

South Orkney Islands

ANTARCTIC CIRCLE

Mount Jackson
10,446 ft (3,184 m)
+

Alexander Island

Antarctic Peninsula

Palmer Land

LARSEN ICE SHELF

Graham Land

E L L S W O R T H   L A N D

Bellingshausen Sea

Amundsen Sea

South Shetland Islands

80°S

70°S

60°S

0   600 Miles
0   600 Kilometers

Azimuthal Equidistant Projection

BENEATH THE ICE lies a rocky continent with mountains, active volcanoes, and valuable minerals, including iron ore, copper, lead, zinc, gold, silver, and oil. Mining, however, is banned by international treaty. Antarctica is the coldest, driest, and windiest continent. East Antarctica is colder than West Antarctica because of its higher elevation. The Antarctic Peninsula has a less severe climate.

THE CONTINENT: ANTARCTICA

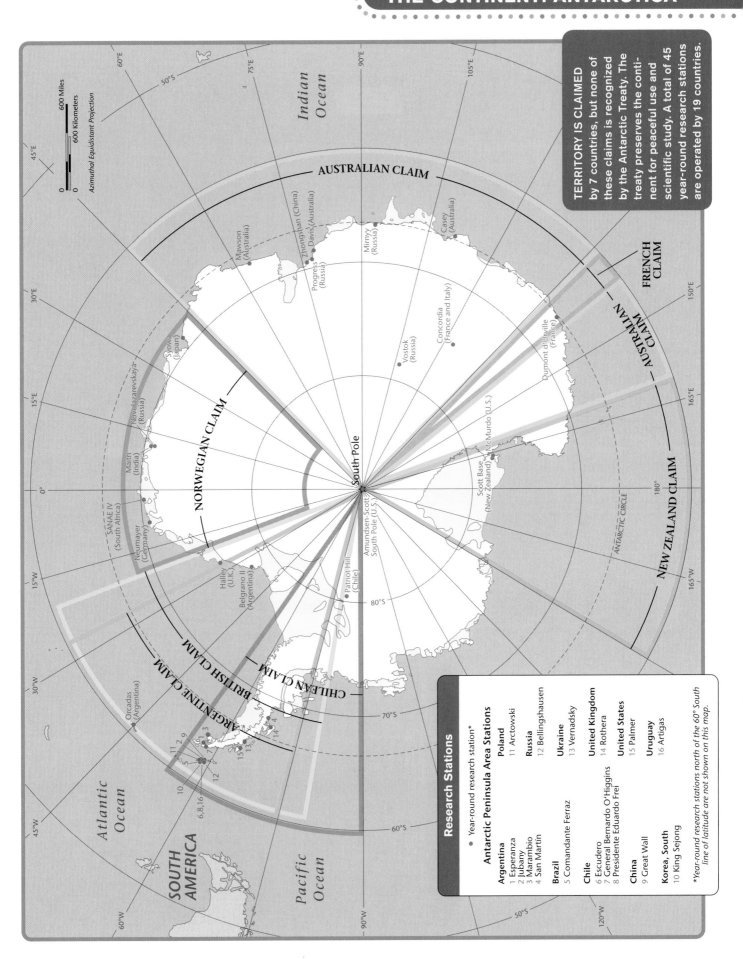

600 Miles
600 Kilometers
Azimuthal Equidistant Projection

TERRITORY IS CLAIMED by 7 countries, but none of these claims is recognized by the Antarctic Treaty. The treaty preserves the continent for peaceful use and scientific study. A total of 45 year-round research stations are operated by 19 countries.

Indian Ocean

AUSTRALIAN CLAIM

Mawson (Australia)
Zhongshan (China)
Progress (Russia)
Davis (Australia)
Mirnyy (Russia)
Casey (Australia)
Concordia (France and Italy)
Vostok (Russia)
Dumont d'Urville (France)

FRENCH CLAIM
AUSTRALIAN CLAIM

Syowa (Japan)
Novolazarevskaya (Russia)
Maitri (India)

NORWEGIAN CLAIM

South Pole

SANAE IV (South Africa)
Neumayer (Germany)
Halley (U.K.)
Belgrano II (Argentina)
Patriot Hill (Chile)
Amundsen-Scott South Pole (U.S.)
Scott Base (New Zealand)
McMurdo (U.S.)

NEW ZEALAND CLAIM

ANTARCTIC CIRCLE

Orcadas (Argentina)

ARGENTINE CLAIM
BRITISH CLAIM
CHILEAN CLAIM

Atlantic Ocean

SOUTH AMERICA

Pacific Ocean

Research Stations

• Year-round research station*

Antarctic Peninsula Area Stations

Argentina	**Poland**
1 Esperanza	11 Arctowski
2 Jubany	
3 Marambio	**Russia**
4 San Martín	12 Bellingshausen
Brazil	**Ukraine**
5 Comandante Ferraz	13 Vernadsky
Chile	**United Kingdom**
6 Escudero	14 Rothera
7 General Bernardo O'Higgins	
8 Presidente Eduardo Frei	**United States**
	15 Palmer
China	
9 Great Wall	**Uruguay**
	16 Artigas
Korea, South	
10 King Sejong	

*Year-round research stations north of the 60° South line of latitude are not shown on this map.

Flags & Stats

The following pages provide a quick glance at flags, facts, and figures for all 194 independent countries, listed in alphabetical order, that were recognized by the National Geographic Society in 2008. An independent country has a national government that is accepted as having the highest legal authority over the land and people within its boundaries.

The flags shown are national flags recognized by the United Nations. Each flag symbolizes the diverse cultures and histories of the respective country. The statistical data, which provide highlights of geography and demography, offer a brief overview of each country. Area figures include land as well as surface areas for inland bodies of water. Population figures are for mid-2007 as provided by the Population Reference Bureau of the United States. The languages listed are either the ones most commonly spoken within a country or official languages of a country. For example, not every language spoken in a specific country can be listed, but those shown are the most representative of that country.

Angola
Continent: Africa
Area: 481,354 sq mi (1,246,700 sq km)
Population: 16,293,000
Capital: Luanda 4,007,000
Language: Portuguese, Bantu and other African languages

Austria
Continent: Europe
Area: 32,378 sq mi (83,858 sq km)
Population: 8,315,000
Capital: Vienna 2,315,000
Language: German

Barbados
Continent: North America
Area: 166 sq mi (430 sq km)
Population: 278,000
Capital: Bridgetown 116,000
Language: English

Antigua and Barbuda
Continent: North America
Area: 171 sq mi (442 sq km)
Population: 86,000
Capital: St. John's 26,000
Language: English, local dialects

Azerbaijan
Continent: Europe/Asia
Area: 33,436 sq mi (86,600 sq km)
Population: 8,581,000
Capital: Baku 1,892,000
Language: Azerbaijani (Azeri)

Belarus
Continent: Europe
Area: 80,153 sq mi (207,595 sq km)
Population: 9,696,000
Capital: Minsk 1,806,000
Language: Belarusian, Russian

Argentina
Continent: South America
Area: 1,073,518 sq mi (2,780,400 sq km)
Population: 39,356,000
Capital: Buenos Aires 12,795,000
Language: Spanish, English, Italian, German, French

Bahamas
Continent: North America
Area: 5,382 sq mi (13,939 sq km)
Population: 334,000
Capital: Nassau 240,000
Language: English, Creole

Belgium
Continent: Europe
Area: 11,787 sq mi (30,528 sq km)
Population: 10,611,000
Capital: Brussels 1,743,000
Language: Dutch, French

Afghanistan
Continent: Asia
Area: 251,773 sq mi (652,090 sq km)
Population: 31,890,000
Capital: Kabul 3,324,000
Language: Afghan Persian (Dari), Pashto, Turkic languages, Baluchi, 30 minor languages

Algeria
Continent: Africa
Area: 919,595 sq mi (2,381,741 sq km)
Population: 34,104,000
Capital: Algiers 3,355,000
Language: Arabic, French, Berber dialects

Armenia
Continent: Asia
Area: 11,484 sq mi (29,743 sq km)
Population: 3,014,000
Capital: Yerevan 1,102,000
Language: Armenian

Bahrain
Continent: Asia
Area: 277 sq mi (717 sq km)
Population: 762,000
Capital: Manama 157,000
Language: Arabic, English, Farsi, Urdu

Belize
Continent: North America
Area: 8,867 sq mi (22,965 sq km)
Population: 311,000
Capital: Belmopan 16,000
Language: Spanish, Creole, Mayan dialects, English, Garifuna (Carib), German

Albania
Continent: Europe
Area: 11,100 sq mi (28,748 sq km)
Population: 3,174,000
Capital: Tirana 406,000
Language: Albanian, Greek, Vlach, Romani, Slavic dialects

Andorra
Continent: Europe
Area: 181 sq mi (468 sq km)
Population: 81,000
Capital: Andorra la Vella 24,000
Language: Catalan, French, Castilian, Portuguese

Australia
Continent: Australia/Oceania
Area: 2,969,906 sq mi (7,692,024 sq km)
Population: 21,000,000
Capital: Canberra 378,000
Language: English

Bangladesh
Continent: Asia
Area: 56,977 sq mi (147,570 sq km)
Population: 149,002,000
Capital: Dhaka 13,485,000
Language: Bangla (Bengali), English

Benin
Continent: Africa
Area: 43,484 sq mi (112,622 sq km)
Population: 9,033,000
Capital: Porto-Novo (constitutional) 257,000; Cotonou (seat of government) 762,000
Language: French, Fon, Yoruba, tribal languages

Bhutan
Continent: Asia
Area: 17,954 sq mi (46,500 sq km)
Population: 896,000
Capital: Thimphu 83,000
Language: Dzongkha, Tibetan dialects, Nepalese dialects

Brunei
Continent: Asia
Area: 2,226 sq mi (5,765 sq km)
Population: 372,000
Capital: Bandar Seri Begawan 22,000
Language: Malay, English, Chinese

Cameroon
Continent: Africa
Area: 183,569 sq mi (475,442 sq km)
Population: 18,060,000
Capital: Yaoundé 1,610,000
Language: 24 major African language groups, English, French

Chile
Continent: South America
Area: 291,930 sq mi (756,096 sq km)
Population: 16,598,000
Capital: Santiago 5,719,000
Language: Spanish

Costa Rica
Continent: North America
Area: 19,730 sq mi (51,100 sq km)
Population: 4,477,000
Capital: San José 1,284,000
Language: Spanish, English

Bolivia
Continent: South America
Area: 424,164 sq mi (1,098,581 sq km)
Population: 9,815,000
Capital: La Paz 1,590,000; Sucre (legal) 243,000
Language: Spanish, Quechua, Aymara

Bulgaria
Continent: Europe
Area: 42,855 sq mi (110,994 sq km)
Population: 7,660,000
Capital: Sofia 1,186,000
Language: Bulgarian, Turkish, Roma

Canada
Continent: North America
Area: 3,855,101 sq mi (9,984,670 sq km)
Population: 32,943,000
Capital: Ottawa 1,143,000
Language: English, French

China
Continent: Asia
Area: 3,705,405 sq mi (9,596,960 sq km)
Population: 1,348,317,000
Capital: Beijing 11,106,000
Language: Standard Chinese or Mandarin, Yue, Wu, Minbei dialects, minority languages

Côte d'Ivoire (Ivory Coast)
Continent: Africa
Area: 124,503 sq mi (322,462 sq km)
Population: 20,237,000
Capital: Abidjan 3,801,000; Yamoussoukro 669,000
Language: French, Dioula, other native dialects

Bosnia and Herzegovina
Continent: Europe
Area: 19,741 sq mi (51,129 sq km)
Population: 3,845,000
Capital: Sarajevo 377,000
Language: Bosnian, Croatian, Serbian

Burkina Faso
Continent: Africa
Area: 105,869 sq mi (274,200 sq km)
Population: 14,784,000
Capital: Ouagadougou 1,148,000
Language: French, native African languages

Cape Verde
Continent: Africa
Area: 1,558 sq mi (4,036 sq km)
Population: 494,000
Capital: Praia 125,000
Language: Portuguese, Crioulo

Colombia
Continent: South America
Area: 440,831 sq mi (1,141,748 sq km)
Population: 46,156,000
Capital: Bogotá 7,764,000
Language: Spanish

Croatia
Continent: Europe
Area: 21,831 sq mi (56,542 sq km)
Population: 4,448,000
Capital: Zagreb 689,000
Language: Croatian

Botswana
Continent: Africa
Area: 224,607 sq mi (581,730 sq km)
Population: 1,753,000
Capital: Gaborone 224,000
Language: Setswana, Kalanga

Burundi
Continent: Africa
Area: 10,747 sq mi (27,834 sq km)
Population: 8,508,000
Capital: Bujumbura 430,000
Language: Kirundi, French, Swahili

Central African Republic
Continent: Africa
Area: 240,535 sq mi (622,984 sq km)
Population: 4,343,000
Capital: Bangui 672,000
Language: French, Sangho, tribal languages

Comoros
Continent: Africa
Area: 719 sq mi (1,862 sq km)
Population: 711,000
Capital: Moroni 46,000
Language: Arabic, French, Shikomoro

Cuba
Continent: North America
Area: 42,803 sq mi (110,860 sq km)
Population: 11,248,000
Capital: Havana 2,178,000
Language: Spanish

Brazil
Continent: South America
Area: 3,300,169 sq mi (8,547,403 sq km)
Population: 189,335,000
Capital: Brasília 3,594,000
Language: Portuguese

Cambodia
Continent: Asia
Area: 69,898 sq mi (181,035 sq km)
Population: 14,364,000
Capital: Phnom Penh 1,465,000
Language: Khmer

Chad
Continent: Africa
Area: 495,755 sq mi (1,284,000 sq km)
Population: 10,781,000
Capital: N'Djamena 987,000
Language: French, Arabic, Sara, over 120 languages and dialects

Congo
Continent: Africa
Area: 132,047 sq mi (342,000 sq km)
Population: 3,801,000
Capital: Brazzaville 1,332,000
Language: French, Lingala, Monokutuba, local languages

Cyprus
Continent: Europe
Area: 3,572 sq mi (9,251 sq km)
Population: 1,023,000
Capital: Nicosia 233,000
Language: Greek, Turkish, English

Czech Republic
(Czechia)
Continent: Europe
Area: 30,450 sq mi
(78,866 sq km)
Population: 10,305,000
Capital: Prague 1,162,000
Language: Czech

Dominican Republic
Continent: North America
Area: 18,704 sq mi
(48,442 sq km)
Population: 9,366,000
Capital: Santo Domingo
2,154,000
Language: Spanish

Eritrea
Continent: Africa
Area: 46,774 sq mi
(121,144 sq km)
Population: 4,851,000
Capital: Asmara 600,000
Language: Afar, Arabic, Tigre,
Kunama, Tigrinya, other Cushitic
languages

France
Continent: Europe
Area: 210,026 sq mi
(543,965 sq km)
Population: 61,725,000
Capital: Paris 9,902,000
Language: French

Ghana
Continent: Africa
Area: 92,100 sq mi
(238,537 sq km)
Population: 22,995,000
Capital: Accra 2,120,000
Language: Asante, Ewe, Fante,
Boron, Dagomba, Dangme,
Dagarte, Akyem, Ga, English

Democratic Republic of the Congo
Continent: Africa
Area: 905,365 sq mi
(2,344,885 sq km)
Population: 62,636,000
Capital: Kinshasa 7,851,000
Language: French, Lingala,
Kingwana, Kikongo, Tshiluba

Ecuador
Continent: South America
Area: 109,483 sq mi
(283,560 sq km)
Population: 13,473,000
Capital: Quito 1,697,000
Language: Spanish, Quechua,
other Amerindian languages

Estonia
Continent: Europe
Area: 17,462 sq mi
(45,227 sq km)
Population: 1,341,000
Capital: Tallinn 397,000
Language: Estonian, Russian

Gabon
Continent: Africa
Area: 103,347 sq mi
(267,667 sq km)
Population: 1,331,000
Capital: Libreville 576,000
Language: French, Fang,
Myene, Nzebi, Bapounou/
Eschira, Bandjabi

Greece
Continent: Europe
Area: 50,949 sq mi
(131,957 sq km)
Population: 11,189,000
Capital: Athens 3,242,000
Language: Greek

Denmark
Continent: Europe
Area: 16,640 sq mi
(43,098 sq km)
Population: 5,454,000
Capital: Copenhagen 1,086,000
Language: Danish, Faroese,
Greenlandic, German, English
as second language

Egypt
Continent: Africa
Area: 386,874 sq mi
(1,002,000 sq km)
Population: 73,418,000
Capital: Cairo 11,893,000
Language: Arabic, English,
French

Ethiopia
Continent: Africa
Area: 437,600 sq mi
(1,133,380 sq km)
Population: 77,127,000
Capital: Addis Ababa
3,102,000
Language: Amharic, Oromigna,
Tigrinya, Guaragigna, Somali

Gambia
Continent: Africa
Area: 4,361 sq mi
(11,295 sq km)
Population: 1,517,000
Capital: Banjul 407,000
Language: English, Mandinka,
Wolof, Fula, other indigenous
vernaculars

Grenada
Continent: North America
Area: 133 sq mi (344 sq km)
Population: 99,000
Capital: St. George's 32,000
Language: English, French
patois

Djibouti
Continent: Africa
Area: 8,958 sq mi
(23,200 sq km)
Population: 833,000
Capital: Djibouti 583,000
Language: French, Arabic,
Somali, Afar

El Salvador
Continent: North America
Area: 8,124 sq mi
(21,041 sq km)
Population: 6,877,000
Capital: San Salvador
1,433,000
Language: Spanish, Nahua

Fiji Islands
Continent: Australia/Oceania
Area: 7,095 sq mi
(18,376 sq km)
Population: 862,000
Capital: Suva 224,000
Language: English, Fijian,
Hindustani

Georgia
Continent: Europe/Asia
Area: 26,911 sq mi
(69,700 sq km)
Population: 4,524,000
Capital: T'bilisi 1,099,000
Language: Georgian, Russian,
Armenian, Azeri, Abkhaz

Guatemala
Continent: North America
Area: 42,042 sq mi
(108,889 sq km)
Population: 13,354,000
Capital: Guatemala City
1,025,000
Language: Spanish, 23 recog-
nized Amerindian languages

Dominica
Continent: North America
Area: 290 sq mi (751 sq km)
Population: 70,000
Capital: Roseau 14,000
Language: English, French
patois

Equatorial Guinea
Continent: Africa
Area: 10,831 sq mi
(28,051 sq km)
Population: 507,000
Capital: Malabo 96,000
Language: Spanish, French,
Fang, Bubi

Finland
Continent: Europe
Area: 130,558 sq mi
(338,145 sq km)
Population: 5,288,000
Capital: Helsinki 1,115,000
Language: Finnish, Swedish

Germany
Continent: Europe
Area: 137,847 sq mi
(357,022 sq km)
Population: 82,254,000
Capital: Berlin 3,405,000
Language: German

Guinea
Continent: Africa
Area: 94,926 sq mi
(245,857 sq km)
Population: 10,112,000
Capital: Conakry 1,494,000
Language: French, ethnic
languages

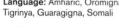

Guinea-Bissau
Continent: Africa
Area: 13,948 sq mi
(36,125 sq km)
Population: 1,695,000
Capital: Bissau 330,000
Language: Portuguese, Crioulo,
African languages

Iceland
Continent: Europe
Area: 39,769 sq mi
(103,000 sq km)
Population: 313,000
Capital: Reykjavik 192,000
Language: Icelandic, English,
Nordic languages, German

Ireland
Continent: Europe
Area: 27,133 sq mi
(70,273 sq km)
Population: 4,369,000
Capital: Dublin 1,060,000
Language: Irish (Gaelic),
English

Jordan
Continent: Asia
Area: 34,495 sq mi
(89,342 sq km)
Population: 5,728,000
Capital: Amman 1,064,000
Language: Arabic, English

Kuwait
Continent: Asia
Area: 6,880 sq mi
(17,818 sq km)
Population: 2,778,000
Capital: Kuwait 2,061,000
Language: Arabic, English

Guyana
Continent: South America
Area: 83,000 sq mi
(214,969 sq km)
Population: 763,000
Capital: Georgetown 133,000
Language: English, Amerindian
dialects, Creole, Hindustani,
Urdu

India
Continent: Asia
Area: 1,269,221 sq mi
(3,287,270 sq km)
Population: 1,131,883,000
Capital: New Delhi 15,926,000
(part of Delhi metropolitan area)
Language: Hindi, English,
212 other official languages

Israel
Continent: Asia
Area: 8,550 sq mi
(22,145 sq km)
Population: 7,347,000
Capital: Jerusalem 736,000
Language: Hebrew, Arabic,
English

Kazakhstan
Continent: Europe/Asia
Area: 1,049,155 sq mi
(2,717,300 sq km)
Population: 15,486,000
Capital: Astana 594,000
Language: Kazakh (Qazaq),
Russian

Kyrgyzstan
Continent: Asia
Area: 77,182 sq mi
(199,900 sq km)
Population: 5,216,000
Capital: Bishkek 837,000
Language: Kyrgyz, Uzbek,
Russian

Haiti
Continent: North America
Area: 10,714 sq mi
(27,750 sq km)
Population: 8,967,000
Capital: Port-au-Prince
2,002,000
Language: French, Creole

Indonesia
Continent: Asia
Area: 742,308 sq mi
(1,922,570 sq km)
Population: 231,627,000
Capital: Jakarta 9,143,000
Language: Bahasa Indonesia
(modified form of Malay),
English, Dutch, Javanese

Italy
Continent: Europe
Area: 116,345 sq mi
(301,333 sq km)
Population: 59,337,000
Capital: Rome 3,340,000
Language: Italian, German,
French, Slovene

Kenya
Continent: Africa
Area: 224,081 sq mi
(580,367 sq km)
Population: 36,914,000
Capital: Nairobi 3,011,000
Language: English, Kiswahili,
many indigenous languages

Laos
Continent: Asia
Area: 91,429 sq mi
(236,800 sq km)
Population: 5,862,000
Capital: Vientiane 746,000
Language: Lao, French,
English, various ethnic
languages

Honduras
Continent: North America
Area: 43,433 sq mi
(112,492 sq km)
Population: 7,106,000
Capital: Tegucigalpa 947,000
Language: Spanish, Amer-
indian dialects

Iran
Continent: Asia
Area: 636,296 sq mi
(1,648,000 sq km)
Population: 71,208,000
Capital: Tehran 7,875,000
Language: Persian, Turkic,
Kurdish, Luri, Baluchi, Arabic

Jamaica
Continent: North America
Area: 4,244 sq mi
(10,991 sq km)
Population: 2,680,000
Capital: Kingston 581,000
Language: English, English
patois

Kiribati
Continent: Australia/Oceania
Area: 313 sq mi (811 sq km)
Population: 96,000
Capital: Tarawa 42,000
Language: I-Kiribati, English

Latvia
Continent: Europe
Area: 24,938 sq mi
(64,589 sq km)
Population: 2,275,000
Capital: Riga 722,000
Language: Latvian, Russian,
Lithuanian

Hungary
Continent: Europe
Area: 35,919 sq mi
(93,030 sq km)
Population: 10,058,000
Capital: Budapest 1,675,000
Language: Hungarian

Iraq
Continent: Asia
Area: 168,754 sq mi
(437,072 sq km)
Population: 28,993,000
Capital: Baghdad 5,500,000
Language: Arabic, Kurdish,
Assyrian, Armenian

Japan
Continent: Asia
Area: 145,902 sq mi
(377,887 sq km)
Population: 127,730,000
Capital: Tokyo 35,676,000
Language: Japanese

Kosovo
Continent: Europe
Area: 4,203 sq mi
(10,887 sq km)
Population: 1,900,000
Capital: Pristina 600,000
Language: Albanian, Serbian,
Bosnian, Turkish, Roma

Lebanon
Continent: Asia
Area: 4,036 sq mi
(10,452 sq km)
Population: 3,921,000
Capital: Beirut 1,857,000
Language: Arabic, French,
English, Armenian

Lesotho
Continent: Africa
Area: 11,720 sq mi (30,355 sq km)
Population: 1,798,000
Capital: Maseru 212,000
Language: Sesotho, English, Zulu, Xhosa

Luxembourg
Continent: Europe
Area: 998 sq mi (2,586 sq km)
Population: 466,000
Capital: Luxembourg 84,000
Language: Luxembourgish, German, French

Maldives
Continent: Asia
Area: 115 sq mi (298 sq km)
Population: 304,000
Capital: Male 111,000
Language: Maldivian Dhivehi, English

Mauritius
Continent: Africa
Area: 788 sq mi (2,040 sq km)
Population: 1,261,000
Capital: Port Louis 150,000
Language: Creole, Bhojpuri, French

Mongolia
Continent: Asia
Area: 603,909 sq mi (1,564,116 sq km)
Population: 2,610,000
Capital: Ulaanbaatar 884,000
Language: Khalkha Mongol, Turkic, Russian

Liberia
Continent: Africa
Area: 43,000 sq mi (111,370 sq km)
Population: 3,750,000
Capital: Monrovia 1,165,000
Language: English, 20 ethnic languages

Macedonia
Continent: Europe
Area: 9,928 sq mi (25,713 sq km)
Population: 2,047,000
Capital: Skopje 480,000
Language: Macedonian, Albanian, Turkish

Mali
Continent: Africa
Area: 478,841 sq mi (1,240,192 sq km)
Population: 12,337,000
Capital: Bamako 1,494,000
Language: Bambara, French, numerous African languages

Mexico
Continent: North America
Area: 758,449 sq mi (1,964,375 sq km)
Population: 106,535,000
Capital: Mexico City 19,028,000
Language: Spanish, Mayan, Nahuatl, other indigenous languages

Montenegro
Continent: Europe
Area: 5,415 sq mi (14,026 sq km)
Population: 626,000
Capital: Podgorica 142,000
Language: Serbian (Ijekavian dialect), Bosnian, Albanian, Croatian

Libya
Continent: Africa
Area: 679,362 sq mi (1,759,540 sq km)
Population: 6,160,000
Capital: Tripoli 2,188,000
Language: Arabic, Italian, English

Madagascar
Continent: Africa
Area: 226,658 sq mi (587,041 sq km)
Population: 18,252,000
Capital: Antananarivo 1,697,000
Language: English, French, Malagasy

Malta
Continent: Europe
Area: 122 sq mi (316 sq km)
Population: 407,000
Capital: Valletta 199,000
Language: Maltese, English

Micronesia
Continent: Australia/Oceania
Area: 271 sq mi (702 sq km)
Population: 108,000
Capital: Palikir 7,000
Language: English, Trukese, Pohnpeian, Yapese, other indigenous languages

Morocco
Continent: Africa
Area: 274,461 sq mi (710,850 sq km)
Population: 31,711,000
Capital: Rabat 1,705,000
Language: Arabic, Berber dialects, French

Liechtenstein
Continent: Europe
Area: 62 sq mi (160 sq km)
Population: 35,000
Capital: Vaduz 5,000
Language: German, Alemannic dialect

Malawi
Continent: Africa
Area: 45,747 sq mi (118,484 sq km)
Population: 13,070,000
Capital: Lilongwe 732,000
Language: Chichewa, Chinyanja, Chiyao, Chitumbuka

Marshall Islands
Continent: Australia/Oceania
Area: 70 sq mi (181 sq km)
Population: 67,000
Capital: Majuro 28,000
Language: Marshallese

Moldova
Continent: Europe
Area: 13,050 sq mi (33,800 sq km)
Population: 3,991,000
Capital: Chisinau 592,000
Language: Moldovan, Russian, Gagauz

Mozambique
Continent: Africa
Area: 308,642 sq mi (799,380 sq km)
Population: 20,359,000
Capital: Maputo 1,445,000
Language: Emakhuwa, Xichangana, Portuguese, Elomwe, Cisena, Echuwabo

Lithuania
Continent: Europe
Area: 25,212 sq mi (65,300 sq km)
Population: 3,376,000
Capital: Vilnius 543,000
Language: Lithuanian, Russian, Polish

Malaysia
Continent: Asia
Area: 127,355 sq mi (329,847 sq km)
Population: 27,160,000
Capital: Kuala Lumpur 1,448,000
Language: Bahasa Malaysia, English, Chinese, Tamil, Telugu, Malayalam, Panjabi, Thai

Mauritania
Continent: Africa
Area: 397,955 sq mi (1,030,700 sq km)
Population: 3,124,000
Capital: Nouakchott 673,000
Language: Arabic, Pulaar, Soninke, French, Hassaniya, Wolof

Monaco
Continent: Europe
Area: 0.8 sq mi (2.0 sq km)
Population: 33,000
Capital: Monaco 33,000
Language: French, English, Italian, Monegasque

Myanmar (Burma)
Continent: Asia
Area: 261,218 sq mi (676,552 sq km)
Population: 49,805,000
Capital: Nay Pyi Taw (administrative) 418,000; Yangon (Rangoon) (legislative) 4,088,000
Language: Burmese, minority ethnic languages

Namibia
Continent: Africa
Area: 318,261 sq mi
(824,292 sq km)
Population: 2,074,000
Capital: Windhoek 313,000
Language: Afrikaans, German,
English

Nicaragua
Continent: North America
Area: 50,193 sq mi
(130,000 sq km)
Population: 5,620,000
Capital: Managua 920,000
Language: Spanish

Oman
Continent: Asia
Area: 119,500 sq mi
(309,500 sq km)
Population: 2,706,000
Capital: Muscat 621,000
Language: Arabic, English,
Baluchi, Urdu, Indian dialects

Paraguay
Continent: South America
Area: 157,048 sq mi
(406,752 sq km)
Population: 6,126,000
Capital: Asunción 1,870,000
Language: Spanish, Guarani

Qatar
Continent: Asia
Area: 4,448 sq mi
(11,521 sq km)
Population: 882,000
Capital: Doha 386,000
Language: Arabic, English
commonly a second language

Nauru
Continent: Australia/Oceania
Area: 8 sq mi (21 sq km)
Population: 14,000
Capital: Yaren 10,000
Language: Nauruan, English

Niger
Continent: Africa
Area: 489,191 sq mi
(1,267,000 sq km)
Population: 14,226,000
Capital: Niamey 915,000
Language: French, Hausa,
Djerma

Pakistan
Continent: Asia
Area: 307,374 sq mi
(796,095 sq km)
Population: 169,271,000
Language: Punjabi, Sindhi,
Siraiki, Pashto, Urdu, Baluchi,
Hindko, English

Peru
Continent: South America
Area: 496,224 sq mi
(1,285,216 sq km)
Population: 27,903,000
Capital: Lima 8,007,000
Language: Spanish, Quechua,
Aymara, minor Amazonian
languages

Romania
Continent: Europe
Area: 92,043 sq mi
(238,391 sq km)
Population: 21,550,000
Capital: Bucharest 1,940,000
Language: Romanian,
Hungarian

Nepal
Continent: Asia
Area: 56,827 sq mi
(147,181 sq km)
Population: 27,828,000
Capital: Kathmandu 895,000
Language: Nepali, Maithali,
Bhojpuri, Tharu, Tamang,
Newar, Magar

Nigeria
Continent: Africa
Area: 356,669 sq mi
(923,768 sq km)
Population: 144,430,000
Capital: Abuja 1,579,000
Language: English, Hausa,
Yoruba, Igbo (Ibo), Fulani

Palau
Continent: Australia/Oceania
Area: 189 sq mi (489 sq km)
Population: 20,000
Capital: Melekeok NA
Language: Palauan, Filipino,
English, Chinese

Philippines
Continent: Asia
Area: 115,831 sq mi
(300,000 sq km)
Population: 88,706,000
Filipino(s)
Capital: Manila 11,100,000
Language: Filipino (based
on Tagalog), English

Russia
Continent: Europe/Asia
Area: 6,592,850 sq mi
(17,075,400 sq km)
Population: 141,681,000
Capital: Moscow 10,452,000
Language: Russian, many
minority languages

Netherlands
Continent: Europe
Area: 16,034 sq mi
(41,528 sq km)
Population: 16,368,000
Capital: Amsterdam 1,031,000
Language: Dutch, Frisian

North Korea
Continent: Asia
Area: 46,540 sq mi
(120,538 sq km)
Population: 23,301,000
Capital: Pyongyang 3,301,000
Language: Korean

Panama
Continent: North America
Area: 29,157 sq mi
(75,517 sq km)
Population: 3,340,000
Capital: Panama City
1,280,000
Language: Spanish, English

Poland
Continent: Europe
Area: 120,728 sq mi
(312,685 sq km)
Population: 38,109,000
Capital: Warsaw 1,707,000
Language: Polish

Rwanda
Continent: Africa
Area: 10,169 sq mi
(26,338 sq km)
Population: 9,347,000
Capital: Kigali 852,000
Language: Kinyarwanda,
French, English, Kiswahili

New Zealand
Continent: Australia/Oceania
Area: 104,454 sq mi
(270,534 sq km)
Population: 4,184,000
Capital: Wellington 366,000
Language: English, Maori

Norway
Continent: Europe
Area: 125,004 sq mi
(323,758 sq km)
Population: 4,702,000
Capital: Oslo 834,000
Language: Bokmal Norwegian,
Nynorsk Norwegian, Sami

Papua New Guinea
Continent: Australia/Oceania
Area: 178,703 sq mi
(462,840 sq km)
Population: 6,331,000
Capital: Port Moresby 299,000
Language: Melanesian Pidgin,
820 indigenous languages

Portugal
Continent: Europe
Area: 35,655 sq mi
(92,345 sq km)
Population: 10,667,000
Capital: Lisbon 2,811,000
Language: Portuguese,
Mirandese

Samoa
Continent: Australia/Oceania
Area: 1,093 sq mi
(2,831 sq km)
Population: 187,000
Capital: Apia 43,000
Language: Samoan
(Polynesian), English

San Marino
Continent: Europe
Area: 24 sq mi (61 sq km)
Population: 31,000
Capital: San Marino 4,000
Language: Italian

Seychelles
Continent: Africa
Area: 176 sq mi (455 sq km)
Population: 86,000
Capital: Victoria 26,000
Language: Creole, English

Solomon Islands
Continent: Australia/Oceania
Area: 10,954 sq mi (28,370 sq km)
Population: 495,000
Capital: Honiara 66,000
Language: Melanesian pidgin, 120 indigenous languages

Sri Lanka
Continent: Asia
Area: 25,299 sq mi (65,525 sq km)
Population: 20,087,000
Capital: Colombo 656,000
Language: Sinhala, Tamil

Suriname
Continent: South America
Area: 63,037 sq mi (163,265 sq km)
Population: 503,000
Capital: Paramaribo 252,000
Language: Dutch, English, Sranang Tongo, Hindustani, Javanese

Sao Tome and Principe
Continent: Africa
Area: 386 sq mi (1,001 sq km)
Population: 155,000
Capital: São Tomé 58,000
Language: Portuguese

Sierra Leone
Continent: Africa
Area: 27,699 sq mi (71,740 sq km)
Population: 5,335,000
Capital: Freetown 826,000
Language: English, Mende, Temne, Krio

Somalia
Continent: Africa
Area: 246,201 sq mi (637,657 sq km)
Population: 9,119,000
Capital: Mogadishu 1,450,000
Language: Somali, Arabic, Italian, English

St. Kitts and Nevis
Continent: North America
Area: 104 sq mi (269 sq km)
Population: 47,000
Capital: Basseterre 13,000
Language: English

Swaziland
Continent: Africa
Area: 6,704 sq mi (17,363 sq km)
Population: 1,133,000
Capital: Mbabane (administrative) 78,000; Lobamba (legislative and royal) NA
Language: English, siSwati

Saudi Arabia
Continent: Asia
Area: 756,985 sq mi (1,960,582 sq km)
Population: 27,601,000
Capital: Riyadh 4,462,000
Language: Arabic

Singapore
Continent: Asia
Area: 255 sq mi (660 sq km)
Population: 4,634,000
Capital: Singapore 4,634,000
Language: Mandarin, English, Malay, Hokkien, Cantonese, Teochew, Tamil

South Africa
Continent: Africa
Area: 470,693 sq mi (1,219,090 sq km)
Population: 47,867,000
Capital: Pretoria 1,336,000; Bloemfontein 417,000; Cape Town 3,211,000
Language: IsiZulu, IsiXhosa

St. Lucia
Continent: North America
Area: 238 sq mi (616 sq km)
Population: 170,000
Capital: Castries 14,000
Language: English, French patois

Sweden
Continent: Europe
Area: 173,732 sq mi (449,964 sq km)
Population: 9,146,000
Capital: Stockholm 1,264,000
Language: Swedish, small Sami- and Finnish-speaking minorities

Senegal
Continent: Africa
Area: 75,955 sq mi (196,722 sq km)
Population: 12,379,000
Capital: Dakar 2,603,000
Language: French, Wolof, Pulaar, Jola, Mandinka

Slovakia
Continent: Europe
Area: 18,932 sq mi (49,035 sq km)
Population: 5,396,000
Capital: Bratislava 424,000
Language: Slovak, Hungarian

South Korea
Continent: Asia
Area: 38,321 sq mi (99,250 sq km)
Population: 48,456,000
Capital: Seoul 9,799,000
Language: Korean, English

St. Vincent and the Grenadines
Continent: North America
Area: 150 sq mi (389 sq km)
Population: 111,000
Capital: Kingstown 26,000
Language: English, French patois

Switzerland
Continent: Europe
Area: 15,940 sq mi (41,284 sq km)
Population: 7,532,000
Capital: Bern 337,000
Language: German, French, Italian, Romansh

Serbia
Continent: Europe
Area: 29,913 sq mi (77,474 sq km)
Population: 7,625,000
Capital: Belgrade 1,100,000
Language: Serbian, Hungarian, Albanian

Slovenia
Continent: Europe
Area: 7,827 sq mi (20,273 sq km)
Population: 2,014,000
Capital: Ljubljana 244,000
Language: Slovene, Serbo-Croatian

Spain
Continent: Europe
Area: 195,363 sq mi (505,988 sq km)
Population: 45,332,000
Capital: Madrid 5,567,000
Language: Castilian Spanish, Catalan, Galician, Basque

Sudan
Continent: Africa
Area: 967,500 sq mi (2,505,813 sq km)
Population: 38,560,000
Capital: Khartoum 4,762,000
Language: Arabic, Nubian, Ta Bedawie, many diverse dialects of Nilotic, Nilo-Hamitic, Sudanic languages, English

Syria
Continent: Asia
Area: 71,498 sq mi (185,180 sq km)
Population: 19,929,000
Capital: Damascus 2,467,000
Language: Arabic, Kurdish, Armenian, Aramaic, Circassian; French and English somewhat understood

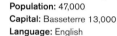

Tajikistan
Continent: Asia
Area: 55,251 sq mi (143,100 sq km)
Population: 7,133,000
Capital: Dushanbe 553,000
Language: Tajik, Russian

Tonga
Continent: Australia/Oceania
Area: 289 sq mi (748 sq km)
Population: 101,000
Capital: Nuku'alofa 25,000
Language: Tongan, English

Tuvalu
Continent: Australia/Oceania
Area: 10 sq mi (26 sq km)
Population: 10,000
Capital: Funafuti 5,000
Language: Tuvaluan, English, Samoan, Kiribati

United States
Continent: North America
Area: 3,794,083 sq mi (9,826,630 sq km)
Population: 302,200,000
Capital: Washington, D.C. 4,338,000
Language: English, Spanish, other Indo-European languages

Venezuela
Continent: South America
Area: 352,144 sq mi (912,050 sq km)
Population: 27,483,000
Capital: Caracas 2,986,000
Language: Spanish, numerous indigenous dialects

Tanzania
Continent: Africa
Area: 364,900 sq mi (945,087 sq km)
Population: 38,738,000
Capital: Dar es Salaam 2,930,000; Dodoma 83,000
Language: Swahili, Kiunguja, English, Arabic, local languages

Trinidad and Tobago
Continent: North America
Area: 1,980 sq mi (5,128 sq km)
Population: 1,387,000
Capital: Port-of-Spain 54,000
Language: English, Caribbean Hindustani, French, Spanish, Chinese

Uganda
Continent: Africa
Area: 93,104 sq mi (241,139 sq km)
Population: 28,530,000
Capital: Kampala 1,420,000
Language: English, Ganda, other local languages, Swahili, Arabic

Uruguay
Continent: South America
Area: 68,037 sq mi (176,215 sq km)
Population: 3,324,000
Capital: Montevideo 1,514,000
Language: Spanish

Vietnam
Continent: Asia
Area: 127,844 sq mi (331,114 sq km)
Population: 85,134,000
Capital: Hanoi 4,377,000
Language: Vietnamese, English, French, Chinese, Khmer

Thailand
Continent: Asia
Area: 198,115 sq mi (513,115 sq km)
Population: 65,706,000
Capital: Bangkok 6,706,000
Language: Thai, English, ethnic dialects

Tunisia
Continent: Africa
Area: 63,170 sq mi (163,610 sq km)
Population: 10,225,000
Capital: Tunis 746,000
Language: Arabic, French

Ukraine
Continent: Europe
Area: 233,090 sq mi (603,700 sq km)
Population: 46,505,000
Capital: Kiev 2,705,000
Language: Ukrainian, Russian

Uzbekistan
Continent: Asia
Area: 172,742 sq mi (447,400 sq km)
Population: 26,499,000
Capital: Tashkent 2,184,000
Language: Uzbek, Russian, Tajik

Yemen
Continent: Asia
Area: 207,286 sq mi (536,869 sq km)
Population: 22,389,000
Capital: Sanaa 2,008,000
Language: Arabic

Timor-Leste (East Timor)
Continent: Asia
Area: 5,640 sq mi (14,609 sq km)
Population: 1,048,000
Capital: Dili 159,000
Language: Tetum, Portuguese, Indonesian, English, indigenous languages

Turkey
Continent: Europe/Asia
Area: 300,948 sq mi (779,452 sq km)
Population: 73,967,000
Capital: Ankara 3,715,000
Language: Turkish, Kurdish, Dimli (Zaza), Azeri, Kabardian, Gagauz

United Arab Emirates
Continent: Asia
Area: 30,000 sq mi (77,700 sq km)
Population: 4,424,000
Capital: Abu Dhabi 604,000
Language: Arabic, Persian, English, Hindi, Urdu

Vanuatu
Continent: Australia/Oceania
Area: 14,707 sq mi (2,190 sq km)
Population: 235,000
Capital: Port-Vila 40,000
Language: over 100 local languages, pidgin (known as Bislama or Bichelama)

Zambia
Continent: Africa
Area: 290,586 sq mi (752,614 sq km)
Population: 11,477,000
Capital: Lusaka 1,328,000
Language: English, Bemba, Kaonda, Lozi, Lunda, Luvale, about 70 other indigenous languages

Togo
Continent: Africa
Area: 21,925 sq mi (56,785 sq km)
Population: 6,585,000
Capital: Lomé 1,451,000
Language: French, Ewe, Mina, Kabye, Dagomba

Turkmenistan
Continent: Asia
Area: 188,456 sq mi (488,100 sq km)
Population: 5,409,000
Capital: Ashgabat 744,000
Language: Turkmen, Russian, Uzbek

United Kingdom
Continent: Europe
Area: 93,788 sq mi (242,910 sq km)
Population: 60,967,000
Capital: London 8,566,000
Language: English, Welsh, Scottish form of Gaelic

Vatican City
Continent: Europe
Area: 0.2 sq mi (0.4 sq km)
Population: 798
Capital: Vatican City 798
Language: Italian, Latin, French

Zimbabwe
Continent: Africa
Area: 150,872 sq mi (390,757 sq km)
Population: 13,349,000
Capital: Harare 1,572,000
Language: English, Shona, Sindebele, numerous minor tribal dialects

Glossary

Note: Terms defined within the main body of the atlas text are not listed below.

Arid climate type of dry climate in which annual precipitation is often less than 10 inches (25 cm); experiences great daily variations in day-night temperatures (pp. 20–21)

Asylum a place where a person can go to find safety; to offer asylum means to offer protection in a safe country to people who fear being persecuted or who have been persecuted in their own country (pp. 34–35)

Bathymetry measurement of depth at various places in the ocean or other body of water (p. 11)

Biodiversity biological diversity in an environment as indicated by numbers of different species of plants and animals (pp. 28, 108)

Boreal forest *see* northern coniferous forest

Boundary line established by people to separate one political or mapped area from another; physical features, such as mountains and rivers, or latitude and longitude lines sometimes act as boundaries (p. 10)

Breadbasket a geographic region that is a principal source of grain (p. 64)

Canadian Shield region containing the oldest rock in North America; areas are exposed in much of eastern Canada and some bordering U.S. regions (pp. 56, 62)

Civil war war between opposing groups of citizens of the same country (p. 53)

Coastal plain any comparatively level land of low elevation that borders the ocean (p. 64)

Continental climate midlatitude climate zone occurring on large landmasses in the Northern Hemisphere and characterized by great variations of temperature, both seasonally and between day and night; continental cool summer climates are influenced by nearby colder subarctic climates; continental warm summer climates are influenced by nearby mild or dry climates (pp. 20–21)

Coordinated Universal Time (UTC) the basis for the current worldwide system of civil (versus military) time determined by highly precise atomic clocks; also known as Universal Time; formerly known as Greenwich Mean Time (p. 13)

Culture hearth center from which major cultural traditions spread and are adopted by people in a wide geographic area (p. 90)

Cybercafé a café that has a collection of computers that customers can use to access the Internet (p. 50)

Degraded forest a forested area severely damaged by overharvesting, repeated fires, overgrazing, poor management practices, or other abuse that delays or prevents forest regrowth (p. 28)

Demography the statistical study of human populations, especially with reference to size and density, distribution, and vital statistics (p. 126)

Desert and dry shrub vegetation region with either hot or cold temperatures that annually receives 10 inches (25 cm) or less of precipitation (pp. 24–25)

Ecosystem term for classifying Earth's natural communities according to how all things in an environment, such as a forest or a coral reef, interact with each other (pp. 10, 15, 68, 79, 120)

Fault break in Earth's crust along which movement up, down, or sideways occurs (pp. 16–17)

Flooded grassland wetland dominated by grasses and covered by water (pp. 24–25)

Fossil fuel a fuel, such as coal, petroleum, and natural gas, derived from the remains of ancient plants and animals (p. 46)

Geothermal energy heat energy generated within Earth (p. 47)

Glacier large, slow-moving mass of ice that forms over time from snow (p. 54)

Global warming a theory about the increase of Earth's average global temperature due to a buildup of so-called greenhouse gases, such as carbon dioxide and methane, released by human activities (p. 29)

Globalization the purposeful spread of activities, technology, goods, and values throughout the world through the expansion of global links, such as trade, media, and the Internet (p. 48)

Gondwana name given to the southern part of the supercontinent Pangaea; made up of what we now call Africa, South America, Australia, Antarctica, and India (p. 16)

Greenwich Mean Time *see* Coordinated Universal Time

Gross domestic product (GDP) the gross national product excluding the value of net income earned abroad (p. 42)

Gross national product (GNP) the total value of the goods and services produced by the residents of a nation during a specified period (as a year) (p. 42)

Groundwater water, primarily from rain or melted snow, that collects beneath Earth's surface, in saturated soil or in underground reservoirs, or aquifers, and that supplies springs and wells (p. 27)

Guerrilla a person who engages in irregular warfare, especially as a member of an independent unit carrying out harassment and sabotage (p. 52)

Hemisphere one-half of the globe; the Equator divides Earth into Northern and Southern Hemispheres; the prime meridian and the 180 degree meridian divide it into Eastern and Western Hemispheres (p. 5)

Highland/upland climate region associated with mountains or plateaus that varies depending on elevation, latitude, continental location, and exposure to sun and wind; in general, temperature decreases and precipitation increases with elevation (pp. 20–21)

Host country the country where a refugee first goes to find asylum (p. 34)

Hot spot in geology, an extremely hot region beneath the lithosphere that tends to stay relatively stationary while plates of Earth's outer crust move over it; environmentally, an ecological trouble spot (pp. 12, 28)

Humid subtropical climate region characterized by hot summers, mild to cool winters, and year-round precipitation that is heaviest in summer; generally located on the southeastern margins of continents (pp. 20–21)

Ice cap climate one of two kinds of polar climate; summer temperatures rarely rise above freezing and what little precipitation occurs is mostly in the form of snow (pp. 20–21)

Indigenous native to or occurring naturally in a specific area or environment (p. 116)

Infiltration process that occurs in the water, or hydrologic, cycle when gravity causes surface water to seep down through the soil (p. 26)

Internally displaced person (IDP) a person who has fled his or her home to escape armed conflict, generalized violence, human rights abuses, or natural or man-made disasters; unlike a refugee, such a person has not crossed an international border but remains in his or her own country (p. 34)

Landform physical feature shaped by uplifting, weathering, and erosion; mountains, plateaus, hills, and plains are the four major types (p. 22)

Language family group of languages that share a common ancestry (pp. 38–39)

Latin America cultural region generally considered to include Mexico, Central America, South America, and the West Indies; Portuguese and Spanish are the principal languages (pp. 36–37)

Llanos extensive, mostly treeless grasslands in the Orinoco River basin of northern South America (p. 72)

Lowlands fairly level land at a lower elevation than surrounding areas (p. 14)

Mangrove vegetation tropical trees and shrubs with dense root systems that grow in tidal mud flats and extend coastlines by trapping soil (pp. 24–25)

Marginal land land that has little value for growing crops or for commercial or residential development (p. 28)

Marine west coast type of mild climate common on the west coasts of continents in midlatitude regions; characterized by small variations in annual temperature range and wet, foggy winters (pp. 20–21)

Median age midpoint of a population's age; half the population is older than this age; half is younger (p. 33)

Mediterranean climate type of mild climate common on the west coasts of continents, named for the dominant climate along the Mediterranean coast; characterized by mild, rainy winters and hot, dry summers (pp. 20–21)

Mediterranean shrub low-growing, mostly small-leaved evergreen vegetation, such as chaparral, that thrives in Mediterranean climate regions (pp. 24–25)

Melanesia one of three major island groups that make up Oceania; includes the Fiji Islands, New Guinea, Vanuatu, the Solomon Islands, and New Caledonia (pp. 112–113)

Melanesian indigenous to Melanesia (p. 116)

Microclimate climate of a very limited area that varies from the overall climate of the surrounding region (p. 22)

Micronesia one of three major island groups that make up Oceania; made up of some 2,000 mostly coral islands, including Guam, Kiribati, the Mariana Islands, Palau, and the Federated States of Micronesia (pp. 112–113)

Micronesian indigenous to Micronesia (p. 116)

Monsoon seasonal change in the direction of the prevailing winds, which causes wet and dry seasons in some tropical areas (p. 94)

Mountain grassland vegetation region characterized by clumps of long grass that grow beyond the limit of forests at high elevations (pp. 24–25)

Nonrenewable resources elements of the natural environment, such as metals, minerals, and fossil fuels, that form within Earth by geological processes over millions of years and thus cannot readily be replaced (pp. 46–47)

Northern coniferous forest vegetation region composed primarily of cone-bearing, needle-leafed or scale-leafed evergreen trees that grow in regions with long winters and moderate to high annual precipitation; also called boreal forest or taiga (pp. 24–25)

Oceania name for the widely scattered islands of Polynesia, Micronesia, and Melanesia; often includes Australia and New Zealand (pp. 110–121)

Pampas temperate grassland primarily in Argentina between the Andes and the Atlantic Ocean; one of the richest agricultural regions in the world (pp. 70, 72)

Patagonia cool, windy, arid plateau region primarily in southern Argentina between the Andes and the Atlantic Ocean (p. 72)

Per capita the total national income divided by the number of people in the nation (p. 27)

Plain large area of relatively flat land; one of the four major kinds of landforms (p. 18)

Plate tectonics study of the interaction of slabs of Earth's crust as molten rock within Earth causes them to slowly move across the surface (pp. 16–17)

Plateau large, relatively flat area that rises above the surrounding landscape; one of the four major kinds of landforms (pp. 18–19)

Polar climates climates that occur at very high latitudes; generally too cold to support tree growth; include tundra and ice cap (pp. 20–21)

Polynesia one of three major regions in Oceania made up mostly of volcanic and coral islands, including the Hawai'ian and the Society Islands, Samoa, and French Polynesia (pp. 112–113)

Polynesian indigenous to Polynesia (p. 116)

Predominant economy main type of work that most people do to meet their wants and needs in a particular country (pp. 44–45, 61, 77, 87, 97, 107, 117)

Province land governed as a political or administrative unit of a country or empire; Canadian provinces, like U.S. states, have substantial powers of self-government (p. 63)

Rain forest see Tropical moist broadleaf forest

Renewable fresh water water that is replenished naturally, but the supply of which can be endangered by overuse and pollution (p. 26)

River basin area drained by a single river and its tributaries (p. 72)

Rural pertaining to the countryside, where most of the economic activity centers on agriculture-related work (pp. 36–37)

Sahel in Africa the semi-arid region of short, tropical grassland that lies between the dry Sahara and the humid savanna and that is prone to frequent droughts (p. 104)

Sampan a flat-bottomed skiff used in eastern Asia and usually propelled by two short oars (p. 98)

Savanna tropical tall grassland with scattered low trees (pp. 24–25)

Selva Portuguese word referring to tropical rain forests, especially in the Amazon Basin (p. 78)

Semiarid dry climate region that experiences great daily variation in day-night temperatures; receives enough rainfall to support grasslands (pp. 20–21)

Silt mineral particles that are larger than grains of clay but smaller than grains of sand (p. 78)

Stateless people those who have no recognized country (p. 35)

Steppe Slavic word referring to relatively flat, mostly treeless, temperate grass-lands that stretch across much of central Europe and central Asia (p. 92)

Subarctic climate region characterized by short, cool, sometimes freezing summers and long, bitter-cold winters; most precipitation falls in summer (pp. 20–21)

Subtropical climate region between tropical and continental climates characterized by distinct seasons but with milder temperatures than continental climates (pp. 20–21)

Suburb a residential area on the outskirts of a town or city (p. 36)

Sunbelt area of rapid population and economic growth south of the 37th parallel in the United States; its mild climate is attractive to retirees and a general absence of labor unions has drawn manufacturing to the region (p. 60)

Taiga see Northern coniferous forest

Temperate broadleaf forest vegetation region with distinct seasons and dependable rainfall; predominant species include oak, maple, and beech, all of which lose their leaves in the cold season (pp. 24–25)

Temperate coniferous forest vegetation region that has mild winters with heavy precipitation; made up of mostly evergreen, needleleaf trees that bear seeds in cones (pp. 24–25)

Temperate grassland vegetation region where grasses are dominant and the climate is characterized by hot summers, cold winters, and moderate rainfall (pp. 24–25)

Territory land under the jurisdiction of a country but that is not a state or a province (p. 57)

Tropical coniferous forest vegetation region that occurs in a cooler climate than tropical rain forests; has distinct wet and dry seasons; made up of mostly evergreen trees with seed-bearing cones (pp. 24–25)

Tropical dry climate region characterized by year-round high temperatures and sufficient precipitation to support savannas (pp. 20–21)

Tropical dry forest vegetation region that has distinct wet and dry seasons and a cooler climate than tropical moist forests; has shorter trees than rain forests and many shed their leaves in the dry season (pp. 24–25)

Tropical grassland and savanna vegetation region characterized by scattered individual trees; occurs in warm or hot climates with annual rainfall of 20 to 50 inches (50–130 cm) (pp. 24–25)

Tropical moist broad-leaf forest vegetation region occurring mostly in a belt between the Tropic of Cancer and the Tropic of Capricorn in areas that have at least 80 inches (200 cm) of rain annually and an average annual temperature of 80°F (20°C) (pp. 24–25, 78–79)

Tropical wet climate region characterized by year-round warm temperatures and rainfall ranging from 60 to 150 inches (150–400 cm) annually (pp. 20–21)

Troposphere region of Earth's atmosphere closest to the surface; where weather occurs (p. 5)

Tundra vegetation region at high latitudes and high elevations characterized by cold temperatures, low vegetation, and a short growing season (pp. 24–25)

Tundra climate region with one or more months of temperatures slightly above freezing when the ground is free of snow (pp. 20–21)

Twenty-foot-equivalent unit (TEU) the standard unit for describing a ship's cargo carrying capacity, or a shipping terminal's cargo handling capacity. A standard forty-foot (40 x 8 x 8 feet) container equals two TEUs (each 20 x 8 x 8 feet) (pp. 98–99)

Universalizing religion one that attempts to appeal to all people rather than to just those in a particular region or place (p. 40)

Upland climate see Highland/upland climate

Urban pertaining to a town or city, where most of the economic activity is not based on agriculture (pp. 36–37)

Urban agglomeration a group of several cities and/or towns and their suburbs (p. 37)

Watershed a region or area bounded peripherally by a divide and draining ultimately to a particular watercourse or body of water (pp. 26–27)

West Bank area bordering the west bank of the Jordan River that, according to a 1993 peace agreement between Israelis and Palestinians, has limited Palestinian autonomy; its future is subject to ongoing negotiations between these groups (p. 35)

Web Sites

Activities and lessons using maps: http://www.nationalgeographic.com/xpeditions/

Antarctica: http://www.nsf.gov/div/index.jsp?div=ANT

Cultural Diffusion: http://www2.geog.okstate.edu/users/lightfoot/lightfoot.html

Earth's Climates: http://www.worldclimate.com

Earth's Vegetation: http://www.earthobservatory.nasa.gov/Library/LandCover/

Environmental Hot Spots: http://earthtrends.wri.org/index.cfm

   Quiz for students: http://www.myfootprint.org/

Flags of the World: http://www.fotw.us/flags/index.html

Globalization: http://www.globalisationguide.org/

Map Projections: http://www.colorado.edu/geography/gcraft/notes/mapproj/mapproj.html

National Geographic Kids Atlases Homepage: http://www.nationalgeographic.com/kids-atlases/index.html

Natural Hazards:

   Earthquakes: http://earthquake.usgs.gov/

   Tsunamis: http://www.tsunami.noaa.gov

   Volcanoes: http://www.geo.mtu.edu/volcanoes/

Political World: http://www.cia.gov/cia/publications/factbook/index.html

Predominant World Economies: http://www.wto.org/english/res_e/statis_e/statis_e.htm

Reading Maps: http://egsc.usgs.gov/isb/pubs/teachers-packets/mapshow/mapshowindexpdf.html

   http://leisure.ordnancesurvey.co.uk/leisure/tscontent/editorial/mapfacts/leaflets/map_reading_made_easy.pdf

Time Zones: http://tycho.usno.navy.mil/tzones.html

Types of Maps: http://erg.usgs.gov/isb/pubs/MapProjections/projections.html

World Cities: http://www.un.org/esa/population/publications/wup2003/WUP2003Report.pdf

World Conflicts: http://www.cnn.com/interactive/maps/world/fullpage.global.conflict/world.index.html

World Energy: http://www.bp.com/productlanding.do?categoryId=6929&contentId=7044622

World Food: http://www.cgiar.org/impact/research/index.html

World Languages: http://www.ethnologue.com/web.asp

   Interactive for students: http://www.ipl.org/div/kidspace/hello/

World Population: http://www.census.gov/ipc/www/idb/

World Refugees: http://www.unrefugees.org

World Religions: http://www.adherents.com/

World Water: http://water.usgs.gov/

Thematic Index

Place-Name Index

Illustration Credits

Published by the National Geographic Society

John M. Fahey, Jr.
President and Chief Executive Officer

Gilbert M. Grosvenor
Chairman of the Board

Tim T. Kelly
President, Global Media Group

John Q. Griffin
President, Publishing

Nina D. Hoffman
Executive Vice President, President of Book Publishing Group

Prepared by the Book Division

Nancy Laties Feresten,
Vice President, Editor in Chief, Children's Books

Bea Jackson, *Director of Design and Illustrations, Children's Books*

Jennifer Emmett, *Executive Editor,
Reference and Solo, Children's Books*

Amy Shields, *Executive Editor, Series, Children's Books*

Carl Mehler, *Director of Maps*

Staff for this Book

Priyanka Lamichhane, *Project Editor*

David M. Seager, Ruth Thompson, *Art Directors*

Lori Renda, *Illustrations Editor*

Steven D. Gardner, Thomas L. Gray, Nicholas P. Rosenbach,
Map Editors

Matt Chwastyk, Steven D. Gardner, Gregory Ugiansky,
XNR Productions, *Map Research and Production*

Martha Sharma, *Writer and Chief Consultant*

Stuart Armstrong, *Graphics Illustrator*

Suzanne Patrick Fonda, *Release Editor*

Debbie Guthrie Haer, *Copy Editor*

Connie D. Binder, *Indexer*

Jennifer Thornton, *Managing Editor*

Grace Hill, *Associate Managing Editor*

Heidi Vincent, *Vice President,
Direct Response Sales and Marketing*

Jeff Reynolds, *Marketing Director, Children's Books*

R. Gary Colbert, *Production Director*

Lewis R. Bassford, *Production Manager*

Susan Borke, *Legal and Business Affairs*

Manufacturing and Quality Management

Christopher A. Liedel, *Chief Financial Officer*

Phillip L. Schlosser, *Vice President*

Chris Brown, *Technical Director*

Rachel Faulise, Nicole Elliott, and Monika Lynde,
Manufacturing Managers

Acknowledgements:
We are grateful for the assistance of
Richard W. Bullington, Jan D. Morris, Karla H. Tucker, and
Alfred L. Zebarth of NG Maps; the National Geographic Image
Collection; and Jo H. Tunstall, Robert W. Witt, and
Lyle Rosbotham, NG Book Division

Founded in 1888, the National Geographic Society is one of the largest nonprofit scientific and educational organizations in the world. It reaches more than 285 million people worldwide each month through its official journal, NATIONAL GEOGRAPHIC, and its four other magazines; the National Geographic Channel; television documentaries; radio programs; films; books; videos and DVDs; maps; and interactive media. National Geographic has funded more than 8,000 scientific research projects and supports an education program combating geographic illiteracy.

For more information, please call 1-800-NGS LINE (647-5463) or write to the following address:

NATIONAL GEOGRAPHIC SOCIETY
1145 17th Street N.W., Washington, D.C. 20036-4688 U.S.A.

Visit us online at www.nationalgeographic.com

For information about special discounts for bulk purchases, please contact National Geographic Books Special Sales: ngspecsales@ngs.org

For rights or permissions inquiries, please contact
National Geographic Books Subsidiary Rights: ngbookrights@ngs.org

Teachers and librarians go to ngchildrensbooks.org

Published by the National Geographic Society
1145 17th Street N.W.
Washington, D.C. 20036-4688

Copyright © 2001, 2005, 2009 National Geographic Society

The Library of Congress has cataloged the 2001 edition as follows:

National Geographic Society (U.S.)
National Geographic student atlas of the world.
p. cm.
Includes index and glossary.
ISBN 978-1-4263-0446-0 (pbk.)
ISBN 978-1-4263-0445-3 (hc.)
ISBN: 978-1-4263-0458-3 (library)
   1. Children's atlases. 2. Earth—remote-sensing images. 3. Physical
      geography—Maps for children. [1.Atlases.] I. Title: Student atlas
      of the world. II. Title.
G1021 .N42 2001
912–dc21   00-030006

Printed in the U.S.A.
09/CK=CML/1

Metric Conversion Tables

CONVERSION TO METRIC MEASURES

SYMBOL	WHEN YOU KNOW	MULTIPLY BY	TO FIND	SYMBOL
LENGTH				
in	inches	2.54	centimeters	cm
ft	feet	0.30	meters	m
yd	yards	0.91	meters	m
mi	miles	1.61	kilometers	km
AREA				
in^2	square inches	6.45	square centimeters	cm^2
ft^2	square feet	0.09	square meters	m^2
yd^2	square yards	0.84	square meters	m^2
mi^2	square miles	2.59	square kilometers	km^2
—	acres	0.40	hectares	ha
MASS				
oz	ounces	28.35	grams	g
lb	pounds	0.45	kilograms	kg
—	short tons	0.91	metric tons	t
VOLUME				
in^3	cubic inches	16.39	milliliters	mL
liq oz	liquid ounces	29.57	milliliters	mL
pt	pints	0.47	liters	L
qt	quarts	0.95	liters	L
gal	gallons	3.79	liters	L
ft^3	cubic feet	0.03	cubic meters	m^3
yd^3	cubic yards	0.76	cubic meters	m^3
TEMPERATURE				
°F	degrees Fahrenheit	5/9 after subtracting 32	degrees Celsius (centigrade)	°C

CONVERSION FROM METRIC MEASURES

SYMBOL	WHEN YOU KNOW	MULTIPLY BY	TO FIND	SYMBOL
LENGTH				
cm	centimeters	0.39	inches	in
m	meters	3.28	feet	ft
m	meters	1.09	yards	yd
km	kilometers	0.62	miles	mi
AREA				
cm^2	square centimeters	0.16	square inches	in^2
m^2	square meters	10.76	square feet	ft^2
m^2	square meters	1.20	square yards	yd^2
km^2	square kilometers	0.39	square miles	mi^2
ha	hectares	2.47	acres	—
MASS				
g	grams	0.04	ounces	oz
kg	kilograms	2.20	pounds	lb
t	metric tons	1.10	short tons	—
VOLUME				
mL	milliliters	0.06	cubic inches	in^3
mL	milliliters	0.03	liquid ounces	liq oz
L	liters	2.11	pints	pt
L	liters	1.06	quarts	qt
L	liters	0.26	gallons	gal
m^3	cubic meters	35.31	cubic feet	ft^3
m^3	cubic meters	1.31	cubic yards	yd^3
TEMPERATURE				
°C	degrees Celsius (centigrade)	9/5 then add 32	degrees Fahrenheit	°F